Aristotle's On The Soul
(De Anima)

By the same author
Aristotle's Metaphysics (1966)
Aristotle's Physics (1969)
Aristotle's Nicomachean Ethics (1975)
Aristotle's Categories and Propositions (1980)
Aristotle's Posterior Analytics (1981)

ARISTOTLE'S ON THE SOUL
(DE ANIMA)

Translation with Commentaries
and Glossary by
HIPPOCRATES G. APOSTLE

THE PERIPATETIC PRESS
Grinnell, Iowa

Copyright © 1981 by H. G. Apostle

Library of Congress catalog card number: 81-86481

Manufactured in the United States of America

cl. ISBN 0-9602870-8-6

pa. ISBN 0-9602870-9-4

To my wife Margaret

Table of Contents

PREFACE

The main concern is to present an accurate translation with commentaries on difficult parts of the text. Textual differences in the various manuscripts present a problem, but no attempt is made here to give textual analysis and state preferences. Where such differences appear or corruption is suspected, however, the translator should follow the principles of translation, such as truth, consistency, and style. Great men of science are likely to state truths and be consistent, and they tend to maintain a constant scientific style. As examples: (1) the common belief that Aristotle said that bodies of greater numerical weight fall faster is untrue because Aristotle said no such thing, for the term βάρος (= "weight"), which has at least two meanings for Aristotle (215a25-9, 217b17-20, 1052b28-9), means density (or specific gravity) in the passages in which he discusses falling bodies of different 'weights', and resistance of a medium through which bodies fall is always included (Aristotle denies the existence of void); (2) in one manuscript of *On the Soul*, the omission of μὴ in line 402b26 is a mistake because it implies an obvious inconsistency in Aristotle's thinking about a relatively simple matter; and (3) the style of the *Constitution of Athens* makes it quite clear that this work was not written by Aristotle, for a host of principles which Aristotle uses in his writings are not used in this work.

Textual analysis by R. D. Hicks and by David Ross appears in their Introductions to *De Anima*.

Perhaps most of the difficulties which arise in understanding the text *On the Soul* are due to one's lack of clear conceptions of the subject, especially of the activities and powers of the rational soul, and perhaps it is for this reason that Aristotle, although attributing accuracy to the subject of this science, adds in lines 402a10-2 that "to attain any conviction concerning the soul is in every way one of the most difficult things". In this respect, one may add, this treatise resembles the *Metaphysics*, for the subject of the latter science is the most universal and abstract and hence the most accurate, yet it is also the most difficult (87a29-37, 982a23-8).

The principles of translation used in *On the Soul* are the same as those in my other translations; they are principles of terminology and of thought, and some of them will be repeated here for the sake of the reader.

Terms common to this and my other translations have the same meanings, with very few exceptions, and their meanings together with the mean-

1

II

ings proper to this treatise are given or indicated in the Glossary. To distinguish in print a vocal or printed or written expression from what it signifies, we enclose it within double (and sometimes within single) quotation marks. For example, "Plato" is a term or name and not a man; it signifies Plato, who was a man and a philosopher and not a term or a name. Thoughts are analogous to expressions, and they too are enclosed within quotation marks. For example, we may truly say that the thought "five is an even number" is false. Sometimes we use the conjunction "that" without the quotation marks, as in "the statement that Aristotle was a philosopher is true". Expressions in Greek are not enclosed within quotation marks, for it is not necessary. For example, we may write: the word μέγεθος is a Greek term and is translated as "magnitude".

Terms in italics with initial capital letters signify first principles posited by philosophers other than Aristotle; for example, the *One* and the *Dyad* are the first principles posited by Plato, the *Odd* and the *Even* are the first principles posited by the Pythagoreans, and *Intelligence* is the first principle posited by Anaxagoras. Terms in italics without initial capital letters are used (a) usually with meanings which are somewhat different from those of the same terms without italics, and (b) occasionally for emphasis. For example, the terms *"substance"* and "substance" have different but related meanings, and those meanings are given or indicated in the Glossary. Expressions appearing within brackets are added for the sake of the reader and are not translations from the Greek.

In the margins of the translation I have inserted the pages and lines of the Bekker text, which are standard. The various works of Aristotle and the Bekker pages containing each of them are listed at the beginning of the Commentaries.

Students who wish to acquire accurately the thought of Aristotle should make full use of the Glossary, for otherwise they will be faced with what appear to be inconsistencies or falsities, which may lead to unfair criticism. The references in the Commentaries to other works of Aristotle, too, are helpful.

I am grateful to Professor Lloyd P. Gerson who examined carefully the entire manuscript and made numerous corrections and suggestions in terminology and in thought, and to Grinnell College for its assistance and encouragement.

Grinnell College   H.G.A.

Summary of On The Soul

BOOK A

SECTION

1. The dignity and importance of the science of the soul, the difficulties faced in choosing a method of investigation and gaining conviction in spite of the accuracy of the subject, and the various problems which arise. 402a1-403b19.
2. An account of the opinions of earlier and contemporary thinkers, i.e., of Democritus, Leucippus, the Pythagoreans, Anaxagoras, Thales, Diogenes, Heraclitus, Alcmaion, Critias, Plato, and the Platonists. Knowledge and the cause of locomotion were the main principles attributed to the soul. 403b20-405b30.
3. Refutation of the doctrine which posits the soul as that which causes locomotion. 405b31-407b26.
4. Refutation of the doctrine that the soul is a harmony. 407b27-408a34. Refutation of the doctrine that the soul can be moved essentially. 408a34-b31. Refutation of the doctrine that the soul is a self-moving number. 408b32-409b18.
5. Refutation of the doctrine that the soul is composed of elements. 408b18-411a7. Refutation of the doctrine that the soul is present in all things. 411a7-24. The soul must have unity, whether divisible into parts or not. 411a24-b30.

BOOK B

SECTION

1. Preliminary definition. The soul is a substance as form and is the first actuality of a natural and organic body which has life. 412a3-413a10.
2. Second definition, in which the cause is included. The cause is the form by which the composite has life. 413a11-414a28.
3. The possible powers of the soul, ordered according to priority in existence, are the nutritive, the appetitive, the sentient, that which causes locomotion, and the *thinking*. Thus if one of these is present in a living thing, those before it are present also. The sense of touch is first and prior to all the other senses. 414a29-415a13.
4. The powers of the soul are defined in terms of their activities, and these are likewise defined in terms of the objects to which they are directed; so the objects should be considered first. 415a14-416b31.

BOOK Γ

SECTION

ON THE SOUL

BOOK A

1

We regard knowing to be noble and honorable,[1] and one kind of it to be more so than another either by virtue of its accuracy[2] or because its objects are better and more wonderful;[3] and for both these *reasons*[4] it is reasonable that we should give a primary place to the inquiry[5] concerning the soul. It is thought, too, that the knowledge of the soul contributes greatly to every kind of truth, and especially to [that about] nature; for the soul is as it were the principle of animals.[6]

Now we seek to investigate and to know, first, both the nature and the *substance*[7] of the soul and, secondly, its attributes, some of which are thought to be proper *attributes* of the soul while others are thought to belong through the soul to animals also.[8] But to attain any conviction concerning the soul is in every way one of the most difficult things. For although the inquiry here is common to that in many other [sciences] also, I mean the inquiry into the *substance* and the whatness of the subject, one might think that there is some one method applicable to every subject whose *substance* we wish to know, as in the case of proper attributes, which are known [by the method] of demonstration.[9] If so, one should inquire what that method is. But if there is not some one, and a common method of coming to know the whatness of things, the matter becomes even more difficult; for we would then have to determine the manner [of inquiry] to be used for each subject. And even if it were evident what that manner is, whether a demonstration or a division[10] or some other method, we are still faced with many problems and uncertainties as to what we should use as starting-points in the inquiry; for different sciences proceed from different principles, as in the case of numbers and of planes.[11]

First, perhaps it is necessary to determine the genus under which the soul falls and the whatness of the soul, that is, whether it is a *this* and a substance, or a quality, or a quantity, or falls under some other of the categories already distinguished;[12] and further, whether it is one of those things which exist potentially or is rather an actuality, for this makes no small difference.[13]

Again, we should consider if the soul is divisible into parts or has no parts,[14] and whether every [kind of] soul is homogeneous or not, and if not homogeneous, whether souls differ in species or in genus;[15] for those who nowadays discuss and make inquiries about the soul seem to limit their investigations to the human soul.[16] We should be careful, too, not to overlook the problem of whether there is a single definition for the soul, such as the soul of an animal, or a different definition for each (e.g., for a horse, a dog, a man, and a god) wherein an animal, taken universally, is either nonexistent or posterior;[17] and similarly for anything which might have a common predicate. Again, if there are not many souls[18] but only parts [of a soul in each thing], there is the problem of whether the inquiry into the whole soul should precede or follow that into the parts of it.[19] And with regard to the parts, too, it is difficult to determine which of them are by their nature distinct from one another.[20] There is also the problem of whether the inquiry into the parts should precede or follow that into their functions, e.g., whether the inquiry into the intellect should precede or follow that into thinking [as an activity], whether the inquiry into the sentient part should precede or follow that into sensing [as an activity], and similarly in the case of the other parts. And if the inquiry into the functions should precede that into the parts, one might still raise the problem whether the inquiry into the objects to which those functions[21] are directed should precede that of the corresponding parts, e.g., whether the sensible object should be sought before the sentient part of the soul,[22] and whether the object of thought should be sought before the thinking [part].[23]

It seems that not only is the knowledge of a *substance's* whatness useful to the investigation of the causes of the attributes of that *substance* (as in mathematics, in which knowledge of the whatness of straightness and curvature and a line and a plane are useful in perceiving the number of right angles to which the sum of the triangle's angles is equal), but, conversely, [knowledge of] the attributes [of the *substance* of a thing] contributes a considerable part to the knowledge of the whatness [of that *substance*]; for whenever we can give an account of all or most of the obvious attributes of a thing, we are in the best position to formulate its *substance*. For the starting point of every demonstration is the whatness of a thing; so if a *definition* fails to make us know by inference those attributes or even facilitate a conjecture about them, then clearly it is in every case so stated as to be dialectical or empty.[24]

The *attributes* of the soul, too, give rise to a problem. Are they *attributes* of that[25] which has the soul also, or is there any one of them which is proper to the soul?[26] This problem must be settled, but it is not easy.

Now in most cases it appears that [such *attributes*] cannot exist unless the body is being affected or is acting, as in anger, courage, *desire*, and sensation in general. Thinking, most of all, seems to be proper to the soul; but if this, too, is a species of imagination[27] or incapable of existing without imagination,[27] then it, too, could not exist without a body. Accordingly, if there is any function or affection of the soul proper to the soul, the soul can be separated [from the body], but if no function or [affection] is proper to the soul, the soul could not be separated from the body but would be just like

the straight. The straight qua straight has many attributes, e.g., it touches
a bronze sphere at a point; but the straight as something separated [in
existence from a body] cannot so touch it, for it is inseparable [from a body]
since it exists always with a body.²⁸

Now it seems that all the *attributes* of the soul, e.g., temper, good temper,
fear, pity, courage, also gladness and love and hate, exist with the body; for
the body is being affected simultaneously with these. This is indicated by
the fact that sometimes when strong or striking affections²⁹ occur, we are
not at the same time irritated or afraid, but at times when the affections²⁹
are weak or obscure, we are moved, and the body is agitated in a manner
similar to that when we are angry. Again, a more evident example is the
fact that we become afraid even if there is no [external] cause of fear.³⁰

If such be the case,³¹ it is clear that the *attributes* of the soul are things
whose formulae include matter.³² So the corresponding definitions will be
as follows: anger, for instance, is a certain motion of such a body or bodily
part or faculty of that body, caused by such and such a mover for the sake
of such and such an end.³³ And because of these facts, it becomes evident
that it belongs to the physicist to investigate the soul, either every [kind of]
soul or such [which is inseparable from a body].³⁴ Accordingly, a physicist
and a dialectician would define each [*attribute* of such a soul] in a different
way. For instance, in stating what anger is, the dialectician would say that
it is a desire to retaliate by causing pain, or something of this sort, whereas
a physicist would say that it is the rise in temperature of the blood or heat
round the heart. Thus the latter would state the matter, the former would
state the form and formula;³⁵ for the formula is the form of the thing, but
that form must be in such and such a matter if it is to exist.³⁶ It is like the
case of a house. Its formula is such as this: a covering which tends to prevent
its contents from being destroyed by wind or rain or scorching heat, but
another would speak of it as being stones and bricks and timber; still another
would speak of it as being the form in these materials for the sake of such
an such an end.

Which of the above three [definitions] will the physicist give? Is it the one
concerned with the matter but overlooks the formula, or the one concerned
with the formula only? Is it not rather the one which includes both [the
matter and the formula]?³⁷ Then what should we call each³⁸ of the other two
[thinkers]? Should we not say (1) that there is no [scientist] who is concerned
[only] with the *attributes* of matter³⁹ which are inseparable and is concerned
with them qua separable,⁴⁰ (2) but that it is the physicist who is concerned
with all [the attributes] which are functions or *attributes* of such and such
a body or matter;⁴¹ and, of the things which are investigated not qua such
attributes, (3) that it is the artist who is concerned with some [*attributes*],
e.g., the carpenter or the physician, if those things happen to be [works of
art],⁴² (4) that it is the mathematician who is concerned with inseparable

attributes but by abstraction and not qua *attributes* of such and such a body,[43] and (5) that it is the first philosopher who is concerned with [things] insofar as they are separate?[44]

But let us return to the point from which we digressed. We were saying that the *attributes* of the soul qua such [*attributes*], as in the case of temper and fear, are inseparable from the physical matter of animals and are not like a line or a plane.[45]

2

20 In our inquiry into the soul we must, while going over the difficulties which should precede their solution, consider also the doctrines of those before us who had something to say concerning the soul in order that we may accept whatever was stated well, but guard ourselves against anything which was not stated well.[1] The starting-point of our inquiry is to lay down
25 before us those things which are particularly thought to belong to the soul by virtue of its nature.

Now that which is animate is thought to differ most of all from that which is inanimate in two ways, by having [self]-motion and by sensing.[2] From our predecessors, too, these two are mainly the things about the soul which were handed down to us. Some declared that soul is particularly and primarily
30 that which causes motion;[3] and thinking that no thing which is not itself in motion can cause another thing to be in motion,[4] they came to the belief
404a that soul is a thing in motion. In view of this, Democritus asserted that soul is a sort of fire and hot. For, of the infinite [kinds of] shapes and atoms, those which are spherical he called "fire" and "soul", these being like the so-called "motes" in the air which appear in the sunbeams entering through windows. And he said that all these seeds [i.e., shapes and atoms] are the
5 elements of the whole of nature (Leucippus, too, speaks similarly) but that those of them which are spherical are souls because elements of such shape are most capable of passing through openings and moving all other things by being themselves in motion. These thinkers regard soul to be that which furnishes animals with motion; and, in view of this, they regard breathing
10 as being the definition of living. For, they think, after the surrounding air presses upon the bodies [of animals] and forces out [atomic] shapes which furnish the animals with motion, because those shapes are never at rest, other such shapes from outside come to the aid by entering the body during respiration, and these prevent the escape of the shapes already in the bodies
15 by compression and solidification; and animals live as long as they are able to do this.

What the Pythagoreans have said, too, seems to amount to the same *thought;* for some of them identified the soul with the motes in the air, others with that which moves these motes. And these motes were referred
20 to because they appear to be continuously in motion, even when the air is completely calm.

The *thinking* of those[5] who say that the soul is that which moves itself,
too, amounts to the same thing. For these thinkers seem to believe that
motion is most appropriate to the soul, and that, while all other things are
moved by the soul, the soul is moved by itself; and it does so because they
observe nothing moving something else which is not itself in motion.

Similarly, Anaxagoras and all others[6] who declare that *Intelligence*[7] caused
the universe to be in motion say that it is the soul which moves other things;
but Anaxagoras does not speak altogether like Democritus. The latter de-
clares that the soul and the intellect are simply the same, for, according to
him, what is true is [the same as] what appears to be;[8] and for this reason
he regards Homer's phrase "Hector lay thinking other thoughts" as well put.
He does not, however, treat the intellect as a certain faculty concerned with
truth but says [merely] that the soul and the intellect are the same. Anaxagoras speaks less clearly about these matters. In many places he says that
Intelligence is the cause of beauty and rightness; in other places he says that
it is the soul, for it exists in all animals, great and small, worthy of honor
and less honorable.[9] But the so-called "intellect", when spoken of with
respect to prudence, does not appear to belong alike to all animals, not even
to all men.[10]

Those, then, who considered the soul from the point of view of the motion
of animate things regarded it as being the most capable of causing motion;
but those who considered it from the point of view of knowledge or sensation of things placed it among the principles, some positing these to be
many, but others only one, [the soul itself]. Thus Empedocles regarded the
soul as being composed of all the [kinds of] elements and each of these as
being a soul. He says:

> By Earth we see Earth, by Water Water,
> By Ether Ether divine, by Fire destructive Fire,
> By Love Love, and Strife by bitter Strife.[11]

In the same manner Plato, in the *Timaeus*, constructs the soul out of
elements; for, according to him, like is known by like, and things are
composed of principles. In [my] treatise *On Philosophy*,[12] too, a similar
description [of Plato's views] is given: Animal Itself is composed of the Idea
of *One Itself*[13] and of the primary Length, the primary Breadth, and the
primary Depth; and the rest are composed in a similar manner.[14] In still
another way, he regards the *Intellect* as the *One*, *Knowledge* as Two (for
this is [arrived at] in one way only), Opinion as the Number of the Plane,
and Sensation as the Number of the Solid.[15] For Numbers, according to him,
are the Forms themselves and the principles [of other things], and they are
composed of elements; and things are apprehended, some by the intellect,
others by *knowledge*, others by opinion, and others by sensation; and the

above Numbers are the Forms of things.[16] And since the soul was thought to be capable of causing motion and of knowing, some thinkers[17] combined these two and declared that the soul is a number moving itself.

But thinkers differ as to what the principles of the soul are and how many of them there are, especially between those who posit them as being corporeal and those who posit them as being incorporeal; and these differ from those who combine these two and declare that the principles are of two kinds. And there are differences as to the number of principles also; for some speak of only one, others of many. The accounts they give of the soul, too, follow from the positions they take [with respect to the principles]; for they regard, not without good reason, the thing whose nature is to cause motion as being among the primary.[18] Thus some are of the opinion that the soul is fire, for fire, too, is [thought to be] composed of the finest particles and [to be] the most incorporeal of the elements; besides, it is in the primary sense both in motion and that which moves other things [according to these thinkers].[19]

Democritus speaks even more precisely than the others by stating the cause of each of the two [traits of the soul just mentioned];[20] for he says that the soul is the same as the intellect, that it is [composed][21] of the primary and indivisible bodies, that it can cause motion because of the smallness and the shape [of the particles] and of the fact that of the various shapes the spherical is the most easily moved, and that such is both the intellect and fire.[22]

Anaxagoras seems to speak of the soul and *Intelligence* as being different, as we have already stated. But he treats them as if they were of one nature, except that he posits *Intelligence* as being the highest principle of all things; at any rate, he says that, of all things, *Intelligence* alone is simple, unblended, and pure. Yet in saying that *Intelligence* set the universe in motion he attributes both knowing and moving other things to the same principle.[23]

Thales, too, judging from the anecdotes related of him, seems to have regarded the soul as something which can cause motion, if indeed he said that the loadstone possesses soul, for it moves iron.

Diogenes, like some others, thinking that [air] is composed of the finest particles and is a principle,[24] [regards the soul as being] air, and for this *reason* he thinks that the soul both knows and causes motion; for he thinks that insofar as it is first [i.e., a principle] and the other things are composed of it, it knows, but that insofar as its particles are the most fine, it can cause motion.

Heraclitus asserts that the principle is soul, if indeed it is an exhalation from which the other things are composed, that it is the most incorporeal and always in a state of flux, and that what is in motion is known by a thing in motion.[25] Both he and many other thinkers think that [all] things are in motion. Alcmaion, too, seems to regard the soul in about the same way as these thinkers,[26] for he asserts that soul is immortal because it seems to be like immortal things, and that is possesses immortality by being always in motion; for, according to him, all divine things, the Moon, the Sun, the stars, and the whole heaven are in a continuous motion.

405b

Of the rather crude thinkers, like Hippo, some went as far as to declare that the soul is water. They seem to have been persuaded by the fact that the seed of all [animals] is moist; for Hippo refutes those who assert that the soul is blood by pointing out that the seed is not blood but is the primary soul. Others, like Critias, regarding sensation to be most appropriate to the soul, declared that soul is blood and that [sensation] occurs because of the nature of blood.

5

Thus each of the elements found its advocate except earth; and no one declared the soul to be earth, unless it be anyone who said that the soul is composed of all the elements or that every element is a soul.[27]

10

Now all thinkers define the soul by three things, so to say: motion, sensation, and incorporeality;[28] and each of these is referred to the principles.[29] It is in view of this that even those who, using about the same language, define it as knowing, posit it to be, with one exception,[30] either an element or composed of elements; for they say that like is known by like and that, since the soul knows all things, it consists of all the principles. Accordingly, those who assert that there is only one cause or one element, such as fire or air, posit the soul, too, to be one; but those who assert that the principles are many posit the soul, too, to be many. Anaxagoras alone says that *Intelligence* cannot be affected and that it has nothing in common with any of the other things. But how *Intelligence*, if it is such, will know and through what cause, he did not say anything, nor is it evident from his writings.[31] Again, those who posit contraries among the principles say that the soul, too, consists of contraries,[32] and, similarly, those who posit one of two contraries, such as the *Hot* or the *Cold*[33] or some other such thing, posit the soul to be that contrary; and, in view of this, these thinkers appeal to language for support of their views. Thus those who posit the *Hot* say that it is because of this principle [and the word ζέω (= "boil")] that the word ζῆν (= "living") is used, and those who posit the *Cold* say that it is because of inhaling and the word κατάψυξις (= "cooling") that the word ψυχή (= "soul") is used.[34]

15

20

25

30

The above, then, are the doctrines concerning the soul which were handed down to us and the *reasons* for which they were so held.

3

First, let us turn our attention to motion; for perhaps it is not only false to say that the *substance* of the soul is such as those claim who speak of the soul as being that which moves itself or can move other things, but also impossible for motion to belong to the soul.[1]

406a

We have stated before that it is not necessary for that which moves something else to be itself in motion.[2] Now everything in motion may be so in one of two ways, (a) directly[3] or (b) indirectly [i.e., in virtue of another thing]. By "indirectly" we mean things, like sailors on a ship, which are in motion by being in other things which are in motion; for sailors are in motion[4] not like the ship. The ship is directly or by itself in motion, but the sailors are in motion by being in the ship which is [directly] in motion. This is clear if we consider the parts of a thing; for walking[5] is a motion appropriate to feet and so to men but not to sailors [when they are in motion indirectly or by something else]. Since "being in motion" has two senses, let us examine if the soul is in motion or[6] partakes of motion[7] by itself or not.

There are four kinds of motion: locomotion, alteration, decrease, and increase; so the soul, if in motion, would have to be moved in one or more or all of these kinds. If it is in motion not as an attribute,[8] then motion would belong to it[9] by its nature; and if so, then place too would belong to it by its nature, for all the kinds of motion just mentioned occur in place.[10] So if the *substance* of the soul is to move itself, motion will belong to the soul not as an attribute, as it does to whiteness or to a length of three cubits. The latter two are in motion also, but as attributes, for it is the body to which they belong that is in motion; and, in view of this, place does not belong to them. But place will belong to the soul if the soul partakes of motion by its nature.

Again, if the soul is moved by its nature, it could be moved by force also, and if by force, then by its nature also. It is likewise with rest. For that towards which it is moved by its nature is also that in which it may be at rest by its nature; and, similarly, that towards which it is moved by force is also that in which it may be at rest by force.[11] But it is not easy to state, even if we wished to make up, any kinds of motion and rest which would belong to the soul by force.

Again, if the soul is to move upward [by its nature], it will be fire; and if downward, it will be earth; for these are the motions of the two bodies.[12] The same applies to the intermediate [motions, places, and bodies].[13] Again, since the soul appears to move the body, it is reasonable for it to produce the [kinds of] motions which it has itself; and if so, then, conversely, it will be true to say that the [kind of] motion produced in the body is the same as that which the soul has.[14] Now a body may be moved by locomotion; so the soul, too, could change as a body by a change of its place, either as a whole or with respect to its parts.[15] If this can be done, then the soul could reenter the body after having departed from it; and it would follow from this that dead animals may be resurrected.[16]

Indirect motion in a thing may be caused by another thing also; for an animal might be pushed [to another place] by force. But that which has self-motion in its *substance* should not be [regarded as being] moved by

another thing, except indirectly, just as that which is good in virtue of itself, or through itself, [should not be regarded as being good] because of some-
10   thing else, or for the sake of something else.[17] One might say, however, that if the soul *as such* is moved at all, it is moved by sensible things most of all.[18]

Moreover, even if [we assume that] the soul moves itself, the soul itself would be moved also; so if every motion is a displacement of a thing in motion qua in motion,[19] the soul too would depart from its own *substance*,
15   unless it moves itself accidentally or indirectly. But motion [according to these thinkers] belongs essentially to the *substance* of the soul.[20]

Some even say that the soul moves the body, in which it exists, in the same way in which it is itself moved. For example, Democritus speaks in about the same way as Philippus, the teacher of comedy; for the latter says that Daedalus caused the wooden Aphrodite to be in motion by pouring into it
20   quicksilver. And Democritus, speaking in a similar manner, says that the indivisible spheres [i.e., atoms],[21] being [always] in motion because it is their nature never to remain still, draw the whole body along with them and cause it to move. But, we may ask, is it these same [atoms] that cause [the body to] rest also? It is difficult, if not impossible, to state how they will do
25   this. In general, it is not in this manner that the soul appears to move the animal but by *intention* of some sort or by thinking.[22]

In the same manner Plato in the *Timaeus* uses the same argument, which belongs to physics,[23] in stating how the soul moves the body; for he says that it is by its motion that the soul moves the body, because it is closely interwoven with it. For, he says, after forming the soul out of the elements and dividing it into parts with ratios according to harmonic numbers so that
30   it may have an innate sensation of harmony and that the universe may move in harmonious revolutions, [the Creator] bent the straight line into a circle; and, after dividing this single circle into two circles touching at two points,
407a   He again divided one of these into seven circles, so as to have the revolutions of heaven be the motions of the soul.[24]

First, the statement that the soul is a magnitude is not well put, for by
5   "the soul of the universe" Plato clearly means that which is called "intel-lect"; for neither the sentient nor the *desiring* power of the soul can be meant since the motion of each of these is not circular.[25] As for the intellect, it is one, and it is continuous like [the process of] thinking; but thinking is [the same as] the concepts, and these are one by being in succession, like the numbers, and not like a magnitude.[26] And it is indeed in view of this that
10   the intellect is not continuous in this way but is either without parts or is continuous,[27] but not like a magnitude; for, if it were a magnitude, how would it think at all with any of its parts? These would be parts either as magnitudes or as points, if points too should be called "parts [of a magni-tude]".[28] Accordingly, if [it thinks an object] by means of its points [as parts], then clearly it will never traverse these, for they are infinite; and if [it thinks

an object] by means of [its parts] as magnitudes, it will think the same thing
many or an infinite number of times. But it appears [that] it can also think
[an object] only once.[29] If it is sufficient [for the intellect] to contact [its
object] with any one of its parts, what need is there for it to be moving in
a circle or even to have a magnitude at all?[30] And if it is necessary for it to
contact [its object] by thinking with its whole circle, what will contact by
its part be?[31]

Again, how will that which has parts think that which has no parts, or that
which has no parts think that which has parts? Now [according to Plato] it
is necessary for the intellect [or *Intellect*] to be this circle. For the motion
of the intellect is thinking, and the motion of a circle is a revolving; so if
thinking is revolving, the intellect too would be a circle, and the revolution
of that circle would be thinking. Then what is that which the intellect [or
Intellect] will always be thinking? For it should be doing this, if the revolution [of this circle] is indeed eternal. Now practical thinking has limits (since
in every case such thinking is for the sake of something else), and theoretical
thinking is limited in a manner similar to that of discourse. But every
formula [in theoretical discourse] is either a *definition* or a demonstration,
and demonstrations proceed from starting-points [principles or premises]
and in a sense have an end, whether this be a syllogism or a conclusion;[32]
and if they do not terminate, still they do not return to the starting-point
but, always taking additional middle or extreme terms, proceed in a straight
line. Circular motion, on the other hand, returns to the starting-point again
and again.[33] As for *definitions*, they are all finite.[34]

Again, if it is the same revolution that is repeated, the intellect [or
Intellect] should be thinking the same thing repeatedly.[35] Again, thinking
seems to be a sort of coming to a rest or a standstill rather than a motion,[36]
and so does a syllogism. Moreover, that which is not easy but forced cannot
be in a blessed state; so if the motion of the soul is not its *substance*, it would
be contrary to the soul's nature.[37] Much effort, too, is required for the soul
to be blended with the body and be incapable of departing from it; and,
besides, this should be avoided if, according to what is usually said and is
thought by many, it is better for the intellect as such not to be with a body.[38]
The cause of the heaven's revolution, too, is not clear; for neither is the
substance of the soul the cause of [that] revolution, since it is indirectly that
it[39] is moved in this manner, nor is the body that cause, but the soul would
be the cause more than the body.[40] Moreover, neither is it stated that [such
motion] is better [for the soul]; yet this is the *reason* why it was necessary
for God to cause the soul to move in a circle, if it is (a) better to move than
to remain still and (b) better to move in this than in any other way.[41] But
since such inquiry is more appropriate to other treatises, let us leave it aside
for the present.[42]

Now there is something absurd both in this and in most of the other

15   doctrines concerning the soul, for they attach the soul to, or place it in, a body, without further specifying the *reason* for this[43] or how the body is related [to the soul];[44] yet one would think that further specification is necessary. For it is because of the association of the two that the one acts while the other is acted upon, and the one moves the other while the latter is moved; and such relation does not exist between any two chance things.

20   Yet the thinkers of these doctrines try to state only what kind of thing the soul is without further specifying the [kind of] body which is to receive it, as if it were possible, according to the Pythagorean stories, for any soul to enter any body; but each [kind of living] body is thought to have its own

25   proper form or *shape*. So, according to them, it is almost as if one said that the art of carpentry enters the flute; but each art should use its own instruments, and each soul should use its own [kind of] body.[45]

4

There is another traditional doctrine concerning the soul which is no less persuasive to many thinkers than those stated above, but which has been

30   aired as if subject to scrutiny even in public discussions. Its upholders assert that the soul is a certain harmony; for they say that harmony is a mixture or composition of contraries, and that the body, too, is composed of contraries.[1]

Now harmony is a certain ratio of the things blended or a composition of them, whereas the soul cannot possibly be either a blend or a composition.[2] Further, moving another thing does not belong to harmony, but all

408a   thinkers, so to say, attribute to the soul motion most of all.[3] It is more fitting to say that health or, in general, each of the bodily virtues is a harmony than to say that the soul is a harmony. This becomes most evident if one were

5   to try to assign the *attributes* and functions of the soul to a harmony; for it is difficult to make them fit.[4]

Again, if we were to speak of harmony from two points of view, then, (a) in the main sense, [we would speak] of the composition of those magnitudes which have motion and position whenever these fit together in such a manner that they do not admit others of their kind between them, and (b) in a secondary sense, we would speak of [just] the ratio of the things so

10   blended. Now in neither of the two senses is it reasonable [to speak of the soul as a harmony]. [To speak of it as] the composition of the parts of the body is quite easily open to doubt upon examination; for the compositions of parts are many and occur in many ways. Of what parts must we believe the intellect or the sentient or the appetitive soul to be a composition, and how? It is likewise absurd to speak of the soul as being a ratio in the blend,

15   for the blend of the elements does not have the same ratio in the case of flesh as in the case of bone. Accordingly, what would follow is that [an animal] has many souls and that these are distributed over the various parts of the

body, if indeed every [part] consists of a blend of elements and the ratio of each blend is a harmony and a soul.[5]

20 Empedocles, too, who says that each part [of the body] exists by virtue of a ratio, might be required to answer the following question: Is the soul the ratio itself, or is it something else which, being distinct, comes to be in the parts? Further, is *Friendship* the cause of any chance blend or of a blend according to a [right] ratio? And, if according to a [right] ratio, is [*Friendship*] the ratio itself or is it something distinct from that ratio?[6]

25 Such, then, are the difficulties which arise from the above [doctrines].[7] On the other hand, if the soul is distinct from the blend,[8] how is it that it perishes at the same time as the essence of flesh and of the other parts[9] of the animal?[10] In addition, if indeed each part has no soul, then, if the soul is not the ratio of the blend, what is that which is destroyed when the soul departs [from the body]?[11]

30 It is clear from what has been said that the soul cannot be such as to be a harmony or to be moving in a circle. As we have stated,[12] however, it is possible for the soul to be moved or to move itself indirectly, that is, for the body in which the soul exists to be moved, but to be moved by the soul; but in no other way can the soul be of such a nature as to be moved with respect to place.[13]

408b Now one might have better reason in raising the problem of whether the soul can be moved if he turns his attention to the following. We say that the soul is pained or glad, courageous or afraid, and also that it is angry or sensing or *thinking*, and all these are thought to be motions; and hence one
5 might think that the soul is moved. But this [conclusion] does not follow. For, however true it is to say that being pained and being glad and *thinking* are motions, that each of these is moved, and that it is moved by the soul (for example, to be angered or to fear is for the heart to be moved in a certain way, and *thinking* perhaps is either to be so moved or to be a motion of some
10 other such thing,[14] and some of these motions are locomotions of certain moving things and others are alterations,[15] but discussions of what kinds of motions these are and how they arise belong elsewhere), still to say that the soul is angered is as if one were to say that the soul is weaving or is building a house. Surely it would be better to say not that the soul pities or learns
15 or *thinks* but that a man does so with the soul, that is, not that the motion is in the soul but that it terminates at or starts from the soul; for example, sensation starts from [sensible objects and terminates at the soul], but recollection starts from the soul and proceeds to the motions or states of rest of the sense organs.[16]

As for the intellect, it seems to come to be in us as a sort of substance and
20 to be indestructible.[17] Now it might be destroyed, if at all,[18] by the feebleness due to old age, but surely what happens here is the same as in the case of the sense organs; for if an old man were to receive an eye of a certain kind,[19]

he would see as a young man sees. So old age is due to the body which has
been affected in a certain way, as in the case of drunkenness or disease, and
not to the soul which is in that body. Thus thinking and speculating, too,
25   are losing their strength while something else within [the body] is being
destroyed,[20] but the [intellect itself] cannot be affected. *Thinking* and also
loving or hating, then, are *attributes* not of the [intellect] but of [that][21]
which has the [intellect], insofar as it has it. And in view of this, when [that][21]
has been destroyed, [man] neither remembers nor loves; for [memory and
love] belonged not to the [intellect] but to that which is shared by both [body
and soul],[22] which has [now] perished, while the intellect is perhaps something more divine and cannot be affected.
30   From the above discussion, then, it is evident that the soul is not of such
a nature as to be in motion; and if it cannot be moved at all, clearly it cannot
be moved by itself.
           Of the above doctrines concerning the soul, by far the most unreasonable
is the one which asserts that the soul is a number which moves itself.[23] The
first impossibilities in this doctrine follow from the assertion that the soul
409a   is in motion, but others of a special nature follow from the assertion that the
soul is a number.
           Now how are we to think of a unit as being in motion, and by what will
it be moved, and in what manner [will it be moved], when it has no parts
and no differentiae? For if it can both cause motion and be capable of being
in motion, it must possess differences.[24]
           Again, since they say that, when in motion, a line generates a plane and
5   a point generates a line, the motions of units, too, will be lines; for a point
is a unit[25] with position, and the number of the soul is [for these thinkers]
somewhere and has position.[26]
           Again, if a number or a unit is subtracted from a number, the remainder
is a different number; but plants and many animals, when divided, continue
10   to live, and each part is thought to have the same kind of soul as the
corresponding whole.[27]
           [Again,] there would seem to be no difference whether we speak of units
or of minute particles of matter; for, even if the spherical atoms which are
posited by Democritus were to become points but retain their [numerical]
quantity, there would still have to be in that [quantity] something which
moves something else and something which is moved, as in that which is
continuous, for what we have just stated happens not because of the difference
15   in the size [of particles] but in virtue of their quantity.[28] In view of this, there
will have to be something to move the units.[29] If the mover in the animal
is the soul, then [for these thinkers] it [must be] in the number also, so the
soul cannot be both a mover and the thing moved but only a mover. But
20   how can this [soul] be a unit?[30] For this unit would have to differ from the
other [units]. But can a point which is unitary differ from another in any

way other than in position? Accordingly, (a) if the units and the points in the body are distinct, the units will be in the same [places] as the points; [for each unit] will occupy the space of a point. But if two [indivisibles, e.g., a unit and a point, occupy the same space], what will prevent an infinity of them from being in the same [space]? For things whose place is indivisible

25 are themselves indivisible. On the other hand, (b) if the points in the body are the soul's number, or if the number of the points in the body is the soul, why is it that not every body has a soul? For points — in fact, an infinite number of them — are thought to exist in every body.[31] Again, how is it

30 possible for souls to be separated or depart from bodies if indeed lines are not divisible into points?[32]

5

Two things, then, follow from what we have stated;[1] (a) in one respect, these thinkers are saying the same thing as those[2] who posit the soul to be

409b a body composed of fine particles, and (b) in another, by agreeing with Democritus, who says that the [body] is moved by the soul, their doctrine is faced with additional absurdities.[3] For if indeed there is soul in every [part of a] sentient body, it is necessary for two bodies to be in the same [place], if the soul is a body; and, for those who call the soul "a number", it is

5 necessary for many points to be at one point, or for every body to have soul if what comes to be in the body is not a different number, [i.e.,] one which is distinct from the [number of] points in that body. It follows, too, that an animal is moved by a number[4] and, as we said, in the same way as Democritus said that it is moved. For what difference does it make whether we call

10 [his atoms] "small spheres" or "large units" or, in general, "units in locomotion"? In either case, it is necessary for them to move the animal by being themselves in motion. Those who combine motion and number into the same thing [i.e., the soul], then, are faced with these and many other such consequences; for this combination is impossible not only as the *definition*

15 of the soul, but also as an attribute of it. This becomes clear if, from this formula, one tries to account for such *attributes* and functions of the soul as judgments, sensations, pleasures, pains, and the like; for, as we stated earlier, it is not easy to even surmise these from [number and motion].[5]

Our predecessors handed down to us three ways of defining the soul:[6] some declared that the soul is the most capable of causing motion by virtue

20 of the fact that it moves itself; others, that it is a body composed of the finest particles or of the most incorporeal particles; and we have described adequately the difficulties and inconsistencies which these two doctrines are facing. It remains now to examine in what way it is stated that the soul consists of the elements of things.[7]

25 Now these thinkers[8] say that the soul [consists of elements] in order that it may both sense [all] things and know each of them, but their doctrine

necessitates many impossibilities; for they posit that like is known by like, as if they are positing the soul to be the things.[9] But these [elements] are not all that exists; there are many other things — or rather, perhaps an infinite number of them — which are distinct from the elements and consist of

30   them. So let it be granted that the soul can both know and sense the elements of each existing thing; then by what will it know or sense the *composite* of each thing [which, besides its elements, has also a form], e.g., by what will

410a   it know or sense what is God or man or flesh or bone or, similarly, any other composite thing? For each of these is not merely its elements regardless of their relation to each other, but those elements in a certain ratio and composition, as Empedocles says of bone:

> The kind earth in its broad-bosomed moulds
> Two parts of eight received from radiant water

5   > Four of fire; and thus came white bones to be

Accordingly, the elements in the soul are of no benefit unless the ratios and compositions [of the things known], too, exist in it; for each [element in the soul] will know its like but nothing will know a bone or a man, unless these

10   too exist in the soul. But the impossibility of these existing in the soul needs no mention; for who would raise the problem whether a stone or a man exists in the soul? In the same way, the good and the not-good [are not in the soul], and similarly for the others.[10]

Again, since the term "being" has many senses (for it means a *this* or a

15   quantity or a quality or a thing under one of the other categories already distinguished),[11] will the soul consist of all of them or not? But no elements are thought to be common to all the categories.[12] Then does the soul consist only of those elements which are the elements of substances? If so, how will it know also each of the other [categories]?[13] Or, will they say that each genus has elements and principles proper to itself,[14] and that the soul consists

20   of all of these? If so, the soul will be a quantity and a quality and a substance [and so on]. But it is impossible [for a thing] which consists of the elements of quantity to be a substance and not a quantity.[15] Those, then, who assert that the soul consists of all the elements are faced with these and other such consequences.

It is also absurd to say, on the one hand, that like is not affected by like

25   and, on the other, that like senses like and like knows like. But they posit that to sense is to be affected and to be moved in a certain way, and similarly in the case of thinking and of knowing.[16]

That there are many difficulties and points hard to handle in saying, as Empedocles does,[17] that each thing is known by corporeal elements and by

30   being related to its like is confirmed by the following argument. The things which are in the bodies of animals and are made simply of earth, such as

410b   bones, sinews, and hair, are not thought to be capable of sensing anything, and hence of sensing what is like; yet [according to these thinkers] they should have been so capable. Again, each of the principles will have more ignorance than intelligence; for each of them will know only one thing and so be ignorant of many, in fact, of all the other things.[18] It follows, too, for

5   Empedocles at least, that God is the most unintelligent of beings; for He alone will not know *Strife*, which is one of the elements, while every mortal being, consisting of all the elements, will know them all.[19] And, in general, why is it that not all things have a soul, if indeed each of them either is an element or consists of one or more than one or all of the elements? For,

10   according to these thinkers, it is necessary for each thing to know one or some or all [of the elements].[20]

    One might raise also the following problem. What is it that produces the unity of each [thing]? For the elements, at least, seem to be [just] matter; but that which holds them together, whatever it be, is the most dominant [principle or cause]. It is impossible for anything to be superior to the soul or to rule it, and even more impossible to be superior to or to rule the intellect; for it is reasonable for the intellect, in virtue of its nature, to be

15   the oldest in origin and the dominant [principle or cause], and these thinkers do say that the elements are prior to all things.[21]

    Now all thinkers, both those who assert that the soul consists of the elements for the sake of knowing or sensing what exists, and those who assert that it is the most capable of causing motion, fail to include every kind of soul. But (1) not all things which can sense can cause motion, for some

20   animals appear to be stationary in place; and, in fact, the soul is thought to move the animal only with respect to place.[22] Again, (2) a similar objection may be brought against those who assert that the intellect or the sentient part is composed of the elements; for plants appear to live without partaking of locomotion or sensation, and many animals have no power of *thinking*.[23]

25   But even if one were to waive these [two objections] and posit the intellect to be a part of the soul (and similarly for the sentient part), he would still fail to include universally every [kind of] soul or a whole soul or even a single soul.[24]

    The objection just raised may be brought against the statement in the so-called "Orphic poems" also; for it is stated there that the soul, [coming] from the whole [universe] and being borne by the winds, enters [the body

30   of an animal] when the animal inhales. This, of course, cannot happen in
411a   the case of plants, nor in the case of some animals, if indeed not all animals breathe; but this fact escaped the notice of those who entertained such belief.[25]

    Now if we are to posit the soul as consisting of elements, there is no need to use all of them; for one of two contrary [elements] is sufficient to judge

5   both itself and its opposite. For instance, it is by the straight that we know

both the straight and the curved; for the [straight] ruler judges both, whereas what is curved judges neither itself nor the straight.[26]

    There are also some who say that the soul is blended in the whole [universe]; and it is perhaps from this view that Thales, too, thought that all things are full of gods. But this doctrine is faced with certain difficulties; for

10   why is it that the soul produces no animal when in air or fire but does so when in a blend of elements, even if it is thought to be in a better state when in air or fire?[27] And one might further inquire as to why it is that the soul is in a better state and more immortal when in air than when in animals. The consequences are absurd or contrary to reason regardless of which of

15   the two contradictory positions one may take; for it is indeed contrary to reason to speak of fire or of air as being an animal, and it is absurd not to call them "animals" when soul is present in them.[28] These thinkers seem to believe that there is soul in these [elements] in view of the fact that a whole is homogeneous with its parts. So, if animals become animate by taking into themselves a part of what surrounds them, it is necessary for these thinkers

20   to say that [their] soul, too, is homogeneous with its parts. But if air, when divided, is homogeneous with its parts, while the soul[29] has parts which differ in kind, it is clear that some part of [this] soul will exist [in air] but some other part will not. But either soul must have homogeneous parts, or soul cannot exist in every part of the whole.[30]

25   From what has been said it is evident that knowing belongs to the soul not because the soul consists of elements, and that the doctrine that the soul is in motion is neither well-expressed nor true.[31]

    Since knowing and sensing and forming opinions, and also *desiring* and wishing and desires in general, all belong to the soul,[32] and since locomotion

30   and growth and maturity and deterioration are all brought about by the

411b soul,[33] does each of these belong to the whole soul or to a different part of it, and do we think and sense and act and are acted upon by every part of the soul or by a different part of it in each case?[34] And does living, too, belong to some one or to more than one or to all [of the parts of the soul],

5   or is there some other cause of it also?[35]

    Some assert that the soul is divisible into parts, and that it[36] thinks with one part but *desires* with another. What is it, then, that holds [the parts of] the soul together if it is by its nature divisible? Certainly not the body; for, on the contrary, it is the soul that is thought to hold the body together. At any rate, when the soul departs, the body evaporates and rots. So if it is some

10   other thing which makes the [whole] soul be one, that thing would be the soul in the highest sense.[37] Then we will have to inquire again whether that thing is single or has many parts. If it is single, why not say at the start that the soul is single? And if it is a whole with parts, reason will ask once more, "What is it that holds that whole together?", and in this manner the process will go on to infinity.[38]

15   Concerning the parts of the soul one might raise also the problem as to
what power each of them has in the body. For if the whole soul holds
together the entire body, then each of its parts, too, should hold together
some part of the body. But this seems impossible; for it is difficult even to
imagine such [bodily] part for the intellect or state how the intellect will
20   hold that part together. It appears that plants and some insects among
animals, too, continue to live after being divided, and in such a way that,
after division, the parts have souls which are the same in species even if they
are not the same in number; at any rate, each of them [in the case of some
animals] has the power of sensation and of locomotion for some time, and
there is nothing strange if it does not last long, for it does not have the
25   necessary organs to preserve its nature. But nonetheless all the parts of the
soul are in each [bodily] part, and they are of the same kind in every such
part and in the whole [animal prior to its division][39]; and while the parts [of
the soul] are not separable from each other, the whole soul is divisible.[40] The
principle in plants, too, seems to be a kind of soul, for it is the one which
is common to animals and plants; and this [principle] can exist apart from
30   the sentient principle, but without it no [living being] can have the faculty
of sensation.[41]

BOOK B

1

412a3   The doctrines concerning the soul handed down to us by our predecessors have been sufficiently discussed. Let us then turn to another starting point, as it were, and try to determine what the soul is and what would be its most common formula.[1]

    Now one genus of things we call "substance", but (1) one kind under this we regard as matter, which taken by itself is not a *this*, (2) another as *shape* and[2] *form*, in virtue of which something is directly called "a *this*",[3] (3) and a third, the composite of the above two kinds.[4] Matter exists as potentiality; form exists as actuality,[5] but in two senses: e.g., (a) as *knowledge*, and (b) as the exercise of *knowledge*.[6]

    Bodies are thought to be substances most of all, especially natural bodies; for the latter are the principles of all the rest.[7] Of natural bodies, some possess life but others[8] do not; and by "life" we mean self-nourishment and growth and deterioration of that body.[9] So every natural body which partakes of life would be a substance of the composite kind. And since there exists such a kind of body (for it has life), the soul would not be a body;[10] for a body[10] is not something which belongs to a subject but exists rather as a subject or as matter.[11] Accordingly, the soul must be a substance as the form of a natural body potential with life, and [such] substance is an actuality.[12] So the soul is the actuality of such a body.[13]

    But actuality is spoken of in two ways, as in the case of *knowledge* and as in the case of the exercise of *knowledge*. Evidently, the soul is an actuality as in the case of *knowledge;* for sleeping and being awake depend on the existence of soul, and being awake is analogous to the exercise of *knowledge*, whereas sleeping is analogous to having [*knowledge*] but not exercising it.[14] Now in the same individual the *knowledge* of a thing is prior in generation to the exercise of that *knowledge*.[15] In view of this, the soul is the first actuality[16] of a natural body with the potentiality of having life; and a body of this kind would be one which has organs.[17] The parts of plants, too, are organs, but they are entirely simple; e.g., the leaf shelters the rind and the rind shelters the fruit, and the roots are analogous to the mouth, for both of these take in food. If, then, there is something common to be said about every [kind of] soul, this would be: "the first actuality of a natural body which has organs".[18] And in view of this, one should not inquire whether the soul and the body are one or not, just as one should not ask whether the wax and its shape or, in general, the matter of each thing and that of which[19] it is the matter are one or not; for, although the terms "one" and "being" have many senses, the dominant sense is that of actuality.[20]

19

10   We have now stated universally what the soul is: with respect to its formula, it is a *substance*,[21] and this is the essence in such and such a body,[22] as in the case of instruments. For example,[23] if an axe were a natural body,[24] its *substance*[25] would be its essence, and this would be its soul; and if that essence were removed, there would no longer be an axe, except by equivo-

15   cation.[26] Now [the essence with the body], here, is an axe; but the soul is the essence and the formula not of such a body,[27] but of such a natural body which has in itself the principle of moving and of stopping.[28]

    What has just been said should be observed in the parts [of a living body] also. If the eye were an animal, its vision would be its soul; for vision is the

20   eye's *substance* with respect to [the eye's] formula. The eye[29] itself is the matter for vision; and if [vision] departs, there is no eye any longer, except equivocally, as in the case of the eye in a statue or a painting.[30] What was stated of the part [the eye] should be taken to apply to the whole living body, for there is an analogy; this part is to that part [in the case of the eye] as the

25   sentient power as a whole is to the whole sentient body qua such.[31] Thus, that which is potentially living is not that which has lost the soul but that which possesses it.[32] As for the seed or the fruit, it is potentially such and

413a   such a body.[33] Now being awake as an actuality is like seeing or cutting, but the soul as [a first] actuality is like vision and the power of the instrument [i.e., of the axe];[34] and the body[32] is that which exists as potentiality. And just as the eye is its vision with its pupil,[35] so the animal is its soul with its body.

    It is not unclear, then, that the soul, or parts of it if by its nature it has

5   parts, cannot be separated from the body; for the actualities in some [living things] are those of the parts themselves.[36] But nothing prevents some actualities[37] from being separable, because they are not actualities of any body. Further, it is not clear whether the soul as the actuality of the body is like the sailor of the boat.[38]

10   In outline, then, let the above distinctions and sketch concerning the soul suffice for the present.

2

    Since what is clear and more known with respect to formula[1] arises from what is unclear but more evident [to us], let us try, by the use of such [method], to go over the soul once more; for the formula which defines the

15   soul should not only make us know the fact, as most definitions do, but also include and make evident the cause.[2] Formulae which are given as definitions nowadays are like conclusions. For instance, what is squaring [of an oblong rectangle]? It is the [construction of an] equilateral rectangle which is equal in area to an oblong rectangle. Now such a definition is a formula of the conclusion. But if a definition states that squaring an oblong rectangle

20   is finding the mean proportional of the sides of that rectangle, it states the cause of the thing.[3]

As a starting-point of our inquiry, then, let us state that an animate thing is distinguished from an inanimate thing by living. The term "living" has many senses; but let us say that a thing is living even if it has in itself only one of the following: the intellect, the power of sensation, the power of producing motion and of stopping with respect to place, the power of moving with respect to nutrition, that of deterioration, and that of growth.[4] Thus all plants, too, are thought to be living; for they appear to possess in themselves such a power and a principle through which they grow and deteriorate in contrary directions, for those which are constantly nourished and continue to live grow [and deteriorate] not only upwards without doing so downwards, but alike in both directions, indeed in every direction, and they do so as long as they are able to take in food.

Now the power of nutrition can exist apart from the other powers, but in mortal beings[5] none of the other powers can exist apart from this power. This fact is evident in plants; for no power other than that of nutrition belongs to them.[6] Accordingly, living belongs to [all] living things because of this principle, but it belongs to animals primarily because of the power of sensation, for even those beings which have no power to be in motion or go to another place but have the power of sensation are called "animals" and not only "living things".[7] Of the sentient powers, that of touch is primary;[8] and just as the nutritive power can exist apart from that of touch or any other power of sensation, so the power of touch can exist apart from any of the other powers of sensation. By "power of nutrition" we mean such part of the soul of which plants partake also; all animals, however, are observed to have the power of touch. As for the cause of each of these facts, it will be discussed later.[9]

At present let us say only so much, that the soul is the principle of the [functions] already stated and that it is defined[10] by the power of nutrition or of sensation or of *thinking* or of producing motion.[11] Whether each of these powers is a soul or a part of a soul,[12] and, if a part, whether it is such as to be separable only in definition or also in place, are problems to be faced.[13] In the case of certain powers the solution is not difficult to perceive; in the case of some others, there are difficulties. For just as in the case of some plants, when each is divided and the parts are separated, each part appears to continue to live, as if the soul of each such plant is actually one but potentially many, so in the case of some insects, when cut into parts, other kinds of soul[14] are observed to continue to live. For each part has both the power of sensation and that of locomotion, and if the power of sensation, it has also the powers of imagination[15] and of desire; for whenever there is sensation, there is also pleasure and pain, and whenever these exist, *desire* too must exist. With regard to the intellect or the speculative faculty, it is not yet evident; but this seems to be a different genus of soul, and [perhaps] it alone can be separated [from the body], just as that which is eternal [can

30

414a

5

be separated] from that which is destructible.[16] As for the other parts of the soul, it is evident from what we have said that they are not separable,[17] in spite of what some thinkers say.[18] But it is evident that they are distinct in definition; for the essence of a sentient power is distinct from the essence of a power of forming opinions, if indeed sensing and forming opinions are distinct, and similarly with each of the other powers mentioned.[19] Further, some animals have all the powers mentioned and some have only some of them, but some [living things] have only one power; and it is from this fact that the differentiae of animals arise.[20] As for the cause of this fact, it will be considered later.[21] Almost the same remarks apply to the powers of sensation; for some animals have all of them, others have some of them, and certain animals have only the one most necessary, and this is the power of touch.

Now the expression "that by which we live or sense" has two meanings, just like the expression "that by which we *know*" (in which the word "that" may mean either *knowledge* or the soul, for we speak of *knowing* by one or by the other) and similarly for the expression "that by which we are healthy" (in which "that"[22] may mean either health or a part of the body, or even the whole body). Further, of these meanings, *knowledge* or health

10

15

20

25

is a *form* or a form of some kind or a formula and, as it were, the *actuality*[23] of the receptive subject, which is the subject which *knows* [in the case of *knowing*] but the subject which is healthy in the case of health (for the *actuality* of that which can act is thought to be in the subject which is affected or is [so] disposed). Accordingly, since the soul is primarily that[24] by which we live or sense or *think*, it would be the formula or the form but not the matter or the subject [of the living thing]. For, as we have already stated, the term "substance" has three meanings, i.e., form, matter, and the composite of these two; and of these three, matter is potentiality, but form is actuality. So since the living thing is the composite of the two, it is not the body that is the actuality of the soul, but the soul that is the actuality of the body, and of a certain [kind of] body.[25] And, because of this, those who think that the soul does not exist without a body or is not a body of any sort have the right belief. For the soul is not a body but something of[26] a body, and, because of this, it exists in a body. But it exists in such and such a body and not as the earlier thinkers thought; they fitted it to a body without further specifying what that body is or what kind of a body it is, although there is no evidence that any chance body can receive any chance soul.[27] According to reason, too, the case is such as the following: each thing's actuality by its nature can exist [only] with the [kind of] potentiality which belongs to that thing or with its appropriate matter.[28]

It is evident from the above remarks, then, that the soul is a certain actuality or formula of that which has the potentiality of being such and such a thing.[29]

3

30   Of the soul's powers mentioned above, namely, those of nutrition, desire,
sensation, locomotion, and *thinking*,[1] some living things possess all, as we
said, others some, and others only one.[2] Plants possess the power of nutrition
414b only,[3] other living things possess this and also the power of sensation.[4] Those
which possess the power of sensation have the appetitive power[5] also. For
the species of desire are *desire* and temper and wish,[6] and all animals have
at least one power of sensation, that of touch; but that which has sensation
5   has also pleasure and pain and is affected by pleasurable and painful objects,[7] and, if so, it has *desire* also, since *desire* is a desire for the pleasurable.[8]
Further, [all animals] have the power of sensing food.[9] Food is sensed by
touch, since all animals are nourished by dry and moist and hot and cold
objects, all of which are sensed by touch; but the other sensible objects are
10   sensed by touch only indirectly;[10] for sounds and colors and odors contribute
nothing to food, whereas flavors are a species of tangible [qualities]. Hunger
and thirst are *desires*, hunger being a *desire* for dry and hot objects, and
thirst for cold and moist objects; and flavor is a sort of seasoning of these
objects. These facts will be made clear later,[11] but at present let us say so
15   much, that those animals which have [the power of] touch have [the power
of] desire also. As for imagination, it is not clear; but it will be examined
later.[12] Some animals possess also the power of locomotion, and others, i.e.,
men and perhaps beings such as men or even more honorable than men,
possess also the power of *thinking* and an intellect.[13]
20   It is clear [from the above discussion], then, that a single formula for a
soul could be given in the same manner as for a figure;[14] for neither does
a figure exist apart from the triangle [and the quadrilateral] and the rest [of
the species of figures], nor does a soul exist apart from the [kinds of] souls
listed above.[15] A common formula for a figure, too, can be given which will
fit all [kinds of] figures, but it will not be proper to any [one kind]; and
25   similarly in the case of the [kinds of] soul mentioned above.[16] In view of this,
it is ridiculous to seek a common formula which will apply to these or other
such cases but fail to be proper to things or appropriate to each ultimate
species, but not seek one which is proper to a thing or appropriate to each
species.[17]
            There is a parallelism in the [kinds of] figures and in the [kinds of] soul;
30   for in both figures and animate things there is a succession in which that
which is prior exists always potentially in that which is posterior. For
instance, the triangle exists [potentially] in the quadrilateral, and the nutritive power exists [potentially] in the sentient power,[18] and so one must seek
the whatness of each kind. For instance, "What is the soul of a plant?",
"What is the soul of man?", "What is the soul of a nonrational animal?".
415a   The *reason*[19] why [the powers of the soul] are related in such succession is
a matter which requires consideration; for the sentient power cannot exist

without the nutritive power, but the latter power can exist without the former, as it does in plants. Again, without the sense of touch none of the other senses can exist; but the sense of touch can exist without any of the other senses, for there are many animals which have neither vision nor a sense of hearing nor a sense of smell at all. Again, of living things which have the power of sensation, some have the power of locomotion but others do not.[20] Finally, some living things — very few — have [also] the power of judging and of *thinking;* for, of mortal beings,[21] those which have the power of judging have all the other powers also, but those which have one of the latter powers do not all have the power of judging, and, of the latter, some do not even have imagination while others live only by imagination.[22] Concerning the speculative intellect, its discussion[23] is of another kind.

It is clear, then, that the formula most appropriate to each of these [powers] is also the formula of each [kind of] soul.

4

One who intends to make an inquiry into the kinds of soul must first grasp the whatness of each kind and then proceed to what follows or what other things should be sought.[1] On the other hand, if one is to state what each of these is, e.g., what the thinking or the sentient or the nutritive power is, prior to this he should state what thinking or sensing [or taking in food] is; for activities or *actions* are prior in formula to the corresponding powers. If so, then, again, since the objects to which the activities are directed should be investigated before the activities, for the same *reason* those objects (e.g., food, sensible object, object of thought) would have to be determined first.[2]

First, then, we should discuss food and reproduction; for the nutritive soul exists in the other kinds of soul and is the primary and most common power of souls,[3] and it is in virtue of this [power] that living[4] belongs to all living things. The function of this soul is to reproduce and to use food. For the most natural function of living things which are perfect and neither defective nor generated by chance[5] is to produce another thing like itself (e.g., an animal produces an animal [of the same kind], and a plant likewise a plant) in order that they may partake of the eternal and the divine as far as they can; for all [living things] 'desire' [the eternal and the divine], and it is for the sake of this that those which *act* according to nature do so. The expression "that for the sake of which", of course, has two senses: (a) that which is done, and (b) that for which it is done.[6] Accordingly, since [such] living things cannot share in the eternal and the divine continuously (because no destructible thing, which is the same and numerically one, can last forever), they partake of the eternal and the divine only as far as they can, some sharing in these more, others doing so less; and what lasts forever is not that which is [numerically one and] the same, but something like it, i.e., something which is one not numerically but in species.[7]

The soul is the cause and the principle of a living body. Now the terms "cause" and "principle" have many senses, and, similarly, the soul is a cause
10   in the three specified senses of "cause"; for it is a cause as a source of motion, and as a final cause, and as the *substance* of an animate body.[8]

Clearly, it is a cause as the *substance* [of an animate body]; for the cause of the existence of each thing is the *substance* of that thing, existence in living things is life, and the cause and principle [in living things] is the soul.[9]
15   Further, the formula of that which exists potentially is its actuality.[10]

It is evident that the soul is a cause as final cause also. For just as the intellect acts for the sake of something, so does nature, and nature's end is a final cause. Such [end] in animals is the soul and [is an end] according to their nature; for all natural bodies are instruments of the soul, and, as in the
20   case of animals, so in the case of plants, [natural bodies] exist for the sake of their soul.[11] And, [as already stated], "that for the sake of which" has two senses: (a) that which is done, and (b) that for which it is done.[12]

Finally, the soul is also a cause as a source of motion with respect to place, but such power does not exist in all living things. Alteration and growth, too, exist [in living things] by virtue of their soul; for sensation is thought to be
25   a species of alteration, and no thing without soul can have sensations. Similar remarks apply to growth and deterioration; for no thing can by its nature grow or deteriorate without taking in food, and no thing can be nourished unless it shares in life.[13]

416a   Empedocles did not speak rightly when he added that the roots of plants grow downwards because the earth [in them] according to its nature travels downwards, and that the [branches] grow upwards because fire [in them according to its nature] travels upwards. First, he did not grasp the terms "up" and "down" rightly, for up and down are not the same for all things as they are for the universe; if the organs of the body are to be called "the
5   same" or "different" according to their functions, then heads are to animals as roots are to trees.[14] Further, what is it that holds together the earth and the fire [in an animal] which tend to travel in contrary directions? They would part from each other, unless there were something to prevent separation; but if there is something, this would be the soul and [also] the cause of growing and of taking in food.[15]
10   Some[16] are of the opinion that fire's nature is without qualification the cause of food and of growth; for, according to them, fire alone of all the bodies or elements appears to nourish itself and to grow. And in view of this, one might come to the belief that it is fire that performs the function of causing growth and nourishment in both plants and animals. Now fire is in some way a joint cause; however, it is not the cause without qualification.
15   It is rather the soul which is the cause. For the growth of fire proceeds indefinitely, as long as there is fuel to be burned; but a thing which is composed by nature of all [the elements] has a limit and a [certain] ratio [of

elements] with respect to both size and growth, and these [i.e., limit and ratio] belong to the soul and not to fire, and to the formula rather than to the matter of that thing.[17]

20 Since it is the same power of the soul that is both nutritive and reproductive, we must specify first what food is; for this power is distinguished from the others by its function of taking in food. Now it is thought that food is a contrary of [another] contrary, though not of every [kind of] contrary, but of that which is generated and also increased in size from its contrary;[18] for, in many cases, one contrary is generated from its contrary, but not all of 25 them are quantities, as in the case of a healthy man from a sick man.[19] But not even the above-mentioned contraries[20] appear to be food to each other in the same way; for water is food to fire, but fire does not nourish water.[21] So it is in simple bodies most of all that one of two contraries is thought to be food and the other to be that which is nourished.[22]

30 Yet there is a difficulty. For some of these thinkers say that like is nourished by like,[23] just as it grows by like; but, as already stated, others have the opposite opinion, namely, that it is a contrary which is nourished by its contrary, since (a) like is not affected by like and food must change and be digested and (b) change in every case proceeds to that which is opposite or 35 intermediate.[24] Again, food is acted upon in a certain way by that which 416b is nourished; but the latter is not acted upon by food, just as the carpenter is not acted upon by his materials; for it is the materials that are acted upon by the carpenter, whereas he himself changes only from inactivity to activity.[25] Now it makes a difference whether food is that which is finally taken or that which is initially taken into the body. If it is food in both cases, the 5 first being undigested but the second digested, then the term "food" would have two meanings; for insofar as food is undigested, it is *contrary* to that which is nourished, but insofar as it is digested, it is *like* that which is nourished. So it is evident that each of the two views is in one sense right but in another sense wrong.[26]

10 Since no thing is nourished unless it partakes of life, that which is nourished would be an animate body qua animate; so food, too, is relative to an animate body and not [just] an accident of it.[27] But to be food and to be a thing which can cause growth are distinct. For insofar as the animate body is a quantity, that which nourishes can cause the body [merely] to grow; but insofar as that body is a certain *this* and a substance, that which nourishes is food, for it preserves the *substance* [of that body], and [that body] contin- 15 ues to exist as long as it can be nourished.[28] And food can also act in the generation not of that which is nourished (for the *substance* of that which is nourished already exists, and a thing which exists preserves itself but does not reproduce itself), but of another [substance] like that which is nourished.[29] So such a principle of the soul is a power of such a nature as to preserve that[30] which has it[31] and to preserve it[32] qua such,[33] while food

provides [the material necessary] for the activity [of that power]. For this
20   reason, an [animate thing] cannot exist if it is deprived of food.

There are three things [in nutrition]: (a) that which is nourished, (b) that
with which a thing is nourished, and (c) that which acts in nourishing. That
which acts is the primary soul,[34] that which is nourished is the body which
has that soul, and that with which [the body] is nourished is food. So since
it is just to name things after the ends [they aim at][35], and since the end [of
25   an animate thing] is to reproduce another thing like itself,[36] the primary soul
would be the soul which can reproduce a thing like itself. Now the phrase
"that with which it is nourished" has two meanings, like the phrase "that
with which one steers"; for the latter may mean either the hand or the
rudder, one of which is both a mover and a thing moved, but the other only
a mover. Thus all food must be capable of being digested, and that whose
activity causes digestion is heat.[37] For this reason, every animate thing has
heat.
30   We have now given an outline of what food is; further clarification will
be taken up later in a treatise[38] appropriate to that subject.

5

Having made the above distinctions, let us discuss what is common to all
the kinds of sensation.[1] Now sensation depends on being moved and being
35   affected, as already stated; for it is thought to be a species of alteration.[2] But
417a   some thinkers say that also like is acted upon by like.[3] How this is possible
or impossible has already been discussed in our general treatise on acting
and being acted upon.[4] There is the problem, however, as to why there can
be no sensation of the sensations themselves as well, and why [the sense
organs] do not themselves produce sensations without the external objects,
5   although there exist in [those organs] fire and earth and the other elements,
which are objects of sensation, whether directly or indirectly through their
attributes.[5]

Now it is clear that the sentient [soul or part] exists not in activity but only
potentially.[6] Thus it is like fuel, which does not itself burn by being fuel,
unless there is something to cause it to burn; otherwise it would cause itself
10   to burn and would have no need of actual fire to set it afire. Then since "to
sense" has two meanings (for (1) that which has the capacity to hear or to
see is said to hear or to see, even if it happens to be asleep, but also (2) that
which is *actually* hearing or seeing), the term "sensation", too, would have
two meanings;[7] it may mean either sensation as potentiality or sensation
when in activity. Similarly, the term "to sense",[8] too, may mean either to
have the potentiality of sensing or to be *actually* sensing.

15   First, let us state that being acted upon and being moved and being in
activity are the same;[9] for motion, too, is an activity, but incomplete, as
stated elsewhere.[10] Now everything which is acted upon or moved is acted

upon or moved by that which can act and *actually* does so. For this reason,
a thing is acted upon in one sense by what is like it but in another sense by
what is unlike it, as already stated;[11] for what is acted upon is unlike [the
agent], but after it has been acted upon, it is like [the agent].[12]

We must distinguish also the senses of "potentiality" and of "actuality",
for up to now we have been using them without qualifying the senses of
each. We call something "a *knower*" (a) in the sense in which we might say
that a man is a *knower*, since he can be a *knower* or have *knowledge*, but
also (b) in the sense in which a man already has *knowledge*, e.g., grammatical *knowledge*. Each of these two men is capable [of *knowing*], but not in
the same manner; the first is capable in view of the fact that his kind and
his matter are of a certain sort,[13] the second in the sense that he can exercise
the *knowledge* [he already has], if he wishes, provided that no external agent
prevents him. But (c) in a third and dominant sense we call a man "a *knower*"
if he is actually exercising his *knowledge* when contemplating a given fact.
The first two men are *knowers* in virtue of a potentiality; but whereas the one
has the potentiality of altering by learning and often by changing from a
contrary habit,[14] the other has the potentiality [of changing] in another way,
e.g., from the inactive possession of sense[15] or of grammar to the exercise of
that possession.[16]

The term "to be acted upon", too, does not have a single meaning. In one
sense, it means a kind of destruction by a contrary, in another, it means
rather a preservation of a thing which exists potentially by a similar thing
which exists actually in a manner in which potentiality is related to actuality; for that which possesses *knowledge* becomes that which exercises that
knowledge, and this becoming, as such, either is not an alteration (for the
progress is towards itself and in its actuality) or is an alteration of a different
kind.[17] In view of this, it is not right to say that a prudent man is changed
in quality when he is judging rightly, just as it is not right to say that a
builder is changed in quality when he is building a house.[18] Accordingly,
it is just to say that that which changes a thing from being potential to the
actuality of that potentiality with respect to thinking or judging rightly is
not teaching but should have some other name, and that which, from being
potential, learns or acquires *knowledge* by that which actually [*knows*] and
can teach, either (a) should not be called "being acted upon," as already
stated, or (b), [if called "an alteration"], this term should be taken in two
senses: (i) as a change to a privative disposition, and (ii) as a change to a
[positive] habit and to the nature [of the thing learned].[19]

In the case of the sentient soul, the first change occurs by that which gives
birth to [the animal with that soul]. When born, the animal now possesses
sensing in a way in which one possesses *knowledge*; and we speak of the
actual [sensing by that being] in the same way as we speak of the exercise
of *knowledge*.[20] But there is a difference. [In the case of sensation], that

which acts in producing *actual* sensation is external to the thing which senses it, and this is the visible or the audible or any of the other sensible objects; and the cause of this is the fact that sensation, when *actual*, is of an individual object.[21] *Knowledge*, on the other hand, is of things universally taken, and these[22] exist in the soul in a certain manner. It is in view of this that thinking depends upon a man whenever he wishes to think; but sensing does not depend on him [alone], for a sensible object must be present.[23] Similar remarks apply to *knowledge* of sensibles,[24] and for the same *reason*, for sensible objects are individuals and are external to man.

25

Further clarification of the above matters will be made later at the appropriate time.[25] At present, it is sufficient to make the following distinctions: just as "to be potentially" has more than one sense, one of them being the sense in which we might say that a boy can lead an army, the other being the sense in which an adult [who is a general] can lead an army, so it is with "the sentient soul". Since there are no names to bring out these differences, but since we pointed out the fact that things which exist potentially may differ and also the manner in which they may differ, we must use "to be acted upon" and "to be altered" as if they were basic names for the two differences;[26] but the sentient soul exists potentially in a way like the sensible object when this already exists in actuality, as already stated.[27] Accordingly, while this soul is being acted upon, it is unlike that object; but after it has been acted upon, it is a likeness of that object and exists in a way like that object.[28]

30

418a

5

6

In dealing with each power of sensation, we should first discuss the corresponding sensible object.[1] The term "sensible object" has three senses, in two of which we say that the object is sensed directly [or essentially or in itself], while in the third we say that the object is sensed [accidentally or] indirectly. In one of the first two senses, the object is proper to one sense, but in the other, it is common to all[2] the senses. By "proper" I mean a sensible object (a) which cannot be sensed by any of the other senses and (b) about which the corresponding sense cannot be mistaken. For example, vision is of color, the sense of hearing is of sound, and the sense of taste is of flavor. In the case of the sense of touch there are a number of differences, yet each sense discriminates the corresponding objects and is not mistaken about those objects.[3] Thus vision is not mistaken about the colors it senses, nor the sense of hearing about the sounds; but each sense may be mistaken as to what the [substance] which has color is,[4] or where it is, or what the [substance] which is sounding is, or where it is. Sensible objects such as these, then, are said to be proper to the corresponding senses.

10

15

The things which are called "common sensibles" are motion, rest, number, shape, and magnitude, for each of them is not proper to any one sense

20   but is common to all; for motion can be sensed by touch, and by vision,
[etc.].⁵

Sensible objects which are said to be sensed indirectly [or accidentally]
are, for example, the son of Diares, if he is white, since it is by way of an
attribute [i.e., whiteness] that man senses him [as a substance]; for what he
senses [directly] is [the attribute] whiteness, which belongs to the son of
Diares. For this reason, vision is not even affected by the sensible object qua
being such a thing [i.e., a substance].⁶

Of the direct sensibles, those which are proper are sensible in the basic
25   sense, and it is to them that the *substance* of each sense [or sensation] is by
its nature related.⁷

7

That to which vision is related is the visible object; and the visible object
is (a) color¹ and (b) an object which may be expressed by a formula but
happens to be nameless.² This will become clear as we proceed. Now the
30   visible object is color,³ and this exists on that [i.e., the surface] which is visible
in virtue of itself; and by "in virtue of itself" I mean not by its formula but
by the fact that it has in itself the cause of being visible.⁴

418b   Now every color can set in motion a transparent medium which exists in
activity, and this is the nature of color. It is indeed for this reason that no
[color] is visible without light, but every color of a thing is visible in light.
So we should discuss first what light is.⁵

There is something which is transparent; and by "transparent" I mean
5   that which is visible, not visible in itself, simply speaking, but visible because
of a color belonging to another kind of object.⁶ Such a thing is air, water,
and many solid bodies; for water or air is transparent not qua water or qua
air, respectively, but by the fact that there is a nature in them which is the
same in both and also in the eternal body of the uppermost region of the
10   universe.⁷ Now light is the activity of what is transparent qua being transparent; and darkness, too, exists in it [the transparent medium], but poten-
tially.⁸ Light, then, is as it were the color⁹ of the transparent medium when
the latter is caused to exist in actuality by fire or a thing such as a celestial
body, for this [body], too, has something which is one and the same [as that
which fire has].¹⁰

We have stated what the transparent¹¹ is and what light is. Light is neither
15   fire,¹² nor a body at all, nor yet something which emanates¹³ from a body
(for, if so, it too would be a body), but the presence in a transparent medium
of something¹⁴ which comes from fire or from some other such thing; for
two bodies cannot exist at the same time in the same place.¹⁵ Now light is
thought to be contrary to darkness; darkness, however, is the privation of
20   such disposition in the transparent (body), so it is clear that the presence of
that disposition is light.¹⁶ So Empedocles, or any one whose doctrine is

similar to his, is not right in saying that light travels and that at some
moment it is somewhere between the Earth and that which surrounds it but
escapes our notice; for this doctrine is contrary both to truth [which follows]
from argument and to what is observed. For if the interval traversed were
short, light [so taken] might escape our notice, but that it does so from East
to West is too big a claim to accept.[17]

That which can receive color is [itself] without color, and that which can
receive sound is [itself] without sound.[18] That which is without color is (a)
the transparent and (b) the invisible or the hardly visible (such as is thought
to be dark); and such is the transparent, but when it exists potentially and
not in actuality, for it is the same nature which is at one time darkness but
at another time light.[19] However, not everything which is visible is visible
in light, but only the appropriate color of each thing; for some things are
not visible in light but produce sensation in darkness, that is, those which
appear fiery or luminous (there is no single name for these), e.g., fungi, flesh,
and the heads, scales, and eyes of fishes; but in none of these is the appropriate color seen. A discussion of the *reason* why these things are thus seen
belongs elsewhere.[20] At present this much is evident, that what is seen in
light is color, and for this reason no color is seen without light; for, as already
stated, to be a color is to be that which causes motion in that which is
transparent when in activity,[21] and light is the actuality of that which is
transparent. This is evident from the following sign. If a colored object is
placed in contact with the eyes, its color will not be seen; but [if the object
is placed at a distance], the color moves the transparent medium, e.g., the
air, and this, being continuously in motion [up to the eye], moves this sense
organ.[22]

Democritus, then, does not speak rightly when he thinks that, if the
intervening space were to become void, one would see an ant distinctly even
if it were in the sky; for this is impossible. Seeing takes place when the
[organ] of sense is affected in a certain way, but the [organ] of sense cannot
be affected [directly] by what is seen, the color itself; what remains, then,
is that it is affected only by what is between the color and the eye, and so
there must be some [medium] between [the eye and the color]. If, on the
other hand, the intervening space were void, it would be true to say, not
that the color will be seen distinctly, but that the color will not be seen at
all.[23]

We have stated, then, the *reason* why color must be seen in light. As for
fire, it can be seen in darkness as well as in light, and this fact is necessary;
for [in darkness] the [potentially] transparent becomes [actually] transparent
by the action of fire.[24]

The same arguments apply to sound and to odor, too, for neither of these
produces sensation when in contact with the corresponding sense organ. So
it is the intervening medium that is moved by odor and sound, and it is by

the intervening medium that the corresponding sense organ is moved. And
whenever the object which produces sound or odor is placed in contact with
30   the corresponding sense órgan, it produces no sensation. Similar remarks
apply to touch and taste, although this does not appear to be the case; but
the *reason* for the [apparent difference] will become clear later.²⁵ The
intervening medium in the case of sound is air. But in the case of odor the
medium has no name; for here there is an *attribute* which is common to
35   air and water, and this *attribute* is related to that which has odor as transparency is related to [that which has] color. For aquatic animals, too, appear
419b   to have the power of sensing odors; but men and other terrestrial animals
which breathe cannot sense odors without breathing air in.²⁶ The *reason* for
this, too, will be discussed later.²⁷

8

5   First, let us make some distinctions concerning sound and hearing. The
term "sound" may mean (1) a certain activity, or (2) a certain power. For
we say that some things (e.g., sponge and wool) have no sound, but that
others (e.g., bronze and other solid and smooth objects) have sound in the
sense that they can make sound, and this means that they can produce
actual sound [in a medium] which is between themselves and the power of
10   hearing.¹ *Actual* sound arises when there is always (a) something [struck]
which is (b) related to something else [which strikes] in (c) something [a
medium]; for that which produces sound is a collision. In view of this, sound
cannot be produced when only one of the above is present. For that which
strikes is different from that which is struck, and so that which is sounding
does so when related to something else; and a collision cannot occur without
locomotion.²

As we said, then, sound is not [produced by] the collision³ of any chance
15   things; for, when struck, wool produces no sound, but bronze and things
which are smooth and hollow do. Bronze produces it by being smooth;
hollow things produce it by the repeated collisions due to reflection after
the first blow, since the [medium] which is moved cannot escape. Further,
sound can be heard both in air and in water, though less loudly [in water].
But the main [mover] of sound⁴ is neither air nor water, for two solids must
20   collide with each other and with the air; and this⁵ occurs when the air struck
stays together and is not dispersed. For this reason, it is when the collision
occurs quickly and with force that the [object struck] makes sound; for the
motion of the striking object should forestall the scattering of the air, just
as if one were to strike at a heap or a mass of sand quickly.
25   An echo is produced when air, [when struck,] kept unified because its
container confines it and prevents it from being scattered, rebounds like a
ball.⁶ It seems likely that echo is always produced but is not distinctly
audible, since surely the same thing happens with sound as with light. For

30   light, too, is always reflected[7] (otherwise it would not exist everywhere[8] but, except for the things illuminated by the Sun, there would be darkness[9]); but, as we define it, it is not reflected in the manner in which it is from water or bronze or any other smooth surface so as to produce a shadow.[10]

    Void is rightly said to be basic to hearing, for air is thought to be void;
35 and air produces hearing when it is moved continuously and in a unified
420a manner.[11] So if that which is struck is not smooth, the air is hardly heard because it is dissipated; but if the surface is smooth, then the air [in activity] becomes unified because of that surface, for the surface of a smooth body is itself one [in kind]. Accordingly, that which can produce sound is that which can move the air in a unified and continuous manner up to the sense of hearing, which is by nature attached to the air [in the ear]. And because
5 hearing depends on air, when the air outside [the ear] is moved, it causes the air inside [the ear] to be moved. For this reason, an animal does not hear with every [part of the body], nor does air go through every [part of the body]; for the animate part which will be moved and has air in it is not any part of the body.

    Now air itself is without sound because it is easily scattered; but when it is prevented from being scattered, its motion is sound.[12] The air in the ear,
10 on the other hand, is built in deeply and tends to be motionless, so that [the sense of hearing] can sense accurately all the differences of the motions [transmitted from the external sounding air].[13] Because of this, we can hear even in water; for water does not enter the air which by its nature is [built in] with the ear.[14] Nor does water enter the ear through the convolutions; but whenever it does, one cannot hear. Nor does one hear if the tympanic
15 membrane is ailing, just as one cannot see if the pupil is ailing. Further, a sign of whether we hear or not is the continuous ringing sound in the ear, as in a horn; for the air in the ear has always a motion which is appropriate to itself,[15] but sound [in external air] is of a different nature and is not proper [to the air in the ear]. And, because of this, it is said that we hear with the void and the resonant; for we hear with that which has air enclosed within it.[16]

20   Which is it that makes sound, the striking body or the body struck? Is it not both, each in its own way? For sound is a [certain] motion of that which can be moved in the manner in which a thing[17] rebounds when it is caused to strike a smooth surface. However, as already stated, not everything that strikes or is struck produces sound, e.g., if a needle were to strike against
25 a needle; but that which is struck should have a flat surface and so enable the air to rebound and vibrate as a unified whole. The differences in the bodies which produce sound are made known by way of *actual* sound; for just as colors are not distinguished by vision without light, so acute [i.e., high] and grave [i.e., low] notes are not distinguished without [*actual*] sound.[18] The terms "acute" and "grave" here are metaphors and are borrowed from

30 terms used for tangible bodies; for a thing is [said to be] acute if it moves the sense much in a short time, but it is [said to be] grave if it moves the sense little in a long time. Now what is acute is not fast, and what is grave is not slow; it is the motion [in the sense organ] which occurs in such a manner, being fast [when one senses the acute] because of its high speed,

420b but slow [when one senses the grave] because of its low speed.[19] And the acute and the blunt in relation to touch seem to be analogous to the acute and grave in relation to sound; for, in a manner of speaking, what is acute stabs but what is blunt pushes by producing motion, the acute acting in a short time but the grave acting in a long time. So it is indirectly that the

5 [acute sound] is fast but the [grave] is slow.[20] Concerning sound, then, let the above distinctions suffice.

 Voice is a certain sound of an animate being.[21] Thus no inanimate thing makes a vocal sound, and it is only in virtue of a similarity that it is said to do so, as in the case of the flute or the lyre or any inanimate thing which has musical range and tune and articulation; for it seems that voice, too, has

10 these traits.[22] Now many animals have no voice, e.g., those which have no blood and, of those which have blood, fish. And this is reasonable, since sound as such is a certain motion of air. Fish which are said to make vocal sounds, such as those in the river Achelous, make sound only with their gills or some other such part.[23] Voice, then, is a sound of an animal, but it is not a sound of any chance part of an animal. And since in every instance of a

15 sounding object there is that which strikes, that which is struck, and that [the medium] in which these occur, the last of which is air, it is with good reason that only animals which take in air should be making vocal sounds.[24]

 Now nature in this case uses the air inhaled for two functions; and just as it uses the tongue for taste and communication, of which taste is necessary for life (and for this reason it exists in many kinds of animals) but convey-

20 ance of thought is for the sake of living well, so it uses breath for internal warmth, which is necessary for life (the cause of this will be discussed elsewhere),[25] but also for voice, which is for the sake of a good life.

 The organ of respiration is the larynx, and this part exists for the sake of the lung; for it is by means of the latter part [of the body, i.e., the lung] that,

25 of all animals, those which are terrestrial are kept most warm. But the primary region of the heart, too, requires respiration; and it is for this reason that during respiration air must be drawn in. So voice is the impact of the air breathed on the so-called "windpipe" and is caused by the soul in these parts of the body. For, as already stated, not every sound made by an animal

30 is voice (sound can be made also by the tongue and when one is coughing), but that which produces the impact should be animate and do so with some image. For voice is a certain kind of sound with meaning and not any sound

421a of the air breathed, like a cough; the animal uses the air breathed to strike the air in the windpipe against the windpipe. A sign of this is the fact that

an animal cannot make a vocal sound while inhaling or exhaling, but only while holding the breath; for it is [only] with the breath held that an animal causes the motion [which makes a vocal sound].²⁶ It is evident, too, why fish
5   have no voice; because they have no larynx. And they do not have this part since they neither take in air nor breathe. As to the cause of this, it is a matter whose discussion belongs elsewhere.²⁷

9

Odor and the object of smell are less easily defined than the [sensibles] already discussed; for the kind of a thing that odor is is not so clear as that of sound or of color. The cause of this is the fact that the sense which we
10   have of it is not accurate but inferior to that of many animals;¹ for man smells odors poorly and does not sense any object of smell unless it be painful or pleasant, and this indicates that the corresponding sense organ is not accurate. It is reasonable to think that hard-eyed animals,² too, sense colors in a similar way, and that differences of color are not clearly sensed by them
15   except when they do or do not cause fear.³ It is in this manner, too, that the race of men are sensing odors; for although there seems to be an analogy⁴ between the sense of taste and the sense of smell and a similarity between the species of flavors and those of odors, men's sense of taste is more accurate [than their sense of smell] because the sense of taste is a species of the sense
20   of touch,⁵ and the sense which is most accurate in men is that of touch. Now with respect to the other senses man is far inferior to the other animals; but with respect to the sense of touch he excels by far in accuracy over the other animals, and for this reason man is the most prudent of all animals.⁶ A sign of this is the fact that, even within the human race, it is by virtue of the organ of this and of no other sense that men are well but others are poorly
25   gifted by nature [for *thought*]; for those with hard flesh are poorly gifted by nature for *thought* but those with soft flesh are well gifted.

Now just as some flavors are sweet but others bitter, so are odors. But some [flavors and odors] have these [qualities, i.e., sweetness, or bitterness] in an analogous manner (I mean that odors and flavors are sweet in an analogous
30   manner), while others have them in a contrary manner. Similarly, too, an odor may be pungent or harsh or acid or oily. But, as we have said, because odors, unlike flavors, are not very clearly sensed, they have taken the names
421b   of these [qualities] from those of the flavors in virtue of their similarity; for instance, the odor of saffron, like the flavor of honey, is called "sweet", and the odor of thyme or of others like it is called "pungent", and similarly in the other cases.⁷

Of the senses, just as that of hearing is of audible and inaudible objects
5   and [vision] is of visible or invisible objects, so the sense of smell is of that which can and that which cannot be smelt. The expression "that which cannot be smelt" may mean an object which cannot have odor at all or an

object which has a slight or a poor odor.[8] Also the term "tasteless" has similar meanings. Smelling, too, occurs through a medium, such as air or water; for also aquatic animals, with or without blood, are thought to smell odors like animals which depend on air, for some of them, affected by scents, travel great distances for their food. And in view of this, a difficulty appears to arise, whether all animals smell in the same way or not; for man smells while inhaling, but not while exhaling or holding his breath, whether the [odorous object] is far or near or even placed inside the nostril and in contact with it.[8] Again, the inability to sense [odorous] objects when in contact with the sense organ is common to all [animals], but the inability to sense them without inhaling is proper to man,[9] and this becomes clear by trying. So since animals without blood do not breathe, they might have a sense different from the above-mentioned. But this is impossible, if it is odors as such that they sense; for the sense which senses an object of smell, whether its odor be foul or fragrant, is that of smell. Further, it appears that these animals are even destroyed by [certain] strong odors just as men are, e.g., by odors of asphalt, sulphur, and the like. So they must be able to smell, but not while inhaling.[11]

It seems, then, that the organ of this sense in a man differs from that in the other animals, just as his eyes differ from those of hard-eyed animals; for man's eyes have a covering, the eyelids, which he uses like a sheath, and he cannot see without moving and raising them, but hard-eyed animals have no such thing but see immediately whatever takes place in the transparent medium. So in these animals the organ of smell, too, seems to be without cover, just as their eyes are, but in [animals] which take in air the organ of smell seems to have a covering which is drawn back during inhalation due to the dilation of the veins and the pores. And it is because of this that animals which breathe cannot smell in water; for to smell they must inhale [air], and they cannot inhale in a liquid.[12]

Odor comes under something which is dry, just as flavor comes under something which is liquid; and the organ of smell is potentially of a thing which is such [e.g., dry].[12]

10

The object of taste is something which is tangible, and it is because of this fact that it cannot be sensed through some other kind of body between it and the organ which tastes it; for contact, too, [takes place without an intervening body].[1] The body in which flavor, which is the object of taste,[2] exists as in a material[3] liquid, this,[4] too, is something which is tangible. For this reason, even if we were to live in water, we would sense a sweet object placed into it; and our sensation of [sweetness] would come not through the intervening medium but by [contact with] the liquid which has become a solution, as in the case of a drink.[5] The way in which color is seen, on the other hand, is not by being blended [with the transparent medium], nor by emanating from another [substance].[6] Accordingly, [in the case of tasting] there is no intervening medium; yet just as the visible object is color, so the object of taste is flavor. But no object produces a sensation of flavor without moisture; [to do so] it must have moisture either *actually* or potentially, as in the case of a salty object, for this can easily be dissolved and act as a solution on the tongue.[7]

20   Now just as vision is of the visible and of the invisible object (for darkness is invisible and it, too, is discriminated by vision), and also of the exceedingly bright object (for brightness, too, is invisible but in a different way from darkness), so the sense of hearing, too, is in a similar way of sound and of silence (the former being the audible object but the latter the inaudible

25   object), and also of a very loud sound, like vision in the case of the [exceedingly] bright object. For just as a slight sound is in a sense inaudible, so is a very loud and violent sound.[8] The term "invisible" has two senses: (a) that which cannot be seen at all, as in other cases in which we speak of the impossible,[9] and (b) that which, though by its nature visible, is not visible or is poorly visible, as in the case of the terms "footless" and "seedless".[10]

30   So, too, with the sense of taste, it is of the object of taste and of the tasteless[11] object; and the latter object has slight or poor flavor[12] or else is destructive of the sense of taste. The starting point[13] here is thought to be the drinkable and the undrinkable object; for it is of each of these[14] that there is taste; but taste in the latter case is poor or even destructive of the sense of taste, while in the former case it is according to its nature.[15] The drinkable object is common to the sense of touch and the sense of taste.[16]

422b   Since the object of taste is moist, it is necessary for the corresponding sense organ, too, to be neither actually a liquid nor incapable of being moistened; for the sense of taste is affected by the object of taste qua such object. So it is necessary for the organ of taste, which can be moistened and still

5   preserve [its nature] but which is not a liquid, to be moistened.[17] A sign of this is the fact that the tongue, when sensing its object, is neither very dry nor very moist; for [taste] in the latter case occurs by contact with the original moisture [in the tongue], as when one tastes a flavor after having first tasted some other strong flavor, or as in the case of a sick person to whom all things appear to be bitter because his tongue is full of such [i.e.,

10   bitter] moisture when he senses them.[18]

The species of flavors, as in the case of colors, are (a) the sweet and the bitter, and these are contraries, which are simple;[19] then follow (b) the oily and the salty, respectively; and between the latter two come (c) the pungent, the harsh, the astringent, and the acid. These are thought to be practically

15   all the different species of flavor. Hence the faculty of taste is that which is potentially such as each of these,[20] and that which can be tasted is that which can actualize that [faculty].

11

Concerning the tangible object and the sense of touch,[1] the same account [will be given]. Now if the sense of touch is not a single [sense] but many, the tangible objects which can be sensed, too, must be many [in species]. So there is the problem (a) whether there is one sense of touch or many, and the further problem as to (b) what the organ which can touch tangible objects is. Is this organ flesh in some animals and something analogous to flesh in others? If not, is the primary[2] sense organ farther inward but flesh the medium between that organ and the tangible object? Moreover, every sense is thought to be a faculty of a single contrariety,[3] e.g., vision is of white and black, the sense of hearing is of high and low pitch, and the sense of taste is of the sweet and the bitter; but in tangible objects there are many contrarieties, e.g., the hot and the cold, the dry and the moist, the hard and the soft, and others such as these.

A partial solution to this problem, however, is the fact that there are many contrarieties in the objects of the other senses also. Thus in voice there is not only high and low pitch, but also loudness and softness, smoothness and roughness, and others such as these; and in colors, too, there are different [contrarieties] of this sort. Still, it is not quite clear what the single subject in the case of touch is which corresponds to sound in the case of hearing.[4]

Is the organ of touch farther inward or is it the flesh which directly [touches the object]? The fact that sensation occurs at the moment when the flesh touches the object is not thought to be a sign [that flesh is the organ of touch]. For it is a fact that if one were to attach something like a stretched membrane to the flesh, the sensation of the object would still be communicated to the sense of touch in a similar way immediately when contact is made; and it is clear [in this case] that the sense organ is not in the [membrane]. And if [the membrane] were to be grown on [to the flesh], the sensation would be transmitted even more quickly. For this reason, it seems that such a part of the body [i.e., the outer flesh] is to the [organ of touch] as air around us would be if air were grown on to us; and in the latter case we would have thought that sounds and colors and odors were sensed by a single [organ], and that vision, the sense of hearing, and the sense of smell were a single sense. As it is, because of the fact that the media through which the motions[5] occur are separated from us, the sense organs are evidently distinct. But in the case of touch it is not at present clear what the fact is.[6]

Now the animate body cannot consist of air [alone] or of water [alone], for there must be some solid material. So the only alternative is that it is a blend of earth and air and water, such as flesh and what the analogue [in animals] tend to be;[7] hence the body [as a medium] which is between the [organ] of touch [and the tangible object] and through which the various [kinds of] sensations [arise], too, must be an organically attached body. That those [sensations are] many [in kind] is clear in the case of the tongue when

it touches its objects; for it is with the same part that it senses all tangible objects and also [all] flavors. So if the rest of the flesh, too, could sense flavors,
20   the sense of taste and the sense of touch would have been thought to be one and the same; but they are in fact two, because they are not convertible.[8]

Here one might raise a problem. Since every body has depth, which is the third dimension, if two bodies have a third body between them, they cannot be touching each other. Now what is moist or wet is not without body
25   but must be or have water;[9] and things which touch each other in water, not having dry boundaries, must have between them water which makes their [touching] extremities[10] everywhere wet. If this is true, it will be impossible for one thing to touch another in water.[11] And likewise for things
30   in air; for air is related to the things in it in a similar way as water is related to the things in it, but we fail to notice this fact, just as aquatic animals fail
423b   to notice that things which touch each other in water have wet surfaces.[12] So the problem arises whether sensation of all [kinds of sensible objects] occurs in a similar manner, or differently for different kinds; for tasting and touching are nowadays thought to occur by contact but the other sensations at a distance. But this is not the case. We sense both hard and soft objects
5   in the same way as we do objects which are sounding and visible and can be smelt, namely, through something else [a medium]; but the latter objects [act] from a distance while the former [act] when they are close to us. For this reason, we fail to notice the fact; for, although we sense everything through a medium, this fact escapes our notice in the case of [objects of touch and of taste]. And indeed, to repeat our previous statement,[13] even if
10   we were to sense all tangible objects through a membrane without being aware that it lies between us and those objects, we would still be related to them in a way similar to the way we are now to objects when we are in air or in water; for we think that we are touching them without an intervening medium. Tangible objects, however, differ from visible and sounding objects in this respect: when we sense the latter, it is the intervening medium which acts upon us in a certain way, but when we sense tangible objects,
15   we are acted upon not by an intervening medium but simultaneous with the intervening medium, as when a man is wounded through a shield; for it is not the shield that strikes after it is struck, but both the shield and the flesh are struck together. In general, it seems that the flesh[14] and the tongue are related to the organs of touch and taste, respectively, as air and water
20   are to the corresponding [organs of] sight, hearing, and smell. Neither in the former nor in the latter cases would there be sensation if the sense organ were touched [by the sensible object], e.g., if one were to place a white body on the extremity [i.e., surface] of the eye; and to this extent it is clear that that which can sense a tangible object, too, lies within.[15] [Sensation of tangible objects], then, should occur in the very same manner as in the other
25   cases; for, the sensible objects in those cases are not sensed if they are placed

on the corresponding sense organs, but tangible objects are sensed when placed on the flesh.[16] Consequently, flesh lies between [the organ] of touch [and the tangible object].

The differentiae of what is tangible are those of bodies qua bodies; and by "differentiae" here I mean those which specify the [four] elements; and they are the hot, the cold, the dry, and the moist, which have been discussed *30* earlier in the [writings] on the elements.[17] The organ of touch which senses these and which is also the primary part in which the so-called "sense of touch" exists is that part which is potentially such [as the tangible objects];[18] *424a* for to sense is to be affected in a certain way. Hence that which makes another thing be something like what it itself is in *actuality* does so if the thing acted upon is potentially like that which acts on it. For this reason we do not sense an object which is as hot or as cold or as hard or as soft [as that which senses it] but only those which exceed it, as if the power of sensing *5* [tangible objects] were a kind of a mean between contraries among sensible objects. And it is because of this that [this] sense discriminates its sensible objects; for the mean has the ability to discriminate, since relative to each extreme it becomes the other extreme.[19] And just as that which is about to sense the white and the black should not be *actually* black or white, respectively, but potentially these (and similarly with the other senses), so in the *10* case of the sense of touch [the organ] should be neither hot nor cold. Further, as already stated, just as vision is in a sense of the visible and the invisible object (and similarly with the other senses, which are of their corresponding opposites),[20] so the sense of touch is of the tangible and the intangible objects; and by "intangible"[21] we mean objects which are tangible to a very slight degree, such as air, or objects which are excessively tangible, like those *15* which are destructive [of the sense organ].

In outline, then, each of the senses has been discussed.

12

Universally speaking, we should bear in mind that every sense is receptive of the forms of sensible objects without their matter, and in a sort of way *20* in which wax receives the impression of a signet-ring without the iron or gold,[1] for the wax receives the impression of the golden or bronze [ring] not qua gold or qua bronze.[2] Similarly, a sense too is affected by a thing which has color or flavor or sound, not insofar as that thing is signified by its name, but insofar as it is such-and-such [i.e., colored or flavored or sounding] and *25* according to the corresponding formula.[3] Now the primary sense organ is that in which such a power [i.e., sense] resides, and it is the same [numerically as the power] but the essence of each of them is different; for that[4] which senses would be a certain magnitude. However, neither the essence of a sense nor the corresponding sensation is a magnitude; they are, respectively, the power [of the sense organ] and a certain formula [in that organ].[5]

From the above discussion it is also evident why objects which are exceed-
30   ingly sensible destroy the sense organs; for if the motion [of the medium]
is stronger than [what] the sense organ [can stand], the formula — and this,
as we saw, is the sense — [of the sense organ] is ruined,[6] like the harmony
and the pitch of instruments when the strings are struck hard. And it is also
evident why plants never have any sensations, although they have some part
as soul[7] and are somewhat affected by tangible objects; for they become cold
424b   or warm.[8] The cause of this is the fact that they have no mean [with respect
to sensible contraries], nor any such principle which can receive the forms
of sensible objects; but they are affected by things along with the matter of
those things.[9]

One might raise the problem whether a thing which cannot smell could
5   be affected in any way by odors, or whether a thing which cannot see could
be affected at all by colors; and similarly in the other cases. But since the
object of smell is odor, if anything produces a sensation of smell, it is odor;
so a thing which cannot smell is not of such a nature as to be affected by
odors (and similarly if the thing lacks any of the other senses), and if it has
a sense, it can be affected by those and only those sensible objects which
10   correspond to that sense. This is clear from the following also. That which
acts upon a body is not light or darkness or sound or odor but the [medium]
in which each of these exists; for instance, what splits the timber is the air
along with its thunderbolt.[10] On the other hand, tangible and flavorous
objects do act [upon bodies]; for, if not, by what would inanimate bodies be
affected or altered?[11] If so, will the other sensible objects, too, act [upon
15   bodies]?[12] Is it not the case that not every body can be affected by odor or
sound, and that those which are affected are indeterminate and do not
remain [so affected], as in the case of air? For air is odorous as if it has been
affected in some way. Then what is smelling if it is not an affection of some
kind? But smelling is also sensing, whereas air, when affected [by odor],
immediately becomes [merely] sensible.[13]

BOOK Γ

1

424b22 That there is no sense other than the five already listed — those of seeing, hearing, smelling, tasting, and touching — one might be convinced by the following arguments.[1]

25 Let the following assumptions be made. We do possess the sense of everything which can be sensed by touch (for all the *attributes* of tangible objects qua tangible are sensed by us through the sense of touch); and, if indeed we lack any sense, we must lack the corresponding sense organ also;[2] and things which we sense by touching can be sensed by the sense of touch, which we happen to possess, but things which we sense through an interven-

30 ing medium and not by touching can be sensed by means of simple elements (e.g., air or water)[3] in the following manner.[4] It is a fact that if sensible things which differ in genus[5] can be sensed through a single medium, the possessor of the corresponding sense organ must be capable of sensing both kinds of sensible objects (e.g., this would be the case if the sense organ were made of air, and if air were the medium for sound and color); but if there

425a are many media for the same sensible object, e.g., if color can be sensed through air and water (for both these are transparent), then the possessor of only one [sense organ, which is composed either of air or water] will still be capable of sensing the things which are sensible through either of the two media. Now each sense organ is composed of only one of the two simple elements (air or water), for the pupil is made of water, [the organ of] hearing

5 is made of air, and [the organ of] smell is made out of one of these two;[6] fire is either in none of the [organs] or in all of them (for no animal can sense without heat), and earth is either in none or, if at all, is blended in [the organ of] touch most of all in a special way.[7] It would remain, then, that there can be no sense organ [which is made of something] other than water or air; and some animals do possess [organs made of air or water]. Consequently, all

10 senses are possessed by animals which are neither incomplete nor maimed; for even the mole appears to have eyes beneath its skin.[8] So if there is no other [kind of] body [besides the four elements] and no *attribute* other than those of these bodies, no sense could be lacking [in a complete animal].[9]

15 Further, it is not possible for there to be an organ proper to the common sensibles, i.e., to motion, rest, shape, magnitude, number, and unity,[10] which we sense indirectly by each sense;[11] for we sense all these by motion.[12] For instance, a magnitude is sensed by motion,[12] and hence shape too is so sensed, for shape is a king of magnitude;[13] rest in a thing is sensed by the absence of motion in it;[14] and a number is sensed by the negation of continu-

20 ity and by the special [senses],[15] for each of these senses a unity.[16] So it is clear

42

that there can be no proper sense for any of these objects, e.g., for motion; for, if there were, we would be sensing them in a way in which we are now sensing a sweet object by vision.[17] But we do this [i.e., we sense a sweet object by vision] by the fact that we happen to possess a sense for each of them [sweetness and color], and in view of this fact we recognize them when they happen to be together;[18] or else, we would not be sensing them at all, except

25   indirectly, as in the case of Cleon's son, whom we sense not as Cleon's son but as white, for this white happens to be Cleon's son.[19]

Now we do have a common [faculty of] sensation[20] of the common sensibles which senses them not indirectly, so there is no proper faculty which senses them; for otherwise[21] we would not be sensing them at all,

30   except in the manner in which we see Cleon's son, as it was stated before. As for the proper senses, they sense each other's objects indirectly; and it

425b   is not qua themselves, but qua one sense[22] when it senses simultaneously [two or more] sensibles in the same [substance], e.g., [when it senses] the bile as being bitter and yellow.[23] For neither one nor the other of the [proper] senses [vision, sense of taste] can state that both [the bitter object and the yellow object] are one object;[24] and for this reason one may be mistaken in thinking, for example, that if the object is yellow, it is bile.

5   One might inquire why we have many senses and not only one. Is it not in order that the [attributes] which accompany [the proper sensibles] and are common, e.g., motion and magnitude and number, be less likely to escape our notice? For if vision were our only sense and whiteness its [only] object, the [common sensibles] would be more likely to escape our notice and all [sensibles] would be thought to be the same thing because, for example, colors and magnitudes accompany each other. As it is, the fact that common

10   sensibles exist also in other [proper] sensibles reveals [to us] that each of the common sensibles is distinct from the others.[25]

2

Since we sense the fact that we are seeing or hearing [or etc.],[1] we must do so either by vision or by some other sense. Then the same sense would be sensing both vision and its object, which is color;[2] so either there would

15   be two senses of the same object, or [vision] would be sensing itself.[3] Further, if the sense which senses vision were different from vision, either the senses would be infinite in number[4] or some one of those senses would be sensing itself. So we should assume that it is the first sense [i.e., vision] which senses itself.[5]

But there is a difficulty; for if to sense by vision is to see, and if that which is seen is color or that which has color,[6] then if a man were to see that which

20   is seeing, that which primarily[7] sees too would have color. It is evident, then, that the expression "to sense by vision" does not have only one meaning;[8] for, even when we do not see, it is by vision that we discriminate both

darkness and light, although not in the same manner. Further, that which sees, too, is in a certain sense colored; for each sense organ is receptive of its sensible object but without the matter of that object.⁹ It is in view of this

25   that sensations and imaginings of those objects exist in the sense organs even when those objects are gone.¹⁰

Now the activity of the sensible object and the activity of the sensation [of it] are one and the same, but the essence of each of them is not the same.¹¹ I mean, for example, that *actual* sound and the *actual* hearing [of it are one and the same]; for a man may have hearing [potentially] and not be [*actually*] hearing, and that which has sound [potentially] is not always

30   sounding.¹² But when that which can hear is *actually* hearing and that which can sound is [*actually*] sounding, then *actual* hearing and [the corre-

426a   sponding] *actual* sounding occur simultaneously; and one might say that these two are *hearing* and *sounding*, respectively. So if a motion and an action and an affection are in that which is acted upon, then both the *actual* sound and the *actual* hearing [of it] must be in that which has the power

5   [of hearing]; for the activity of that which can act and cause motion comes to be in that which is being affected.¹³ In view of this, it is not necessary for that which causes motion to be moved.¹⁴ Accordingly, the activity of that which can sound is sound or *sounding*, and the activity of that which can hear is hearing or *hearing*; for "hearing" has two meanings, and so does "sound".¹⁵ The same account may be given of the other senses and their

10   sensible objects. For just as action and [*actual*] affection are in that which is being affected and not in that which is acting, so the activity of the sensible object and of that which can sense is in that which can sense.¹⁶

Now in some cases the activities have names, e.g., "*sounding*" and "*hearing*", but in others there is no name for one or the other; for the activity of vision is called "seeing", but that of the color¹⁷ has no name, and the

15   activity of the sense of taste is called "*tasting*", but that of flavor¹⁷ has no name. And since the activity of a sensible object and of the corresponding sense is one, although the essence of each of the two [activities] is different, it is necessary for hearing and sound, taken as activities, to cease to exist or to continue to exist simultaneously; and similarly with flavor and taste and the others. But if they are taken as potentialities, there is no such necessity.

20   The earlier natural philosophers, thinking that neither whiteness nor blackness can exist without vision, nor flavor without the sense of taste, did not state the facts well; for in one sense they were right, but in another wrong. For, since each of the terms "sensation" and "sensible objects" has two meanings, they were right if the terms mean *actual* sensation and

25   sensible object in activity, respectively, but they were wrong if the terms mean potential sensation and sensible object in potency, respectively. But these thinkers were using terms which have more than one meaning without distinguishing the two meanings.¹⁸

If harmony is a vocal sound, and if voice and hearing are one and the same in one sense, although not so in another,[19] and if harmony is a formula,[20] then hearing too must be a formula[20] of some sort. And it is because of this fact that excessive pitch, whether high or low, destroys the sense of hearing; and similarly, excessive flavors destroy the sense of taste, extremely bright or dusky colors destroy vision, and strong odors, whether sweet or bitter, destroy the sense of smell, and these facts indicate that each of the senses is a formula. And it is in view of this, too, that sensible objects which are pure and unblended, e.g., the acid or the sweet or the salty, are pleasurable whenever they are brought into a [proper] proportion; for then they are pleasurable. In general, however, that which is a blend [or a] harmony is more [pleasurable] than a high or a low tone, and, in the case of touch, that which can be heated or cooled [is more pleasant than the hot or cold; for] each sense is a formula, and [a sensible object] in excess causes pain or destroys [the corresponding sense].[21]

Now each sense is relative to its own sensible object,[22] it exists in a sense organ qua such organ, and it discriminates the differences in that object; thus vision discriminates whiteness and blackness, the sense of taste discriminates sweetness and bitterness, and similarly in the other cases. But since we discriminate also between whiteness and bitterness and [in general] between a sensible object of one kind and a sensible object of another kind, by what [power] do we sense also the fact that the two sensible objects differ?[23]

We must do so by a sense;[24] for both objects are sensible. From this fact it is also clear that flesh cannot be the ultimate sense organ; for, if it were, it would be necessary for that which discriminates [any two sensible objects] to do so by contact [with those objects].[25] Nor again can we judge that sweetness is distinct from whiteness [by each of the two corresponding organs or senses] separately, but both these objects should be made known to a single [faculty]; for, otherwise, it would be as if my sensing one object and your sensing an object [of a different kind] could make it clear [to you, or to me] that the two objects are distinct from each other. Only a single [faculty], then, should assert that the two objects are distinct; for sweetness is distinct from whiteness. So it is the same [faculty] that asserts this; and just as it asserts [this distinction], so it thinks[26] it or senses it.[27]

It is clear, then, that it is not possible to judge separately by separate [faculties] the fact that [sensible objects of different senses are different];[28] and from what follows it is also clear that it is not possible to discriminate such difference at separate times. For just as it is the same [faculty] which asserts that goodness is distinct from evil, so when [that power] asserts that A differs from B it asserts also that B differs from A, and the time [when A and B are asserted to be different] is not accidental as it is, for example, if I now assert that A differs from B, but not that it now differs from B. It asserts the difference both (a) now and (b) as being a difference now; and so [it asserts that it is] at the same time [that A is distinct from B]. Hence it is an inseparable [faculty that distinguishes A from B], and it [asserts that the distinction exists] at an indivisible time.[29]

30

427a

On the other hand, [one may say that] it is impossible for the same thing, qua undivided, to have contrary motions in an undivided time. For if [a sensible object] is sweet, it moves the sense or thinking in one way, if it is bitter, it moves it in the contrary way, and if it is white, it moves it in a [generically] different way. Then is the discriminating sense, which is indivisible numerically and inseparable, at the same time divided in essence? In one sense, it is the divisible which senses divided objects, but in another

5

sense [it does so] qua indivisible; for in essence [that which senses] is divisible, but locally and numerically [that which does this] is indivisible.[30][31]

Is not this impossible? For, although the same indivisible thing may be potentially both contraries, in essence it cannot be [these contraries]; it is when in *actuality* that it is divisible [into these contraries]. An object, for example, cannot be both white and black at the same time; so if the corresponding sensing or thinking is a thing such as that object, it cannot be acted

10

upon by the forms of these [i.e., of black and white at the same time]. But the [discriminating sense] is like the so-called "point", which may be taken either qua one or [qua] two; and this is the manner in which [this sense] is divisible. So qua indivisible, the discriminating sense is one and judges simultaneously; but qua existing as divisible, it uses the same point of reference twice at the same time. Accordingly, insofar as it uses the limit twice, it makes two separate judgments as if of two separate things; but insofar as it uses it only once, it [judges it] by one [judgment] and at one time.[31]

15

Concerning the principle by means of which we speak of animals as being capable of sensing, let the above distinctions suffice.

3

The principal differentiae by which thinkers define the soul are two, (a) motion with respect to place and (b) thinking and discriminating and sens-

20

ing.[1] Both thinking and judging rightly[2] are thought to be like a sort of sensing, for [according to these thinkers] in each of these two[3] cases the soul discriminates something and knows things; and the ancient thinkers, too, went as far as to assert that judging rightly and sensing are the same. Thus Empedocles said "For thought in men increases with what is before them",[4] and elsewhere, "whence it befalls them ever to change their right judgments

25

too";[5] and Homer, too, had in mind the same thing when he said "such is the nature of man's thought".[6] For all these thinkers believed that thinking, like sensing, is corporeal, and that like is sensed or judged rightly by like, as we explained at the beginning of this treatise.[7] But these thinkers should

427b   have discussed at the same time the fact that errors occur; for errors are
        more appropriate to animals, and their souls are subject to error the greater
        part of their existence. So either all appearances must be true, as some
        thinkers assert,[8] or an error must be an apprehension of what is unlike, for
5   such apprehension is contrary to knowledge of like by like; but it is thought
        that it is the same science that knows two contraries and the same disposition
        that is erroneously disposed to those contraries.[9]
            Now it is evident that sensing and judging rightly are not the same thing;
        for all animals share in the former, but only few of them in the latter.[10]
        Thinking, too, which may be right or wrong (right thinking is prudence or
10   science or true opinion, but wrong thinking is the contrary of each of these)
        is not the same as sensing; for sensation of the proper sensibles is always true,
        and it exists in all animals, but *thinking* may be also false, and it belongs
        to no animal which has no power of reasoning.[11] Imagination, too, differs
15   from sensation and from *thought;* but without sensation there can be no
        imagination, and without imagination there can be no belief.[12]
            Evidently, thinking is not the same as believing. For this affection [i.e.,
        thinking] is within our power, whenever we wish to be thinking (for we can
        bring it about before our eyes, as those do who use mnemonic devices and
20   form images); but forming opinions is not up to us, for an opinion must be
        either true or false.[13] Again, whenever we are faced with the opinion that
        something is dangerous or fearful, we are also affected immediately, and
        we do so likewise whenever something inspires courage; but whenever we
        imagine these, we are disposed towards them like spectators looking at
25   dangerous or encouraging objects in paintings.[14] Belief itself, too, has differen-
        tiae; the species of belief are *knowledge*, [true] opinion, prudence, and the
        contraries of these, but the discussion of their differences belongs to another
        treatise.[15] As for thinking, since it differs from sensing, and since one [spe-
        cies] of it is thought to be imagination and the other to be belief, we must
        discuss belief after having specified what imagination is.[16]

428a   If imagination is that[17] in virtue of which an image is formed in us, but
        not something spoken of in a metaphorical way,[18] it [may be] some power
        or habit by which we discriminate, whether truly or falsely; and such are
5   [the powers or habits of] sensation, opinion, *knowledge*, and intellect.
            That it is not sensation[19] is clear from the following. Sensation is either
        a faculty, like vision, or an activity, like seeing; but images may be formed
        even if neither the one nor the other is present, as in sleep.[20] Again, sensa-
        tion[21] is always present [in animals], but not imagination. And if *actual*
10   sensation were the same as imagination, the latter would exist in all the
        nonrational animals; but it is thought not to exist in all of them, e.g., not in
        ants or bees or worms. Again, sensations [of proper sensibles] are always true,
        but most imaginations turn out to be false.[22] Once again, when we are
        sensing a sensible object accurately, we do not say, for example, that it

15 appears to us to be a man; we do so rather when we are not sensing the object distinctly, and it is only then [that our statement may be] true or false.[23] Finally, as we said earlier, visual impressions appear to occur even when our eyes are closed.[24]

Further, imagination is none of those [powers or habits] which are always true, such as *knowledge* or the intellect; for imagination may be also false.[25]

It remains, then, to see if imagination is opinion; for an opinion may be 20 true or false. But opinion is attended by conviction (for a man cannot have an opinion of objects if he is thought not to be convinced of them); and, although most nonrational animals have imagination, none of them has conviction. And, we may add, every opinion is accompanied by conviction, which follows when one has been convinced, and that which causes a man to be convinced is reason; but although some nonrational animals have 25 imagination, none of them has reason.[26] It is evident, then, that imagination cannot be opinion aided by sensation, nor opinion through sensation, nor yet a combination of opinion and sensation,[27] both because of the above arguments[28] and clearly in view of the fact that opinion is of nothing but of the object which is also sensed (and by "a combination" here I mean, for example, an imagination which is a combination of the opinion concerning 30 the white and the sensation of the white, certainly not a combination of the 428b opinion concerning the good and the sensation of the white). Now to appear to be is to have an opinion of that which is sensed as such but not indirectly.[29] But one may have also false appearances of things of which he has at the same time true belief; for instance, the Sun appears to be a foot in diameter, but one may be convinced that it is greater than the inhabited world.[30] So 5 it turns out that, while a thing remains unchanged, (a) a man, without having forgotten or having changed his conviction, has abandoned his true opinion which he had of that thing, or else, (b) if he still has that opinion, his [opinion of that thing] is both true and false. But a [true opinion] would become false only when the thing would change to its contrary without being noticed. So imagination is neither one of these [opinion, sensation] nor a combination of them.[31]

10 Now (1) since it is possible, when one thing has moved, for another thing to be moved by the first,[32] and (2) since imagination is thought to be a species of a motion,[33] to occur not without sense[34] but in sentient beings, and to be of objects which can be sensed, and (3) since motion can be produced by the activity of a sense[35] and must be, if so produced, similar to a [correspond- 15 ing] sensation,[36] such motion could neither occur without sensation nor exist in beings which are not sentient; and, according to such motion, (a) the possessors of it do and are affected by many things, and (b) that motion may be true or false [of what it denotes] and occurs for the following *reasons*.

First, the sensation of proper sensible objects is true or has the least 20 possible falsity.[37] Second, there is the sensation of the objects[38] of which these

[proper sensibles] are attributes, and in this case one may now *think* falsely;
for, as to [the sensation of] the whiteness of an object, there is no falsity, but
as to whether the [substance which is sensed as being] white is this thing or
some other thing, there may be falsity. Third, there is the sensation of the
common sensibles (e.g., of motion and of magnitude) that accompany the
[substances] which are accidental to (the proper sensibles)[39] and to which the
25   proper sensibles belong; and it is about these [the common sensibles] most
of all that sensation may be mistaken.[40]

    Now the motion brought about by the activity [of sense] differs from the
three kinds of sensations listed above.[41] The first kind is true whenever the
[corresponding] sensation is present;[42] but the other [two] kinds, whether [the
sensation is] present or absent, may be false, and especially when the sensible
object is at some distance from the sentient being. Accordingly, if no thing
429a   other than imagination has the things stated above,[49] then imagination
would be a motion produced by the activity of sense. The name
φαντασία (imagination), too, is derived from φάος (light); for vision is the
sense in the highest degree, and without light it is not possible to see. And
5   because imaginations persist in us and are similar to the corresponding
sensations, animals do many things according to them, some (i.e., nonrational animals) because they possess no intellect, and others (i.e., men) because
their intellect is sometimes clouded by passion or disease or sleep.

    Concerning imagination, what it is and why[44] it exists, let the above
discussion suffice.

4

10   Concerning the part of the soul with which the soul knows and judges
rightly,[1] whether it is separable with respect to magnitude or not so separable but [only] with respect to definition,[2] we should consider what its differentia is and how thinking takes place.[3]

    If thinking is indeed like sensing, then it would either be a process of
15   being affected in some way by the object of thought or be some other thing
such as this.[4] So [the thinking part of the soul] should be incapable of being
affected but capable of receiving the form [of the object of thought] and be
potentially such as that [form] but not the [form] itself; and the intellect
should be related to the object of thought in a manner similar to that in
which a sense is related to its sensible object. And, since the intellect [can]
think every [object of thought], it must exist without being blended [with
something else] in order that, as Anaxagoras says, "it may rule", that is, in
20   order that it may know. For, if it appears along [with some other thing], the
[latter will] prevent or obstruct [the knowledge of] another kind [of thing];
hence it is necessary for [the intellect] to be of no nature other than that of
[mere] potentiality.[5] So the part of the soul which is called "intellect" (by
"intellect" I mean that [part] by which the soul [can] *think* and believe)[6] is

actually none of the things prior to thinking. In view of this, it is not even
25 reasonable that it should be blended with the body, for it might then acquire
some quality, e.g., coldness or heat, or there might be even an organ [for
it], as there is for the sentient power; but, as it is, there is no [such organ].[6]
So those who say that the soul is a place of forms speak well, except that it
is not the whole soul but only the thinking part of it, and that [that part]
is not actually but potentially the forms [of things].[7]

30   It is evident from the sense organs and the corresponding sensations that
the impassivity of the sentient [soul] is not similar to that of the thinking
429b [soul].[8] For a sense loses its power of sensing immediately after [it is acted
upon by] a very strong sensible object, e.g., it cannot hear sound immediately after very loud sounds, it cannot see immediately after very bright colors,
and it cannot smell immediately after very strong odors. The intellect, on
the other hand, immediately after having thought a very highly intelligible
object, can think objects which are less intelligible not less but even more;
5 for the sentient soul cannot exist without a body, whereas the intellect is
separable.[9] And whenever the intellect becomes each particular [intelligi-
ble object] in the sense in which we speak of a scientist when he is *actually*
a scientist (and this occurs when a scientist can exercise [his *knowledge*] by
himself), even then it exists somehow potentially and in a similar manner,
although not in a manner like that prior to having learned or discovered [the
object it knows];[10] and it is [only] then that it is capable of thinking of itself.[11]

10   Since there is a difference between magnitude[12] and the essence of a
magnitude, between water[12] and the essence of water, and so too in many
other cases, but not in all (for in some cases [a thing and its essence] are the
same[13]), the [soul] discriminates flesh and the essence of flesh either by
different [powers] or [by the same power] but differently disposed towards
them;[14] for flesh[15] exists not without matter[15] but as *this* snubness in *this*
15 [nose]. Accordingly, it is by the sentient power that the [soul] discriminates
the hot and the cold and the things whose formula is flesh; but it is by a
different power, one which is either separate[16] or related to it as a bent line
when straightened out to the bent line itself,[17] that the soul discriminates
the essence of flesh. Again, of things which exist by abstraction, the straight[18]
is like the snub, for it exists with that which is continuous; but its essence,
20 if it is different from the straight, [is discriminated] by a [power] different
[from that which discriminates the straight]. For let [that essence] of the
straight be duality. Then [the soul discriminates duality] by a different
[power] or else by the same [power which discriminates the straight] but
when this power is differently disposed. In general, then, as [certain] things
are separable from matter, so are those concerning the intellect.[19]

One might raise this question: if the intellect is simple and not capable
of being affected and has nothing in common with anything else, as Anax-
25 agoras says, how will it think, if thinking is a species of being acted upon?

For it is thought that it is insofar as two things have something in common that one of them acts and the other is acted upon.[20] Again, [one may raise the problem] whether the intellect itself, too, is intelligible. For, if the intellect is intelligible not with respect to something else and if what is intelligible is one in kind, then either it will belong to the other things [also] or it will be blended with something which makes the intellect intelligible as it does the other things.[21]

30   But we stated earlier when we distinguished the [two] senses of "to be acted upon in virtue of something common" that the intellect, prior to thinking, is in a certain way potentially the intelligible objects but is none of them actually;[22] and it should [be regarded potentially] as [being] in a 430a   tablet which has no actual writing.[23] This is indeed the case with the intellect. Moreover, the intellect itself is intelligible like the [other] intelligible objects.[24] For, in the case of objects without matter, that which thinks and that which is being thought are the same,[25] for theoretical *knowledge* and 5   its *knowable* object are the same;[26] and as for the *reason* why [the intellect] does not think always, this matter should be examined.[27] But in the case of objects which have matter, each of them is potentially intelligible. Consequently, intellect will not belong to the latter objects (for it is a potentiality of such things but without [their] matter); but it will belong to an intelligible object.[28]

5

10   Since in each genus of things there is something, e.g., matter, as in every case of [things by] nature (and matter is that which is potentially each of these things), and also something else which, by producing those things, is the cause and is capable of acting, as in the case of art in relation to its material, these different [principles] must belong to the soul also.[1] And one 15   [principle] is an intellect of the sort that can become all things,[2] but the other is such that, like a sort of disposition,[3] it can make all things, as in the case of light; for in a certain sense[4] light, too, makes potential colors be *actual* colors.[5] And the latter intellect is separable and cannot be affected by or be blended with anything, and in *substance* it exists as an *actuality*;[6] for that which acts is always more honorable than that which is acted upon, and the principle [of a thing which has matter is always more honorable] than the matter [of that thing].[7]

20   *Actual knowledge* is the same as the thing [*known*];[8] potential *knowledge*, however, is prior in time [to *actual knowledge*] in an [individual],[9] but, as a whole, it is not [prior] in time.[10] But the [active intellect] is not[11] at one time thinking and at another not thinking.[12] When separated [from the body], it is *as such* just that [i.e., intellect], and only this [part of the soul] is immortal and eternal.[13] But we do not remember[14] in view of the fact that, although this [part of the soul] cannot be affected, the intellect which can be affected 25   is destructible, and without it [it[15]] cannot think.[16]

52

6

The thinking of indivisibles is among things[1] concerning which there can be no falsity;[2] but objects to which truth or falsity may belong are combinations of concepts already formed,[3] like unities of things, and as Empedocles said: "where sprang into being many neckless heads", which were then put together by *Friendship*.[4] These separate [concepts], too, are combined in the same way, as in the case of "incommensurability" and "the diagonal [of a square]". If [thinking] is of past or future objects, it includes also time in the combination.[5] Now falsity exists always in a composite; and even if one [says] "the white is not-white", he has combined "not-white" [with "the white"]. One may, however, state every composite as being a division also.[6] At any rate, truth or falsity belongs not only, for example, to the [thought] "Cleon is white", but also to "Cleon was white" and "Cleon will be white". As for that which produces a unity [of concepts] in each case, it is the intellect.[7]

Since things may be indivisible in two ways, potentially or *actually*, nothing prevents [the intellect] from thinking the indivisible when, for example, it thinks a length;[8] for [a length] is *actually* indivisible and [is thought] in an indivisible time, since time is divisible or indivisible in a way similar to that in which a length is.[9] Accordingly, it is not possible to state in each half of that time what [part of the length] it is thinking; for if [the length] is not divided, it does not exist [*actually* as many], but only potentially.[10] But if [the intellect] thinks each half [of the length] separately, then it divides the time [along with the length] also; and in this case [the two parts] are as it were [two *actual*] lengths.[11] And if [the intellect thinks the length] as being composed of two parts, then [it does this], too, in the time taken [to so think] the two parts.[12] As for the indivisible not in quantity but in kind, the intellect thinks it in an indivisible time and by an indivisible [thought or act] of the soul.[13] But [it does so] indirectly, not insofar as these (i.e., the object thought[14] and the time taken) are divisible, but insofar as they are indivisible; for in these, too, there is something indivisible which, being perhaps not separable, makes each of them (e.g., the length [thought] and the time [taken]) one. And this exists similarly in everything continuous, whether this be time or length. As for a point or any division or whatever is indivisible in this manner, it comes to be known just as a privation is known; and similarly for others [of this sort]. For instance, how does one know evil or black? In a sense, he knows each by its contrary.[15] But that which [so] knows [each of these] should exist potentially and should be included in that [i.e., in its contrary].[16] If, however, there is among causes a thing in which there can be no contrary, then [this thing] knows itself and exists in *actuality* and is separate.[17]

An assertion, like an affirmation, is of something about something else, and in every case it is [either] true or false. But the intellect is not in every

case [of this sort]. If it is of whatness with respect to essence, it is [always]
true, and it is not [a thought of] something about something else; and just
30   as seeing a proper [sensible] is [always] true, whereas [believing] that the
white thing seen is a man (or is not a man) is not always true, so it is with
things which are without matter.[18]

7

431a   *Actual Knowledge* is the same as the object [of *knowledge*]; potential
knowledge, however, is prior in time in any single [individual], but, as a
whole, it is not [prior] in time, for all things which come into existence do
so from things which exist actually.[1]
5   Now it is evident that the sensible object causes the faculty of sensation
when existing potentially to become *actual;* for [this faculty] is neither
affected nor altered.[2] In view of this, [its *actuality*] is a different kind of
motion; for, as stated elsewhere, motion [in the usual sense] is the *actuality*
of that which is incomplete, but the *actuality* of what is complete, being
unqualified, is distinct [from such motion].[3] Accordingly, sensing is like
mere naming or [mere] conceiving;[4] but whenever [the sensible object] is
10   pleasant or painful, [the soul], as if affirming or denying,[5] pursues or avoids;
and to be pleased or pained [for the soul] is to be in activity with the sentient
mean towards the good or the bad, respectively, qua such;[6] and *actual*
aversion and *actual* desire[7] are, respectively, just that.[8] And the parts [of the
soul] which can desire and can avoid are not different from each other or
from the sentient part, except in essence.[9]
15   Images are to the *thinking* soul like sense impressions.[10] But when the
[*thinking* soul] affirms or denies them as good or bad, it pursues or avoids,
respectively, and for this reason the soul never thinks without images;[11] [they
are] like the air which affects the eye in a certain way, while the eye in turn
[affects] something else, and similarly in the case of hearing. And the last
20   thing [to be affected] is a single thing and a single mean, but it is many in
essence.[12]
We have stated earlier what it is that judges the difference between the
sweet and the hot; here, too, let us discuss this matter as follows. There is
a single [*thinking* faculty which judges], and [it exists] in a manner like a
boundary.[13] And the [images of the sweet and the hot], too, being one by
analogy and numerically, are to each other as the others [the sensations of
the white and the black] are to each other.[14] For what is the difference
between asking how [the soul] discriminates things not[15] in the same genus
25   and how it discriminates contraries, such as [the sensation of] whiteness and
the [sensation of] blackness. So let C and D be related to each other as A,
[the sensation of] whiteness, and B, [the sensation of] blackness, are related
to each other.[16] Then, by alternation, it follows that [A:C :: B:D].[17] Now if
C and D are to belong to a single [subject], then this subject, like the subject

431b to which A and B belong, will be one and the same numerically but not in
essence. The same may be said if A were to be sweet and B were to be white.

The thinking part, then, thinks the forms in the images;[18] and just as what
is to be pursued and what is to be avoided [when sensible objects are present]
is determined for it[19] by the corresponding [sensations], so it is moved when
5 images are before it and there is no sensation. For example, sensing a beacon
as being fire, it knows by the common faculty of sensation that the enemy
is approaching when it sees the beacon in motion.[20] At other times, it forms
judgments and deliberates about future objects relative to present objects
by means of images or thoughts[21] as if it were seeing these objects; and
whenever it asserts that [certain objects imagined] are pleasurable or pain-
10 ful, it pursues or avoids [those objects] as it does when it senses objects;[22] and
it does so in *actions* in general.[23]

Objects which are outside of the sphere of *action*, too, i.e., the true and
the false, come under the same genus, namely, that of good and evil; they
differ, however, [by being good or evil] either without qualification or in a
qualified way.[24]

As for the so-called "objects by abstraction",[25] the [thinking faculty]
thinks them as if it were thinking of the snub-nosed;[26] for in thinking of the
snub-nosed qua snub-nosed, it does so not as something separated [from
matter], but in thinking it qua concave, if it were to *actually* so think it, it
15 would think it apart from the flesh in which concavity is present.[27] So
whenever the [thinking faculty] is thinking [physical objects], it thinks the
mathematical objects [in them] as if they were separate objects, although
they are inseparable [from physical objects or from physical matter].[28]

In general, then, the intellect when in *actuality* is the objects[29] which it
thinks. But whether the intellect, which is not separate from magnitude, can
or cannot think any separate object is a matter to be considered later.[30]

8

20 We may now sum up the main points concerning the soul under one
heading and state once more that the soul is all things, but in a certain sense;
for things are either sensible or intelligible, and in a certain sense, *knowledge* is the objects *known* while sensation is the sensible objects.[1] We should
inquire, then, in what sense this is the case.

Knowledge and sensation may be so marked off as to correspond to
25 things; and if [*knowledge* and sensation] exist potentially, [they correspond]
to things existing potentially, but if actually, to things existing actually.[2] The
knowing and sentient [powers] of the soul are potentially these things,
namely, the *knowable* and sensible objects, respectively; and they must
either be those things themselves or [their] forms.[3] Certainly, they cannot
be the things themselves; for it is not the stone [itself] which is in the soul
432a but the form[3] of the stone.[4] The soul, then, is like the arm of a man; for just

as the arm is an instrument of instruments, so the intellect is a form[3] of forms and the faculty of sensation is a form[3] of sensible objects.

Now since, as it is thought, no thing exists apart from sensible magni-
5   tudes,[5] then intelligible objects, both those which are said to exist by abstrac-
tion and the dispositions and *attributes* of sensible objects, [must] exist in the forms of sensible objects. And it is because of this that (a) no one can ever learn or *understand* anything without sensing anything, and that (b), when speculating, one must do so along with an image; for images are like
10   sense impressions, except that they are without matter.[6] Imagination, how-
ever, is different from assertion and from denial; for truth or falsity is a combination of concepts. In what way, then, will the primary concepts differ from images? Surely neither they nor the other [kinds of thoughts] are images, although they cannot exist without images.[7]

9

15   The soul of animals has been defined by two powers, (A) that of dis-
criminating, whose function is *thought* and sensation, and also (B) that of causing motion with respect to place.[1] The power of sensation and the intellect have been sufficiently specified by the above discussions. Let us now consider what it is in the soul that causes motion, whether it is some
20   one part of the soul and is separable, in magnitude or in definition,[2] or the whole soul; and if it is a part, whether it is some special part distinct from the ones usually discussed or those enumerated,[3] or some one of these.[4]

An immediate problem may be raised here as to the manner in which we should speak of parts of the soul and the number of such parts,[5] for in some sense[6] there appear to be an indefinite number of them and not only (1) the
25   estimative part and the parts concerned with temper and *desire*, as some thinkers specify, or (2) the part which has reason and the irrational part,[7] as other thinkers specify; for, according to the differentiae by means of which these thinkers separate these parts, there will appear also other parts, already mentioned, which are much further apart from each other than these.[8] For instance, such will be: (a) the nutritive part, which belongs to
30   plants as well as to all animals; also (b) the sentient part, which one could not easily posit as being nonrational or as having reason;[9] again, (c) the
432b   imaginative part, which is distinct in essence from all the other parts but presents much difficulty as to whether it is the same as or distinct from any of them, if one were to posit separate parts of the soul;[10] lastly, (d) the appetitive part, which would be thought to be distinct from all the others
5   both in definition and in what it can do. It is indeed absurd, too, to tear the last-mentioned part away from the other parts, for wish occurs in the estimative part, and both *desire* and temper come under the nonrational part;[11] and if the soul is [divided into] three parts [as in (1)], there will be desire in each of those parts.[12]

Returning to the subject concerning which our present discussion arose, let us inquire what it is that causes an animal to move from one place to another.[13] Now one would think that growth and deterioration, which are motions belonging to all [living things], are caused by the reproductive and nutritive parts, which exist in all [those things]; and as for inhaling and exhaling and sleep and waking, they will be examined later, for these too present considerable difficulty.[14] As for the part concerned with locomotion, let us consider what the mover is which causes an animal to travel.

Clearly, it cannot be the nutritive power. For this motion occurs always for the sake of something and is accompanied either by imagination or by desire; for, if not forced, no animal moves [with respect to place] unless it desires or avoids something. Besides, plants too would be capable of causing [loco] motion and so would have organic parts to bring about such motion.[15]

Similarly, it cannot be the sentient part [of the soul]; for there are many [kinds of] animals which have the faculty of sensation but are stationary and motionless till the end of their lives.[16] So since nature does nothing in vain[17] and leaves out nothing which is necessary [for an end],[18] except in cases of defect or incompleteness,[19] such [i.e., the stationary] animals are complete and not defective, as confirmed by the fact that they can reproduce and reach maturity and deteriorate, and so they would have possessed also organic parts for travelling.[20]

Nor again can that mover be the estimative part or the part which is called "intellect".[21] For the speculative part does not think of anything which is to be *acted* upon and does not assert anything about what should be avoided or pursued,[22] whereas [loco] motion exists in that which avoids or pursues something; and when this part speculates about a matter[23] [to be *acted* upon], even then it does not directly bid avoidance or pursuit. For instance, many times it *thinks* of something fearful or pleasurable, but it does not bid us to be afraid; it is the heart which is moved [if the object is fearful], or some other part if the object is pleasurable.

Again, [a man] is not [necessarily] moved even if the intellect gives the order and *thought* asserts that something should be avoided or pursued, as in the case of the incontinent man who *acts* according to *desire*.[24] And, in general, we observe that the possessor of medical science does not [necessarily] cure, and this shows that the authoritative [moving principle] which causes action in accordance with *knowledge* is some other [part of the soul] and not the part which has *knowledge*.[25]

Finally, desire too is not the authoritative [principle] which produces this kind of motion; for continent men have desires and *desire* certain things, but they follow the intellect and do not *act* to attain the objects of their desire.[26]

10

There appear, then, to be at least two [possible] movers here, desire and
10   the intellect,[1] provided that one were to posit imagination as being a kind
of thinking. For many [*actions*][2] which are against *knowledge* follow imagination; and in the other animals there is neither thinking[3] nor judgment, but
[only] imagination. So both of these — intellect and desire[4] — [appear to]
have the power of causing locomotion.

Now the intellect[5] [meant here] is that which judges for the sake of
15   something and is practical;[6] and it differs from the speculative intellect with
respect to the end in view. Every desire, too, is for the sake of something;[7]
for it is for the object of desire which is the starting-point of the practical
intellect, and the last [step reached by the practical intellect] is the beginning of *action*.[8] So it is with good reason that these two — desire and
practical *thought* — appear to be the moving causes; for what causes motion
20   is the appetitive [soul],[9] and it is through this that *thought* causes motion,
for the starting-point of [this] *thought* is the appetitive [soul].[9] Imagination,
too, when it causes motion, does so not without desire. One thing which
causes motion, then, is the appetitive [soul];[9] for if there were two, the
intellect[10] and desire, they would cause motion according to some common
form.[11] As it is, the intellect does not appear to cause motion without desire;
for wish is a [species of] desire, and whenever a man is moved according
25   to judgment, he is moved according to wish also.[12] But desire [may] cause
motion in violation of judgment [also]; for *desire* is a [species of] desire.[13]

Now the intellect [is] in every case right;[14] but desire or imagination [may
be] right and [may be] wrong.[15] In view of these facts, what always causes
motion is the object of desire;[16] but this object may be either the good or
the apparent good, although not every [kind] but that which is practicable,
30   and what is practicable may exist now in one way and now in another.[17] It
is evident, then, that the power of the soul which causes [loco] motion is that
which is called "desire".[18]

433b   As for those who distinguish the parts of the soul, if they are to distinguish
them or separate them according to powers, a great many parts will arise:
the nutritive, the sentient, the thinking, the deliberative, and also the appetitive part; for these differ from one another more than the *desiring* part does
from the part concerned with temper.[19]

5   Now since desires may arise which are contrary to each other, and this
takes place whenever reason[20] and *desire* are contrary to each other and
arise in [animals which] have a sense of time[21] (for the intellect bids us to
resist for the sake of the future but *desire* [bids us to pursue] for the sake
of the present, and what is pleasurable now may appear to be pleasurable
without qualification and good without qualification because one may not
10   look to the future[22]), there can be [only] one mover[23] in kind, the appetitive
[part] qua appetitive, while the first mover in all cases is the object of desire

(for this causes motion by being thought or imagined and is not in motion),[24] but numerically [there can be] many movers.[25]

Now in motion there are three things [which may be distinguished]: (1) the mover, (2) that by which it moves, and (3) that which is moved; and a mover may be either (a) that which is immovable, or (b) that which causes motion but is also moved.[26] The immovable mover here is the practicable good,[27] the mover which is also moved is the appetitive part[28] (for that which is in motion is moved qua desiring, and its [kind of] motion is a species of desire taken as an activity[29]), and that which is in motion [only] is the animal.[30] The instrument with which desire causes motion is at this point corporeal; and, for this reason, its study comes under the treatise which investigates the functions common to body and soul.[31] At present, we may briefly say that the mover which causes motion instrumentally lies where a beginning and an end coincide, as in a ball-and-socket joint; for here the convex and concave sides [coincide], the one being an end and the other a beginning. For this reason, one of them is at rest but the other is in motion; and they are different in definition but not separate in magnitude,[32] for all things are moved by being pushed or pulled.[33] Thus, something should remain fixed, as in a [rotating] wheel, and it is from this thing that motion should begin.

In general, then, as already stated, an animal causes its own motion qua being appetitive, and it cannot be appetitive without imagination. Now imagination may be either with judgment or [merely] sentient; and [not only man but] all the other animals partake of sentient imagination.[34]

11

434a We must consider also what the mover is in imperfect animals, [i.e.,] those which have only the sense of touch,[1] [and] whether imagination[2] and *desire* can belong to them or not. Now it appears that they can be pained or pleased; and, if so, they must also have *desire*. But how can imagination be in them? Must we not say that, just as their motions are indefinite, so these [*desire* and imagination] exist in them but in an indefinite way?[3]

Sentient imagination, as we have stated,[4] exists in all other animals also, but deliberative imagination exists [only] in animals which use reason in practical matters. For, in the latter case, whether one will *act* in this or that manner is a function of judgment; and a man must make the measurement by a single [principle], for he pursues the greater [good].[5] Consequently, one must be able to produce a unity out of many images.[6] And this is the *reason* why it is thought that [sense imagination] has no opinion, seeing that it does not have [the power] to connect [images], whereas [opinion] includes imagination.[7] In view of this, desire does not have the power to deliberate.[8] Now sometimes desire [i.e., *desire*] overpowers and displaces wish,[9] and this happens whenever incontinence prevails; at other times, however, it is the

[wish] that does this to [*desire*]. Thus each [kind of] desire [overpowers and displaces] in turn the other, as one sphere [does to another]).[10] By its nature,

15   however, the higher[11] [desire, i.e., the wish] is always the higher principle, and it prevails [over the lower, i.e., over *desire*]; hence there arise three kinds of locomotion.[12] As for the [part of the soul] that *knows*, it is not moved but remains still.[13] So since one belief or statement is universal but the other is of a particular (for the former [merely] asserts that such a kind of man should do such a kind of thing, whereas the latter asserts that this thing before me is of such a kind and I am such a kind of man),[14] it is the latter

20   opinion which causes the motion and not the universal; or else, it is both, but the universal is rather at rest whereas the other is not.[15]

12

Now everything which is living and has a soul from the time it is generated till it is destroyed must, as such, possess the nutritive soul, for that which is generated must grow and reach maturity and deteriorate, and these are impossible without food; so it is necessary for the nutritive power

25   to exist in everything which grows and deteriorates.[1] But it is not necessary for the power of sensation to exist in all living things. For a thing whose body is simple cannot have the sense of touch, and an animal cannot exist without

30   this sense; and things incapable of receiving forms without matter cannot [have this sense].[2]

Animals, on the other hand, must have a sense, if nature does nothing in vain;[3] for all things existing by nature are for the sake of something, or else they will be coincidences of [things which are] for the sake of something.[4] Accordingly, if every body which can travel from one place to another did

131b   not have a power of sensing, it would be destroyed and would not attain its end, which is [its] nature's function.[5] For how will it be nourished? Stationary [living things] take nourishment from the source at which they have grown; but a body which is not stationary and has been generated with a soul or an intellect capable of judgment cannot [be nourished] without the

5   faculty of sensation. (As for [a body] which is ungenerable, it cannot have [the power of sensation]. For, why should it have it?[6] [Perhaps because it would be] better for its body or for its soul. But, as it is, this cannot be the case; for neither will its [soul] think any more [by having sensation], nor will its body, [being ungenerable], exist more because of [sensation]). No [generable] body which is not stationary, then, can have a soul without the power of sensation.

Further, if a thing has the power of sensation, it must be either simple

10   or a blend. It cannot be simple; for then it will not have the sense of touch, which is necessary [for sensation]. This is clear from the following.[7] Since an animal is an animate body and every body is tangible, and since a tangible body is sensible by the sense of touch, the body of an animal must

be capable of sensing by touch [other bodies] if the animal is to save itself.
15 For the other senses (i.e., sense of smell, vision, sense of hearing) are sensing
[their objects] through other [external media], whereas if [the body of an
animal] touches an object but has no power of sensing it, it will not be able
to avoid some tangible objects and accept others, and in such a case the
animal cannot save itself.[8] It is in view of this, too, that tasting is a sort of
20 touching, for it is of food, and food is a tangible body;[9] but sounds and colors
and odors do not nourish [the body of an animal], nor do they make it grow
or deteriorate. So the sense of taste too must be a species of touch, because
it is a sense of tangible and nourishing objects. Accordingly, these two senses
[of touch and of taste] are necessary for an animal, and it is evident that no
animal can exist without the sense of touch.

As for the other senses, they exist also for the sake of living well,[10] and,
25 we may add, they must exist not in any chance species of animals but in
certain species, i.e., those which can travel from place to place. For if these
are to save themselves, they should sense not only objects which they can
touch but also objects at a distance;[11] and sensation of objects at a distance
is possible if sensation through an intervening medium can take place when
that medium is acted upon by the sensible object and the sense is acted upon
30 by that medium. For just as the mover of an object in locomotion acts till
the change is made (as when A pushes B and causes it to push C and so a
motion through an intermediate object is produced, in which case the first
mover pushes without being pushed, the last object C is pushed without
pushing another, but the intermediate object B both pushes and is pushed,
435a and [there may be] many intermediates), so it is in the case of alteration,
except that the [mover] causes alteration while remaining in the same
place.[12] Thus, if one were to dip an object into wax, motion would occur just
so far as the object is dipped; [if one tries to dip the object into] a stone, there
will be no motion at all; [if in water], the water will be moved far [beyond
5 the object dipped]; [and if in air], the air will be moved the furthest and will
both act and be acted upon, if it remains unified.[13] It is in view of this that
in reflection, too, instead of saying that vision proceeds [i.e., travels] from
the eye out and is reflected, it is better to say that the air is acted upon by
the shape and color [of the object seen], while remaining unified as far as
it proceeds. Now the air remains unified after [striking] a smooth surface,
and so upon returning it moves one's vision;[14] and this is as if[15] the impres-
10 sion in the wax had penetrated through to the other side [of the wax].

13

It is evident, then, that the body of an animal cannot be simple; I mean,
for instance, that it cannot be made of fire alone or of air alone. For, without
the sense of touch, an animal cannot have any other sense since, as already
stated,[1] every animate body [of an animal] has a sense of touch. Now the

15   other elements, with the exception of earth, might become sense organs, but
      each of them produces sensation through something else, an intervening
      medium;[2] but the sense of touch [produces sensation] by the direct touching
      [of its objects],[3] and it is in view of this that it has [received] its name.[4] And
      although the other organs, too, sense by touch, they do so through something
      else;[5] but only the sense of touch is thought to sense [its objects] through
20   itself.[6] Consequently, no body of an animal is made of [only one of] those
      other elements [fire, air, water].
          Nor can such body be made of earth [alone].[7] For the sense of touch is
      like a mean between all tangible objects, and its organ can receive not only
      all the differentiae of earth, but also those of hot and cold and the other
25   tangible objects.[8] So it is because of this that we cannot sense by our bones
435b or hair or such parts of the body, for these are made of earth; and it is
      because of this that plants, too, have no sense, for they are made of earth,
      and without the sense of touch no other sense can exist.
          The organ of touch, then, is not made of earth [alone] or of any other
5   single element. Hence it is evident that animals which are deprived of this
      one sense must die; for neither a thing which is not an animal can have this
      sense, nor is it necessary for an animal, which must have this sense, to have
      any of the other senses.[9] It is because of this fact, too, that the excesses of
      the other sensible objects, e.g., of colors and sounds and odors, destroy only
10   the corresponding sense organs and not the animal, except indirectly, e.g.,
      when an [excessive] sound is accompanied by a thrust or a blow, or when
      [excessive] odors or objects of sight set other things in motion which in turn
      destroy the sense of touch. Flavors, too, destroy the sense of touch in this
      manner, i.e., insofar as they happen to act excessively as objects of touch.
      But the excesses of tangible objects [qua tangible], e.g., of hot or cold or hard
15   objects, destroy the animal; for the excess of every sensible object destroys
      the corresponding sense organ, and so such object of touch too destroys the
      sense of touch, in virtue of which living [for an animal] is defined, since it
      was shown that an animal cannot exist without the sense of touch. It is in
      view of this that the excess of tangible objects destroys not only the organ
      of touch but also the animal, since [the sense of touch] is the only sense which
      an animal must have [if it is to live].[10]
20   An animal possesses the senses other than that of touch not for the sake
      of existing but for the sake of living well, as already stated. For instance,
      it has vision so that it may see [objects at a distance], for [it lives] in air or
      water or, in general, in a transparent medium; it has the sense of taste
      because of what is pleasant or painful to taste, so that it may sense [the
      pleasant] in food, *desire* it, and move itself [towards it]; but it has the sense
      of hearing, so that it may be informed [by others through sound]; and it has
25   a tongue, so that it may convey information to others.[11]

COMMENTARIES ON THE SOUL

The references given in the Commentaries and in the Glossary are to the standard pages (sections) and lines according to the Bekker's edition of Aristotle's works (Berlin, 1831). In particular, pages 402a1-435b25 cover the treatise *On the Soul*, and these pages (and lines) appear as such in the margins of the translation. The Bekker pages covering each of Aristotle's works are as follows:

Categories: 1a1-15b33.
Propositions (De Interpretatione): 16a1-24b9.
Prior Analytics: 24a10-70b38.
Posterior Analytics: 71a1-100b17.
Topics: 100a18-164b19.
Sophistical Refutations: 164a20-184b8.
Physics: 184a10-267b26.
On the Heavens: 268a1-313b23.
On Generation and Destruction: 314a1-338b19.
Meteorology: 338a20-390b22.
On the Universe, To Alexander: 391a1-401b29.
On the Soul: 402a1-435b25.
On Sensation and Sensibles: 436a1-449a31.
On Memory and Recollection: 449b1-453b11.
On Sleep and Wakefulness: 453b11-458a32.
On Dreams: 458a33-462b11.
On Divination from Dreams: 462b12-464b18.
On Longevity and Shortness of Life: 464b19-467b9.
On Youth, Old Age, Life, and Death: 467b10-470b5.
On Respiration: 470b6-480b30.
On Breath: 481a1-486b4.
A Treatise on Animals: 486a5-638b37.
On Parts of Animals: 639a1-697b30.
On Motion of Animals: 698a1-704b3.
On Locomotion of Animals: 704a4-714b23.
On Generation of Animals: 715a1-789b20.
On Colors: 791a1-799b20.
On Objects of Hearing: 800a1-804b39.
Physiognomy: 805a1-814b9.
On Plants: 815a10-830b4.
On Reported Marvels: 830a5-847b10.
Mechanics: 847a11-858b31.

Problems: 859al-967b27.
On Indivisible Lines: 968al-972b33.
Positions and Names of Winds: 973al-b25.
On Xenophanes, Zeno, and Gorgias: 974al-980b21.
Metaphysics: 980a21-1093b29.
Nicomachean Ethics: 1094al-1181b23.
Great Ethics: 1181a24-1213b30.
Eudemean Ethics: 1214al-1249b25.
On Virtues and Vices: 1249a26-1251b37.
Politics: 1252al-1342b34.
Household Management: 1343al-1353b27.
Rhetoric: 1354al-1420b4.
Rhetoric for Alexander: 1420a5-1447b7.
Poetics: 1447a8-1462b18.

BOOK A

1

1. Knowing is to knowledge as activity is to potentiality or to power, and activity is better than the corresponding power among good things. So "knowing" rather than "knowledge" should be used, as the Greek term indicates. Perhaps the primary kind of knowing is meant, i.e., that which is pursued or chosen for its own sake. The terms "noble" and "honorable" suggest this. Such knowing is noble, for what is noble is a good in itself and is pursued for its own sake. Again, such knowing is honorable, for we honor things which are noble or good in themselves, just as we honor great deeds or great men. 1362b7-9, 1364b27-8, 1366a33-5.

The usual translations of καλός as "beautiful" here are mistaken. An alternative to "noble" is "fine".

2. That which is more accurate is better known, and that which is better known is more noble and more honorable. One kind of knowledge is more accurate than another in three ways: (a) by being of the fact and its cause rather than of the fact alone, if that fact has a cause; (b) by being more abstract or universal, for only thus can the cause and maximum universality be viewed without irrelevant facts; (c) by proceeding from relatively fewer principles. 87a31-7, 1078a9-14. See also the commentaries on 87a31-7 in my *Aristotle's Posterior Analytics*.

3. Other things being equal, one science is better than another if the objects of the first are better than those of the second. For example, ethics is better than the science of fish, for ethics is concerned with happiness, which is better than fish or knowledge of fish. 157a9-11, 1064b3-6.

4. Few would doubt the importance of man's soul as a subject for a science; yet there is some doubt as to the accuracy of a science of soul. But an accurate science is not necessarily easy, otherwise first philosophy, which investigates things most universally, would be easy. So the difficulties that some thinkers, like the behaviorists, have in getting concepts and doing so accurately in psychology are due to their lack of intuition.

5. Why the use of the term ἱστορία (= "inquiry") rather than the term for "science"? Is this work preliminary to the science of soul, as R. D. Hicks thinks? Perhaps ἱστορία is the genus of which ἐπιστήμη is the species and inquiry is more valuable into these matters even if it is not scientific.

6. Of natural things, animals are better than inanimate objects, and so their soul or their nature as form — and form is prior to matter — is better than the corresponding nature of inanimate things. Further, *knowledge* of man's parts of the soul, which are concerned with science and the principles of science, contributes to truth, whether theoretical or practical or produc-

tive. Such knowledge may be of the whatness or properties or functions of those parts, even of thought itself; and it is considered in this treatise, in *Ethics* (Book Z), and in the *Organon,* although differently. As Aristotle states in the *Metaphysics* (1005b2-5), one must have *knowledge* of analytics before proceeding to the objects of a particular science, such as mathematics; and to know analytics is to know something about the soul, for analytics as given in print is a substitute for thoughts as existing in the soul.

7. The term "nature" has many senses (1014b16-5a19) and is limited mainly to principles of things existing by nature. It is used also metaphorically. The term *"substance",* on the other hand, does not apply to every sense of "nature" 1017b21-3. It is not limited to principles existing by nature, for it applies also to the prime mover (1074b21-3). Perhaps the two terms refer to the two problems raised in lines 402a22-b1: (a) Is the soul a form or matter or a composite of the two; and (b) is it a substance or a quantity or a quality, etc.? Both problems are discussed.

8. The term "attribute" is more universal than the term *"attribute".* The expressions "some are thought" and "others are thought" are used because at this stage it is not yet clear whether there are any proper *attributes* of the soul at all. One may think that all attributes assigned to the soul are attributes of the composite of soul and body, as in the case of sensation, which is impossible without a bodily organ, and in the case of anger, in which the body too appears to participate (403a26-7, 436a6-11). This opinion is indicated by the second part of this sentence.

One must not confuse the distinction between "essential element" and "attribute". Triangularity and magnitude are essential elements but not attributes of a scalene triangle; and concurrence of the angle bisectors is an attribute of that triangle, although not a proper *attribute.* In general, the essential elements of a thing are known through its definition alone; the proper *attributes* of the thing are demonstrated by the use of that definition and the axioms and hypotheses concerning that thing. These matters are discussed in the *Posterior Analytics.*

9. The first problem in the science of the soul is laying down the definition of the soul, which is the subject of that science; for the definition signifies the nature or *substance* of the soul. Is there a single method of reaching that definition or not? The problem of getting the proper *attributes* is secondary and simple; it is secondary because those attributes cannot be attained without the definition, and it is simple because, in a science, all attributes are reached by a single method, namely, by demonstration.

The scientists in Aristotle's time either assumed the subject of their science, or made it known by sensation, or laid down its definition hypothetically, or described it in some way or other, without discussing the nature, the whatness, or the existence of their subject. Thus, many ways were used in making the subject of a science known. 1025b7-16.

10. Plato used the method of division in order to arrive at a definition. For example, is a man an animal or inanimate? He is an animal. Is he aquatic or terrestrial? He is terrestrial. Is he footed or footless? and so on. So a man is an animal, terrestrial, footed, etc. Aristotle rejects this method of demonstrating or arriving at a definition. 46a31-b37, 91b12-27.

11. Let the method of arriving at the definition of man be Plato's division. One might start by asking whether he is a quality or not a quality, or whether he is terrestrial or aquatic, or whether he is footed or footless, or whether he is a self-mover, or not, etc. What, then, is the starting-point? So even if a given method is used, the starting points may be different not only for things investigated by different sciences, whose principles are different and many, but also for a given thing within a science.

12. The genus meant here is the ultimate genus, i.e., the category, and there are ten different categories. These are discussed in the *Categories*. The whatness of the soul, as given in the definition of it, includes the differentia also. Evidently, one should seek the genus first, and then the differentia. If one asserts that the genus of man is quality, it is useless to proceed to seek the differentia, for no differentia of a quality is a differentia of a substance; but if he asserts that the genus of it is substance, he can then proceed to seek the differentia. This kind of priority is used in seeking the definition of virtue (1105b19-6a15), of intention (1111b4-3a14), and of other things.

13. Potentiality and actuality are two different modes of existence. For example, the power to see differs from actual seeing, and the power to walk differs from actual walking. If one defines the soul as the activity or activities of its powers, then a man who is sleeping, not being in activity, would be without a soul and therefore dead. So if we are to reject this and other absurd conclusions, it makes no small difference whether we define man's soul in terms of his powers or in terms of the activities of those powers. In general, confusion of potentiality with actuality leads to absurd results. 1046b29-7a24.

14. The term "part" has many meanings (1023b12-25), and it will be shown later that in one sense the soul has parts but in another sense it does not (407a2-32, 411b5-30, 413b10-4al, 432a22-b7).

15. Is man's soul the same in kind as the soul of a horse? Are the parts of man's soul the same in kind as the whole soul? These are different questions. Lines 402b5-8 and 414b19-5a13 are related to the first question, lines 411a16-b30 to the second.

16. The problem here is one of adequacy. One may so define the soul that it applies to men only. If, however, some attributes of this soul belong to other things also, e.g., to plants and animals, they are not properties of man or of his soul; but science should investigate only properties if it is to investigate the causes of things. Those attributes as attributes of other things also, then, would be left out of the investigation. It follows, then, that the definition of the soul should not be so restricted as to apply to men only.

17. If a definition is primarily of an ultimate species, then the formula for a genus will be a qualified definition; for a genus is related to a species of it as matter to form (1016a24-8, 1024b11-5), and the essence of a thing is revealed in a definition through a genus and also a differentia. An animal, universally taken, does not exist apart from animals, otherwise we are faced with Plato's Ideas and the ensuing absurdities; but it exists, if at all, as a term or a thought, and as such it is not a substance but something present in a substance. But a substance is prior in existence to what is present in it; and so an animal, taken universally, would be posterior in existence to animals. In another sense, however, "animal" is prior in existence to, say, "man" or "Socrates", if we inquire logically and attend to the things of which these are predicable; for if a man or Socrates exists, so does an animal, but the converse is not necessarily true (15a4-7, 1069a26-8).

18. Perhaps "many souls" here means many separate souls in each living thing, and the opposition would be between "many actually" and "many potentially", the latter term signifying many parts.

19. Given a whole, does one begin his inquiry with that whole or with its parts? In one sense, the part is prior to the whole; for if 5 exists, so does a unit in it, but if that unit exists, 5 does not necessarily exist (14a29-34). In another sense, the whole is prior to a part of it, for a part cannot exist as a part without the whole, and it is defined in terms of the whole, as in the case of a hand, which can neither exist nor be defined without the soul; for a dead hand is not a hand except equivocally (1253a18-25). In Book B Aristotle begins to define the soul as a unity or a whole, in general terms; then he considers the parts.

20. For example, problems might arise as to whether vision, the sense of hearing, and imagination are distinct from and not dependent on each other. Vision can exist without the sense of hearing, and conversely, but imagination without any of the senses is impossible. So it appears that there are parts of the soul which are dependent on other parts and also parts which are not so dependent.

21. Aristotle uses the term "opposites" here for what we translate as "objects related to those functions". The term "opposites" has four meanings: contraries, contradictories, privation and possession, and relatives (11b16-31). Here, it means relatives, and these are objects in relation to the functions of the soul.

22. This part is the faculty (or power, if you wish) of sensation.

23. Behaviorists are not interested in the faculties and the activities of the soul, for these cannot be sensed; so they limit their investigations to the objects corresponding to those faculties and activities. Evidently, Aristotle includes behaviorism as one of the three things to be investigated in psychology, i.e., (1) faculties, (2) functions, and (3) objects. His criticism of the behaviorists would then be: they are limited in scope, for (a) they deny the

existence or avoid the study of the form and functions of the soul, (b) they use behavioristic definitions of pain and anger and the like, which are not definitions of the things as understood and experienced, and (c) they use principles, hypotheses, logical inferences, and, in general, terms and expressions with universal meanings, all of which cannot be arrived at behavioristically, and without which there can be no science.

24. In a science, the investigation of properties of a thing through the cause proceeds by demonstration from principles, and the whatness or definition of that thing must be used, as in the case of a triangle, which is a plane figure bounded by three straight lines and whose existence can be demonstrated from indemonstrable principles. Thus the properties arrived at in this manner reveal the causes, as stated analytically in the *Posterior Analytics*. But in the investigation of the definition of the soul, when one does not yet possess the first principles which are indemonstrable, another method must be used. Nowadays we call this method experimentation, using this term in a somewhat inclusive manner; Aristotle had his own terminology and analysis corresponding to what we now call "experimentation".

We know some attributes of a thing, say B, and we are in the best possible position to arrive at the definition of B if we know as many of these attributes as we can under the circumstances; for if from a proposed definition such attributes follow and are not contradicted, then the definition proposed has some probability of expressing what B is, and this probability increases as the number of known attributes increases. If all the facts about B are known (which is not likely), the definition — assuming it does not contradict the principles of a definition — becomes a certainty. The known attributes of B, of course, are not known through the cause, for we do not yet know the definition of B, and knowledge of this definition is necessary for the knowledge of those attributes through the cause; yet knowledge of many such attributes contributes greatly, although indirectly, to arriving at the right definition of B.

It follows, too, that if from a proposed definition of B facts can be proved which contradict one or more of the known facts about B, then the proposed definition of B must be rejected. Applying this truth repeatedly later in Book A, Aristotle rejects the various definitions of the soul given by his predecessors by showing that some facts which can be proved from those definitions contradict known facts about the soul or even facts which these thinkers themselves posit concerning the soul. Further, if known facts about B cannot be proved or contradicted, whether with ease or difficulty or at all, by the use of a proposed definition, then that definition is empty or dialectical. It is empty, if it signifies something which has little or nothing to do with the soul as usually known; and this would be the case if one were to define the soul as "a three-sided plane figure", or, to some extent, if he were to define it as "a self-moving number", as Plato did. It is dialectical, if it signifies the soul to some extent but fails in one or more ways as a definition; for it may be vague, or incomplete, or too wide, or a property rather than a definition, or in terms of what is *known to us*, etc.

The knowledge of facts demonstrated by the use of the definition of B is knowledge *by nature* or knowledge of those facts through the nature of B; but knowledge of facts about B prior to knowledge of the definition of B is knowledge *known to us*, and such knowledge is undemonstrated. Evidently, what is *known to us* about a thing is usually or always prior in time to what is known about that thing *by nature*, for knowledge, chronologically, proceeds from sensation to experience and finally to universals and principles, and knowledge *by nature* proceeds from principles.

An alternative to "obvious" in line 402b23 is "according to imagination", which is more literal. If so, the meaning may be this: if from the proposed definition the object imagined appears to lead or somehow contain or imply all or most of the known attributes of the thing, we are in the best position to formulate its *substance*.

25. That which has the soul is the animate substance, whether an animal or a living thing in general, and it is a composite of body and soul.

26. An *attribute* proper to the soul would be a property of the soul not requiring a body for its existence. If so, the soul would be separable from the body, for, if not, the *attribute* would require the body for its existence.

As stated in lines 402a8-10, some thinkers are of the opinion that there are attributes, such as thinking, which are proper to the soul, and hence that thinking does not require the body. But thinking, as we shall see later, is impossible without the body; further, thinking presupposes sensation and images, which are impossible without the body 427b16-8.

27. "Imagination" here means imagining, which is an activity, like thinking. So an alternative to "imagination" is "imagining". 429a1-2, 433a9-10.

28. The term "the straight" is a noun; it stands for anything which is straight or has straightness, or even for a straight line. In either case, the straight touches a bronze sphere qua being straight (or having straightness), otherwise it would not always so touch it; and, in either case, it exists always with a body, for it is a quantity, which is an attribute of a natural substance, and all attributes are present in substances (i.e., incapable of existing apart from substances). Further, touching is an attribute of a physical body and not of a quantity. 1a20-9, 2b6-8, 226b18-23. A mathematician studies straight lines *as such*, but in so doing he separates them only in thought and not in existence; for he cannot detach the straightness of a ruler from that ruler and exhibit it as something separate. Straightness or a straight line is not a substance, and only substances exist or can exist separately from other things. 1077b17-8b6.

The similarity indicated is as follows. The straight qua having straightness has the *attribute* of touching a bronze sphere, but it always exists in a physical body and is inseparable from that body. Similarly, the soul has *attributes* and functions, but it cannot have these unless it exists with a body from which it is inseparable; for having any of these *attributes* necessitates the existence of the body with which it exists, and if the soul were to exist apart from that body, it would not have any of these *attributes*.

29. Perhaps these are affections of the body caused by external agents. The next sentence, which gives a second example, suggests that the affections in the first example are caused by external agents.

30. The dialectical argument by means of examples in the two sentences goes as follows. If all the bodily affections of a man (or an animal) were caused by external agents, then similar agents would produce similar affections of the body of a man. But this is not so with bodily affections which occur simultaneously with mental affections such as anger and fear. Hence the agent causing bodily affections in these cases is the soul or a part of the soul; and so anger and fear and other affections (some or all) are attended by affections of the body.

31. In other words, if this is so in all cases of *attributes* of the soul, then such *attributes* cannot exist without the corresponding affections of the body, and hence they cannot exist without the body itself.

32. In other words, the *attributes* of the soul cannot exist without matter, and hence their nature or whatness and also their definition must include matter.

33. All the four causes are included in this definition. The form or formal cause is signified by "a certain motion", the matter or material cause by "such a body or bodily part or faculty of the body", the moving cause by "such and such a mover", and the final cause by "for the sake of such and such an end." The causes are given in a somewhat general form, but this is sufficient for illustrative purposes. The expression "a certain motion" need not be further specified, and similarly for the other expressions. One might raise problems such as whether the genus is motion or affection or desire or whether "faculty" can be a material cause at all (in a qualified way, it can); but these problems, too, do not affect the fact that all four causes are included.

34. In the case of man, the active intellect, as a part of his soul, does not depend on the body, and so it can exist apart from the body. 430a10-25. The term "physicist" for Aristotle is wide enough to include psychology.

35. Many questions arise. Is "formula" the correct translation? If so, what does it mean? Is the formula with the thing, like the form of the thing, or of the thing, like a definition, which is of a thing and not with it? How does the formula of a thing differ from its form? Also, manuscripts differ, and perhaps there is some corruption in the text.

36. There is a problem here. Why is the definition of anger, which states

the form alone, dialectical? If a physicist is concerned with all four causes (198a22-4), and if form is prior to matter (1049b4-50b1), he would be even less of a physicist by stating the matter alone than by stating the form alone (1037a16-7). Each definition gives only one cause, and all must be used in physics. Perhaps the form given by the dialectician's definition is not the form of anger; for it may be generally accepted — in which case it is dialectical — but perhaps not every angry man desires to retaliate, or perhaps anger is a motion and not a desire (assuming that desire is not a motion). Aristotle raises the problem concerning the two partial definitions later in 403b7.

37. This is Aristotle's position. Both form and matter should be considered by the physicist, and elsewhere Aristotle's definition adds also the mover and the final cause, for the physicist must consider all the four causes (198a22-4).

38. One of them would be concerned with matter alone, while the other would be concerned with the formula alone.

39. Aristotle here is referring to proximate matter and not to prime matter. A man's soul must be with the kind of matter which is appropriate to his soul, and the same applies to vision and such attributes as seeing and being pained. 1044a15-9.

40. For example, one who investigates seeing is not a scientist unless he includes the appropriate matter in the definition of seeing; for as seeing exists, so it must be defined.

41. In other words, the physicist must include the appropriate matter in the investigation of the affections or functions of natural substances. Moving and final causes are not mentioned, perhaps because not all attributes investigated by the physicist require these causes. The simple elements — fire, air, water, air — appear to have no final cause, or else to have very little of it (390a3-4). So perhaps the term "body" suggests or includes animals or physical things which have moving and final causes but "matter" applies rather to physical things without those causes (1040b5-10). Consequently, chemistry would come under physics and would be a branch of physics, and so would botany, biology, and psychology (if man's active intellect is excluded).

42. Substances existing by nature may or may not be made into works of art; but if they do so, art or the artist is their moving cause, and their *attributes* qua works of art are not attributes according to their nature. The materials of a house become a house by the architect, and a sick man becomes well after the physician performs surgery.

43. Since quantities are ultimately attributes of natural substances, *attributes* of quantities are inseparable from those substances, which have matter; and it would appear that they should be defined in terms of matter, like sensation and anger and the like. But there is a difference. Sensation and anger and the like use moving and final causes and they require specific

physical matter in their definition; they exist in animals only, not in plants or stones or water. Mathematical *attributes* have no such requirements; they are immovable and are treated as such, and they are alike *attributes* of natural bodies, regardless of the specific matter in each of those bodies. It makes no difference whether the surface of a triangle is present in a wooden or an iron natural body; its *attributes* are the same. So the mathematician abstracts in thought quantities from natural and sensible bodies, i.e., he does not assert that they exist separately from those bodies but treats them in themselves or as if they were separate without reference to the kind of bodies in which they are present or to the kind of sensible matter in those bodies. Quantities so abstracted and the *attributes* which belong to them *as such* are said to be intelligible, and so is their matter, e.g., surface and line and volume. 431b12-6, 1036a8-12, 1061a28-b3.

Aristotle sometimes uses the phrase "objects by abstraction" for the mathematical objects. 81b3, 299a16, 429b18, 431b12, etc.

44. Substances exist separately, and it is the philosopher who considers them qua such, but universally, i.e., he considers being qua being. Quantity, quality, priority, part, whole, unity, definition, cause, and the like, which are considered in Book Δ and elsewhere, are *attributes* of substances; and they are attributes of other things, if at all, only secondarily and in a qualified way. Some substances are eternal, like the prime mover, others are not.

45. The study of lines and planes and their *attributes* does not depend on specific physical matter qua such, i.e., qua sensible or movable. But this is not the case with temper and fear and the like; so the study of these must include the specific physical matter on which they depend.

2

1. After laying down the soul as the subject and listing the problems concerning the soul, Aristotle now proceeds to discuss the difficulties dialectically, examining at the same time the various views of his predecessors in order that he may profit from what has been truly stated but discard what has been falsely stated. He uses this method in his *Metaphysics, Ethics, Politics,* and, in general, in treatises which are concerned with subjects discussed by others to some extent. If the subject of the science is new or hardly dealt with, as in *Prior Analytics, Posterior Analytics,* and *Propositions,* there is little or no necessity for this method.

2. This is a dialectical premise, i.e., one which is generally accepted as true.

3. According to these thinkers, the soul causes motion primarily, for it causes its own motion and that of others, whereas other things cause motion not by themselves but by being moved by the soul. So, as a mover, the soul is first and hence prior in existence to other things. Perhaps "most of all"

signifies motion to the highest degree. The case is similar to primary substances as underlying subjects; for primary substances, compared with the
various secondary substances as underlying subjects, are substances most of
all. 2b7-28, 1032a18-9, 1034a4.

4. Aristotle denies this principle, for a thing which moves another thing
need not be in motion, as in the case of the prime mover. 1012b31.

5. Plato is among these. 1071b37-2a3, *Laws* 894-6, *Phaedrus* 245.

6. Perhaps Hermotimus is included. 984b18-20.

7. The term *"Intelligence"* instead of "intellect" may be used here, for
Anaxagoras uses what is translated here as "intellect" as a first principle; and
for first principles posited by thinkers other than Aristotle we use capitalized
terms in italics, as in the *Metaphysics*.

8. It would follow from this statement that for Democritus the intellect
and sensation are the same; and this is confirmed by 1009a38-b17 and by
Philoponus.

9. 984b8-31, Frag. 12D.

10. If *Intelligence* or the intellect is the cause of beauty and rightness,
it appears to be a final cause; and if it is the cause as a mover of what is done
beautifully or rightly, it seems to include somehow both the moving and the
final cause. (984b11-22). But these thinkers are not so clear or definite in
their statements concerning the causes (988a20-3, 993a15-6), and they are
using the terms "soul" and "intellect" without making the appropriate
distinctions. For there is intellect with respect to truth, as in the principles
of science, and intellect with respect to prudence, i.e., for things done
according to what is good for oneself or a state. The latter kind of intellect
exists in some living things but not in others, so one is faced with a difficulty
if he identifies the intellect with the soul; for some living things, not being
prudent, would have no soul, or they would have one kind of soul but not
another kind of soul.

11. Frag. 109D, 1000b6-9.

12. A lost work.

13. According to Plato, Animal Itself is an Idea; and Ideas are eternal and
the causes of perishable things which share the same name and participate
in the corresponding Ideas. Aristotle's criticism of Ideas is in many of his
works, depending on the treatise to which a given problem belongs. A
general account of the Ideas followed by a criticism of them is given in the
Metaphysics, 987a29-993a-10, and in greater detail in 1076a8-1093b29. (To
guard against confusion of terms, see my *Aristotle's Metaphysics*, the Peripatetic Press).

14. 1090b20-4.

15. The *One* is Plato's first principle as form, and the *Dyad* is the principle
as matter. Two is the first Number formed by the action of the *One* upon
the *Dyad*. Three is formed from the *One* and Two, etc. The primary Length

is formed when Two acts on the *Dyad*, the primary Breadth is formed when Three acts on the *Dyad*, and the primary Depth is formed when Four acts on the *Dyad*. Plato regards the *Intellect* as the *One*, perhaps because the *Intellect* conceives the essence or nature of a thing, and an essence or nature is one thing and not many. In a similar way, *Knowledge* is of the primary Length, something which has two things; for, like a statement, *knowledge* of a fact has a subject and a predicate, and these are two, and a length is determined by two points, or else it requires the motion of a point to be formed. Analogous remarks may be made concerning Opinion and Sensation, which are Ideas, for these require additional principles; opinion in men is not fixed but may or may not be true, and sensation is even further from opinion (*Timaeus* 53C-57D, *Laws* 894). Aristotle regards Plato's theory of Ideas and their formation as fictitious and contradictory; for things which resemble each other only in some respects are not identical in nature, Plato's two principles are inadequate, generation of eternal things (Ideas are posited as eternal and immutable) is impossible, and many other difficulties arise. Books M and N of the *Metaphysics* give a detailed criticism of Plato's Ideas.

16. Numbers, as already stated, are generated from the *One* and the *Dyad* as principles and elements; and the others, which are the mathematical objects and the sensible objects, are generated from Numbers and those two principles. Plato's early theory did not identify Numbers with Ideas (or Forms); the identification was posited later. 987b20-5, 991b9, 1083a17-9.

17. Perhaps Xenocrates and some other Platonists.

18. For Aristotle, that which can cause motion without being caused to move is a first mover or a primary mover, and hence a principle. So these thinkers had good reason, at least in principle if not in application, to say that the soul is the first principle which causes motion; for it seems that a man, who has a soul, can initiate such motion but a rock, which is inanimate, cannot do so.

19. We have inserted the bracketed expressions because Aristotle would reject or qualify the assumptions in this sentence.

20. What are these two traits? Some say that they are (a) being composed of the finest particles and (b) being in motion and causing motion; others, that they are (a) knowing and (b) causing motion; still others, that they are (a) being in motion and (b) causing motion.

It appears that the text favors the last alternative. The preceding sentence speaks of fire, which Democritus here identifies with soul, as being primarily in motion and primarily the cause of motion, that is, as being most easily moved and as being the first in causing motion in others; and to state the cause of these is to give the middle term. Now Aristotle uses the word διὰ for what we translate as "cause" or "through" or "because", depending on idiomatic English, and in the next part of this sentence Aristotle gives the middle terms as follows: "because of the smallness . . . moved". So, since for Democritus the soul and fire and the intellect are the same, the two middle terms may be stated in the following: (a) the soul is the smallest of particles; the smallest of particles is the primary cause of motion; hence the soul is the primary cause of motion; (b) the soul has a spherical shape; what has spherical shape is most easily moved; hence the soul is most easily moved.

21. Some manuscripts add ἐκ after εἶναι, in which case the correct translation would be "is composed" and not "is". The two alternatives lead to the next commentary.

22. It is not clearly stated whether each particle is a soul, and whether many particles can make up one soul, as in a man. Perhaps Aristotle merely states what Democritus says, in which case the lack of clarity is due to Democritus.

23. In saying that *Intelligence* is the cause of beauty and rightness and also of the first motion of the universe (404a25-7, 984b18-22), and that it alone is simple and unblended and pure, Anaxagoras seems to distinguish *Intelligence* as the first cause from the soul of a man or of an animal; for the soul of a man or of an animal did not start the motion in the universe and may not be intelligent (404b5-7), and it is blended with the body. But in speaking of the soul as being an intellect (404b1-5) and as both knowing and causing motion (405a17-9), he treats it as if it had the same nature as that of *Intelligence*.

24. 984a5-7.

25. According to Heraclitus, the principle of all things is fire, which is always in motion or a state of flux (987a32-4), and that all other things are composed of fire (984a7-8). Here, this principle is called "exhalation", perhaps a term which Heraclitus used at times for "fire".

26. Thales, Diogenes, and Heraclitus.

27. Such a thinker would be one who posited a finite number of elements, like Empedocles, or an infinite number of them, or else a follower of such a thinker.

28. Perhaps "incorporeality" should be so taken as to include least corporeality or possession of finest particles, as indicated by lines 404b31, 405a6, 22, 27, and 409b20-1.

29. In other words, each of these is regarded as being a trait of the principle (fire, or air, or blood, etc.) taken as being the soul or a part of the soul.

30. The exception is Anaxagoras; for he regards *Intelligence* as being simple, unmixed, pure, and distinct from all other things, and so for him like is not known by like. 405a13-7, 429b22-4.

31. To sense or to know is to be affected in a certain way. So since *Intelligence* cannot be affected, how is it possible for it to know? Besides,

what moving cause can affect it? Another *reason* why it cannot be affected is given in 429b22-9.

32. For the Pythagoreans, the principles of all things are the *Odd* and the *Even*, which are contraries; for Empedocles, they are *Friendship* and *Strife;* and similarly for other thinkers.

33. For Heraclitus, the principle is *Fire*, which is hot; for Hippo, it is *Water*, which was considered to be cold.

34. The Greek terms for "to cool" and "soul" differ only in one letter, and breathing was regarded by some as taking in air to cool the blood or body.

3

1. Falsity differs from impossibility. If we assume that the soul moves itself or causes other things to move, it does not follow that self-motion or causing motion is its *substance;* for self-motion or causing motion may be only an attribute and so different from the *substance* of the soul, or it may be only one of the elements of that substance, like the appetitive element, which can cause motion. The impossibility arises when motion is attributed to the soul, whether as its *substance* or an element of that *substance* or even an attribute which follows from that *substance.*

2. 258b4-9, 1012b30-1, 1072a25-6.

3. A thing which is directly or essentially in motion must be a body having matter and form and be subject to the three principles of motion, as stated in the *Physics*, Book A; it cannot be just a form or an attribute of a substance which has matter. 224a21-34, 254b7-22, 1067b9-11.

4. By "sailors in motion" here he means sailors who are at rest in a ship but in motion relative to stationary objects external to the ship.

5. Walking is a species of locomotion, which is in motion with respect to place. 639b2-3.

6. An alternative to "or" is "and".

7. Perhaps the expression "is in motion or partakes of motion" indicates two alternatives; for the soul may be considered as being essentially in motion either always or sometimes. In either case, the soul would have place essentially and so be a body; for only bodies can be in place essentially.

8. An alternative to "as an attribute" is "indirectly". A thing which is in motion as an attribute is either a form or an attribute of a substance which has matter and form, as stated in Comm. 3.

9. That is, motion would belong to the soul either always or sometimes, as suggested in Comm. 7.

10. That which alters is in place, even if it does not change with respect to place. Thus stationary milk may turn sour, and a sick man in bed may be in the process of becoming healthy.

11. 276a22-6.

12. Such will be the motions of fire and of earth if each of these is not in its proper place.

13. The bodies meant are water and air. Water is up relative to earth and down relative to air, and air is down relative to fire. Bodies which are mixtures or blends of the four elements have corresponding relative places.

14. The two premises put forward are dialectical.

15. The term μεθισταμένη means changing place or going elsewhere, and this necessitates locomotion, whether of a thing as a whole, or of any part or parts relative to other parts or to the place of the thing, or of all the parts, as in the case of a revolving spherical body about its axis; and the position of this term, which indicates locomotion, is guided by grammatical construction. So it is evident that the kind of change which is assumed for the soul here is locomotion; and the attempts by many commentators to introduce variants or regard this text as corrupt or find fault with it have no basis.

16. Since resurrection is impossible, the soul cannot be a body as posited by these thinkers.

17. Certain animals, for example, are of such a nature that they can be moved by themselves, and they are physical bodies; but they can also be moved by other things by force. These animals, however, are not in motion always, although they have the power to move themselves and to be moved by external causes. But the soul as posited by these thinkers cannot be moved by another thing; for its *substance* is to be causing its own motion. So it must always be in motion and cannot be changed by another thing from rest to motion, except indirectly. For example, a container which has a soul might be moved by an external agent, so one might say that the soul is moved by that agent; but such motion is indirect or accidental to the soul and does not change the soul from rest to motion, for it is already in motion.

Perhaps the analogy of motion to goodness is as follows. That which is good because of itself is not good because of something else, otherwise its goodness would be caused by two causes of the same kind, e.g., by two final causes, and this is impossible. Man's final cause is happiness, which is a good, and no other cause causes this. Similarly, an act of generosity is a good in virtue of itself, and it is pursued for its own sake and is not a means to something else; for even if we act generously *because* of something else (happiness), a generous act is still good in *virtue of itself* (1096b16-9). Similarly, that whose *substance* is to cause its own motion can have no other cause of that motion.

18. This statement is yet to be discussed and developed when Aristotle's own theory of the soul is considered.

19. This statement is not a definition of motion but something which follows from the definition. The departure indicated is from that which the thing is to that which it will be after the motion. The terms "actuality" and "potentiality", which are included in the definition of motion, are not needed for the argument. 201a10-1.

20. If the *substance* of the soul is to cause itself to be moved, then the soul

causes a change not in the quantity or quality or some other attribute of itself but in the *substance* of itself. So if self-motion is that *substance*, then self-motion would have to be changed, either partly or wholly. In either case, the *substance* of the soul would be changed and so the soul would be destroyed; for, whether the soul changes qua a cause of its motion or qua in motion, there would be no soul which causes its own motion.

In his argument Aristotle considers the change in the soul to be that of its motion. Perhaps he does this because if the soul changes as the cause of its motion, the motion too will change, and so there will be no soul which causes its own motion.

21. As stated in 403b31-4a5, Democritus identified these spheres with soul.

22. If these indivisible spheres are always in motion, they should be always causing a living body to move. But that body also stops and rests; and it appears that *intention* or thought causes the body to move or to rest. So it is difficult, if not impossible, for such spheres to be the cause of motion in a living body. In 433b10-2 Aristotle states that that which causes the animal to move is the desiring part of the soul, and that the primary mover is the object of desire, which is unmoved but causes motion by being thought, as is usual in men, or imagined, as in the other animals.

23. Arguments belonging to physics are those whose terms belong to physics, but such arguments need not be true.

24. *Timaeus* 34B-36E.

25. By "the soul of the universe" Plato cannot have meant a sentient soul or a *desiring* soul; for he regards these as aberrations or distortions from the soul in the universe, and these souls or parts of a soul were generated later, according to him, and they do not move continuously in a circle, for they have a beginning, a middle, and an end. The soul of the universe, on the other hand, always has truth, which is *knowledge* and true opinion (*Timaeus*, 42-3). In view of this, Plato must have regarded the soul of the universe to be what was usually called "intellect", which is always the same, never false, and a form and not matter or something with matter. If this be the case, then the soul cannot have magnitude; for only natural bodies (things with physical matter) have magnitude. Magnitudes may be abstracted from natural bodies and studied in themselves, but they are attributes of such bodies and cannot exist apart from them (1077b17-8a31). But the soul, which is a form, cannot be or have magnitude.

Aristotle's disagreement, of course, rests partly on his own principles; and one may raise an objection to these. On the other hand, if truth is the aim, and if Plato's principles lead to contradictions, then one should first refute Aristotle's premises, some or all, before raising an objection to his criticism of Plato.

26. One may consider thinking in two ways: (a) as a process, which takes

time and is an attribute and not an essential element of the intellect, and
(b) as a nature or in respect to its contents, which are concepts. Thinking
as a process is a motion and takes time, and in this way it is continuous; for
motion is continuous, and so is time (if taken not as a number but as that
which may be measured by a unit of time, 219a10-4). But thinking in
respect to its *substance* or contents consists of concepts as combined or
separated, and such concepts are not magnitudes and hence not continuous;
they are like numbers, to which succession may apply. In respect to concepts, the thought that three is odd is not continuous; it signifies oddness as
a trait with or of three; and "oddness" or "three" as a concept is indivisible
and not continuous. Even "circle" as a concept is not continuous, although
what it signifies is continuous; and a circle, although a magnitude divisible
as a quantity, is actually one and is indivisible in respect to its form. The
problem is considered with greater detail in 430a26-b31.

27. Perhaps continuous in sense (a), as stated in the preceding commentary.

28. A point cannot be a part of a line but only a limit or division of a line;
for a line is not made up of points, nor is it divisible into just points as its
matter. As a limit of a line, a point is analogous to an attribute or trait of
a subject or substance, e.g., a point is to a line as whiteness is to a body which
has whiteness. In a qualified sense, however, a point may be a part. Thus
in the definition of a finite straight line, the term "point" — but not the
point itself — appears as a part. So just as a solid cannot be reduced to
surfaces as its material parts, so a surface cannot be reduced to lines and a
line cannot be reduced to points. 141b3-9, 220a18-20.

29. If a moving point takes time to think an object, then an infinity of such
points in a circle will take infinite time to think that object; for different
points think or make contact with the object of thought at different times
and cannot think the same object simultaneously. If the parts of a moving
circle, as magnitudes, think an object, then the circle will be thinking the
same object an infinity of times, either because parts of a circle as magnitudes may be finite or infinite (for a magnitude is finitely or infinitely
divisible into magnitudes), or because the circle (and so its parts) is revolving
eternally and so makes an infinity of revolutions in the same way. But man,
having intellect, may think an object only once; so his intellect cannot be
a moving circle or an imitation of it.

30. If not the whole circle but only one — any one — of its parts thinks
or makes contact with the object, there is no necessity for the circle to
revolve or to be a magnitude; for the contact, once effected, does not require
motion to be eternal, and the part which is in contact need not be a
magnitude, for it may be a point.

31. If the circle as a whole contacts or thinks an object, what will a part
of the circle do? The circle and the object may be so different in their nature

or structure that it is difficult or impossible to conceive contact by a part of the circle with a part of the object; and some objects do not even have parts. Further, if "contact" is taken literally, then the *Intellect* or intellect, being a circle, will be unable to think most things; for only physical bodies may be in contact.

32. If thinking is revolving, since thinking is the proper activity of the intellect (or *Intellect*) and revolving is the proper activity of this circle, then the intellect must be this circle. So since this circle is posited as always revolving, and since this revolving is always the same, thinking should be always of the same thing. But practical thinking is not of this sort, for it has an aim, which is a final cause and an end; and theoretical thinking, too, is not of this sort, for its aim is to reach a conclusion from premises, whose terms are finite, and the conclusion is an end; and the intellect, which thinks, is either practical or theoretical.

33. Let "AB" mean that all B is A, as in all triangles inscribed in a semicircle are right. Then, in a science, from AB and BC, where C is a term, the conclusion AC follows demonstratively; and this conclusion is an end. And if one posits CD as an additional premise, the conclusion AD follows in the same way. Additional premises may be posited; but the resulting demonstration will still proceed along a straight line, so to say, without ever yielding AB as a conclusion. For if AB were both a premise and a conclusion, there would be a circular argument, and the same premise would be both a cause and an effect; and this is impossible. But the eternal motion of the circle returns to the same thing, and, being identical with thinking, would return to the premise AB; and this situation contradicts the nature of demonstration 72b5-73a20, 78a14-21.

34. 82b37-83a1, 994b20-31, 1043b32-6.

35. Man's intellect, being like the circle which Plato posits as being the *Intellect* of the universe, or being an imitation of that circle, is certainly not thinking always of the same thing, whether continuously or repeatedly.

36. Thinking, like seeing and *acting* and being happy, is an activity which is complete in itself and an end in itself and not in the process of becoming, like becoming healthy and going to the store to buy something, which are motions, i.e., incomplete activities. As a complete activity, then, thinking is more like resting than like moving toward something. 1048b18-34, 1066a20-2.

37. If the motion of the circle were the *substance* of that circle, it would contradict the perfection and happiness which Plato attributes to the circle (i.e., the soul of the universe, *Timaeus* 34). For motion is incomplete activity and is painful or requires an effort (1050b26-8, 74b25-9), and such activity proceeds to something better or to something worse; but in either case, the thing in motion cannot be perfect and happy throughout the duration of that motion. If the circle's motion is not the circle's *substance*, it would still

be contrary to the nature of the soul, for it would interfere with the soul's perfection and happiness. This conclusion follows not just from Aristotle's definition of motion but also from the generally accepted opinion about motion and from what Plato himself considers motion to be; for Plato attributes motion only to the material principle (the *Dyad*) but regards the principle as form (the *One*) and the Ideas as eternal and immovable and perfect, and he attributes the change in perishable things to the further involvement of the *Dyad* and not to the *One* or to the Ideas. Thus Aristotle's argument is both dialectical (i.e., it proceeds from generally accepted opinions) and logical (i.e., it indicates a contradiction in Plato's own statements).

38. This argument, too, is logical and dialectical. It is better for the soul of the universe to be by itself than to be always with the body of the universe; for, according to Plato himself, the proper function of the soul is impeded when it is with a body and has to attend to the body's desires.

39. Does "it" refer to the soul or to the heaven?

For Aristotle, of course, the soul cannot be moved, except accidentally, that is, if the body is moved; and then it is not essentially that the soul is moved but in virtue of the body, for no attribute or form can be in motion essentially since only things with matter can be in motion essentially (224b11-3). For Plato, the soul is defined as a substance or a number which moves itself. If this definition stops here, it would be by accident that the soul's motion is a revolution, but if lines 406b25-407a2 are added in the above definition, the soul's motion for Plato becomes a revolution.

If "it" refers to the heaven, then, even if one regards the motion of the soul as being a revolution, there is the problem of whether such motion can cause the heaven to revolve; for additional assumptions are needed, such as "the soul's revolution causes the heaven in which it exists to move in the same manner."

40. Aristotle's objection in this sentence is not spelled out. We may offer an interpretation. The cause of the heaven's revolution is not clear; for neither can the soul cause that revolution, since it cannot even cause its own motion (whether a revolution or not) except accidentally, nor can the heaven as a body (apart from the soul) cause it, since (for both Aristotle and Plato) the cause of motion is a form rather than a body. 335b10-6.

41. There are two assumptions: (a) it is better for the soul to move than to be at rest, and (b) it is better for its motion to be a revolution.

Aristotle would reject (a) because motion is incomplete activity, in which case no moving thing can be perfect and blessed. Aristotle's prime mover is not in motion but is just activity (1073a3-5), which is complete; and such activity, remaining always the same, is closer to rest than motion is, for motion changes the thing in motion, and no perfect thing admits of change.

Perhaps Aristotle would be somewhat sympathetic to (b). For the circle is the most complete of lines, and so is the sphere in the case of bodies; and the same applies to the motion of the circle or of the sphere relative to all other motions (286b10-26, 915a33-6, 1016b16-7, 1018b37-8). So since God is most perfect and most unified and always the same, then, of all figures and motions, circles and spheres and their motions would be the closest to God and his activity because of their greater perfection and unity and sameness. Any motion, however, causes a change, either in the thing as a whole or in its parts, and no thing can be perfect during a change.

42. Whether it is better to move than to remain still and better to move in a circle than in any other way are problems requiring the definition or intuition of motion, rest, activity, perfection, happiness, final cause, and the like; and these things are considered in *Metaphysics*, *Physics*, *On the Heavens*, *Ethics*, and perhaps in other places. Some references have been given in the preceding Commentary.

43. The *reason* why the soul, which is a form, should be attached to or be placed in or exist with a body is that it must have a body, as a material cause, to perform its function, which is its final cause.

44. Should there be a relation of a body to the soul in it? If so, it should be specified. Now each kind of soul or part of a soul has its own proper function to perform and so must use as a material cause a body appropriate to that function. Seeing requires an eye, smelling requires a nose, and so on with the others. Consequently, there must be a relation between the soul and its parts, on the one hand, and the body and its parts, on the other.

45. That which can act is relative to that which can be acted upon (1020b26-30), and that which can cause motion is relative to that which can be caused to be in motion; and to each kind of action there corresponds a distinct kind of affection, and likewise for motion. Further, that which can act or cause motion on a certain thing cannot be any chance thing, and similarly for that which can be acted upon or caused to move (323b29-324b24). A quality does not act or move a quantity or a relation; it is a physical body that can be acted upon or caused to be in motion; and it is not rocks or cyanide that can be acted upon by the nutritive soul or the stomach but only what is called "food". So, in a living thing, it is the soul (a form) or a part of it which is the primary thing that acts or causes motion and the body which is acted upon or is moved, whether the body itself as an instrument acts on or moves another thing (a physical body) in turn or not. Accordingly, the soul of a man cannot enter the body of a worm or a tree, for each of these lacks certain bodily parts as instruments necessary for a man's soul to perform the corresponding functions (415b18-20, 642a9-13). A worm does not have the required bodily parts to think mathematically or to construct a house. Conversely, a worm's soul in a man's body would make certain parts of that body (eyes, etc.) useless, for the corresponding faculties of those parts are not in a worm's soul, and nature does nothing in vain (291b13-4).

4

1. According to Aristotle, these thinkers mistake similarities for identities, for their arguments amount to this: all A is C, all B is C, hence A and B are the same, where C is a mixture or a composition of contraries. But the conclusion does not follow.

2. Arguments of a general nature may be given against the position that the soul is a harmony. A ratio is a relation but the soul is a form or a substance and not a relation. A composition of things blended is a substance having matter and form but the soul has no matter. Arguments of a more detailed nature are given in lines 408a5-18.

3. Ability to cause motion is not a necessary trait of harmony or of that which has harmony, but it is generally thought by these thinkers to be a necessary trait of the soul; so the soul cannot be a harmony.

4. Harmony is generally thought to belong to bodily virtues and not to virtues of the soul, and if one identifies the soul with harmony, difficulties follow. For example, pain and vices and evil actions and inconsistent thoughts are *attributes* or functions of the soul; but it is ridiculous to attribute them to harmony.

5. It is generally held that harmony has two senses, (a) and (b), and that (a) is the main sense; so this opinion is dialectical. It also appears that sense (a), which is a composition (whether a mixture or blend) of material parts or elements and so a composite, has matter and form, as in the case of flesh or bone, but that sense (b), which is a ratio, is just an attribute, or else the form according to these and other thinkers, of that composition or composite. To speak of the soul in sense (a) or in sense (b) is unreasonable. First, how could one believe that the soul, which has no matter, is a composition? Besides, compositions may differ in two ways, in the ratios of the elements or material parts or in the nature of the parts themselves; for the ratio 3:2 may have fire and earth as parts in one case, but earth and water in another, and relative positions of the parts may also differ. Second, the ratios of the various material parts (flesh, bone, blood, etc.) of an animate body differ, at least in some cases; so if the soul is a ratio, there would be many and different souls distributed over the various parts of the same animate body.

6. Empedocles posited four elements: earth, water, air, and fire; and he declared that *Friendship* brings things together but *Strife* draws them apart, thus positing these two principles as movers and, in a sense, as principles of what is good and what is bad.

The three questions raised imply difficulties in the theory of Empedocles. (a) If the soul is the ratio itself, then there are as many souls in a man as parts; and if it is not the ratio, we are not told what it is, except that we know earth by earth, water by water, etc., a position which seems to allow only knowledge of the elements and not of other things (404b8-15), such as sensation and relation and things in other categories, and to suggest that the soul is identical with each of the four elements but without a unity. (b) If *Friendship* is the cause only of blends according to right ratios, Empedocles fails to supply a moving cause for blends according to other ratios, which are wrong ratios; and if *Friendship* causes blends according to any ratios, it will cause good as well as bad things, contrary to his intended position (985a4-10). (c) If *Friendship* is the ratio itself of a thing (e.g., of a bone), then prior to the existence of the bone there is no moving cause to bring that thing into existence; and if it is not the ratio, we are back to the difficulty in the second part of (a).

7. Difficulties arise if, according to Empedocles, the soul is posited to be a harmony, whether as a composition or a blend or a ratio.

8. Perhaps by "distinct from the blend" he means not the blend or the ratio or anything in the blend but something else.

9. An alternative translation of "and of the other parts" is "or of [any of] the other parts".

10. An alternative translation of "how is it . . . animal?" is "how is it that, along with the destruction of the essence of flesh, the other parts of an animal are destroyed also?". Some commentators interpret the meaning of the Greek text to be that of this alternative; I prefer the first alternative.

Perhaps the meaning of this sentence is as follows. If the soul is distinct from the blend, as indicated in Comm. 8, then there is no reason for it to perish when the flesh or bone or blood of the body perishes; so it appears that the soul is more closely connected with these parts of the body than these thinkers hold. Aristotle considers the nature of this connection in Book B.

11. Hicks interprets this question (or objection) as implying that it is the body which decays when the soul departs; and he adds that the two questions raised here suggest the mutual connection of body and soul. Now it is a fact that the body disintegrates when the soul departs; but bones along with their ratio do not, nor does flesh along with its ratio, at least for some time. If so, the second question might have taken such form as this: "Why is the body destroyed when the soul departs?" If Hicks is right, then perhaps the question in the manner raised is concerned not with the fact that the body is destroyed but with the nature of that body; for that body is not just flesh and bones, etc., and what is destroyed is not any kind of body but a living body, and without the soul there would be no living body, and conversely, as suggested later in lines 412a19-22.

12. 406a3-b10, 259b16-20.

13. In short, the soul cannot be moved essentially; it is immovable. But it can be moved indirectly; and this is done when it (or a part of it) moves the body, and the body is moved with respect to place. It is in this way that the attributes of the body, too, are moved, e.g., the color and the shape and the volume of the body.

14. Perhaps by "thing" he means the brain, as held by some thinkers.

15. The motions of the heart are locomotions, but sensations are alterations; and both are motions of bodily parts. 415b24, 459b4-5.

16. Pitying and learning and sensing, and even *thinking*, which is impossible without images (431b2), are motions, and motions belong to subjects
which have matter and form, as discussed in the *Physics*, Book A. Thus it
is not the color of a colored thing that is moved or changes, but the thing
itself with respect to color. Now the soul is just a form of a certain physical
body, and hence it cannot be moved. So, although in ordinary language we
say that the soul is moved, analysis of motion shows that such statement is
not literally true. Sensing, then, belongs to a man or an animal, which is a
composite of matter and form; and similarly for pitying and the other
motions. The soul, of course, plays a part in these motions. If the motion is
caused by the soul, as when we recollect or desire or start thinking about
something, then the soul (or a part of it) acts as a mover from which that
motion starts; but if the mover is outside, like an object's color which acts
on the medium, which in turn acts on the sense organ, then the last motion
caused is in the sense organ and terminates at the soul (i.e., the power or
faculty of that organ, which is a part of the soul), at which point we say that
we are sensing something.

17. Is this the active or the passive intellect, i.e., the potential intellect
which can become all things or the *actual* intellect which can cause those
things to be in the passive intellect? From 430a10-25 it appears that it is the
active intellect, and this is confirmed by what follows and by 413b24-7 and
736b27-8.

18. The Greek term, translated here as "if at all", makes the possible
destruction of the intellect only a hypothesis, which is later denied.

19. An eye of a young man is understood.

20. Thinking or speculating is in one sense like sensing; for just as sensing
is impossible without sense organs, which have matter, so thinking or speculating is impossible without phantasms, which are like sense impressions and
cannot exist apart from the composite of body and soul, 432a3-14. And just
as the deterioration of the body tends to enfeeble the sensations and sense
impressions, so it tends to enfeeble thinking and speculating; for these
require phantasms, and these require sense impressions, which in turn
depend on the composite of body and soul.

21. It is not clear from the text whether "that" refers to the living body,
which is the proximate matter of the composite, or to the composite itself.
Perhaps it refers to the latter, for thinking and loving must include the
composite in their definition. On the other hand, although the composite as
composite is destructible, the active intellect in it is not. Perhaps the first
alternative is correct.

22. The literal translation is "that which is common". Perhaps "that

86

which is shared by both body and soul" means the same thing, but more explicitly.

23. This doctrine is attributed to Xenocrates, a Platonist who headed the Academy during Aristotle's later years.

24. Ancient mathematicians regarded a unit as having no parts, units as not differing from each other in quantity or quality, and a number as having units as parts. Euclid defined a unit as that in virtue of which each thing is called "one", and a point as that which has no parts, thus neglecting to add position to a point. Aristotle discussed at length and philosophically the terms "one" and "unit" in the *Metaphysics* (1015b16-1017a6, 1052a15-1057a17); and he regarded a unit as without parts and without position and a constituent principle of a number, and a point as indivisible but with position.

How are we to think of a unit in motion? It is demonstrated in the *Physics* (240b8-241a26) that no thing without parts can be moved; and a unit has no parts. Besides, only things in place can be moved, for motion can belong only to a body, which has place; but a unit has no position, and hence no place.

By what will a unit be moved? It cannot be moved by itself. For that which moves itself has at least two parts, one of them causing motion and the other being caused to be in motion, and cause and effect cannot be identical; but a unit has no parts. Neither can one unit be moved by another unit; for the unit which causes motion would differ from the unit which is caused to be in motion, but units do not differ in their nature or definition, and what one can truly say about them is that they are just numerically distinct, that is, one unit is not another unit, and that the two may be parts of the number two or a greater number.

In what manner can a unit be moved? Not by contact, for it has no position and hence no place, and things are in contact if they are in the same place (226b23). Again, it cannot be moved with respect to quantity, since it can have no length or volume, nor with respect to quality, for units do not differ in quality (1083a1-10), nor yet with respect to place, for they have no position.

In this treatise, the term "number" means what is nowadays called "a natural number greater than 1".

25. Perhaps Aristotle uses "unit" here as a genus of a point and a unit in the narrow sense, as in line 409a20, for he does this sort of thing for the terms "chance", "disposition", and some others to avoid coining new terms; or else, perhaps he allows these thinkers to regard a unit like a point for the sake of argument, thus saving them from a contradiction.

26. If, according to these thinkers, the soul is a self-moving number and each unit, like a point, generates a line when in motion, then the soul will be in place and will always be generating a line — an absurd conclusion.

27. If a unit or some number is subtracted from a number, say 10, then the result, which is 9 or some other number, differs in species from 10. But if a plant when divided continues to live, it remains a plant with a soul of the same species as before. Hence the soul cannot be a number.

28 . A number of things is meant, not a magnitude.

29. Since the atoms posited by Democritus, although material and with magnitude, are regarded by him as indivisible, they function like points or units, as far as their number is concerned; hence they are not subject to the divisibility which applies to magnitudes as posited by Aristotle and by the ancient mathematicians. So, if there is to be motion, some of the atoms will cause motion and others will be caused to be in motion, as Aristotle has shown in the case of divisible bodies in motion (257b26-258a27); for if a man is in motion, that which is moved is the body or a part of it, but that which causes motion is the soul, or else another part of the body which is itself caused by something else to be in motion. Thus, divisibility into that which causes motion and that which is caused to move is necessary, whether that which is in motion is a number of units or a number of atoms.

30. Since that which causes motion and is in motion is divisible (257b26-258a27), only part of the number as soul for these thinkers will have to be a mover but the other part will not; and the mover may be a unit or a smaller number. But Aristotle posits it here as being a unit; and various commentators suggested a correction, either in the Greek text or in Aristotle's thinking. Logically, however, it has to be a unit; for if the mover is a smaller number, the objection against the original number may be repeated, and we finally arrive at a unit as the only mover.

31. But a unit as mover and a unit as moved show a difference, whereas mathematicians treat all units as not differing in quantity or quality or any other way; and if the units in the soul are posited in any other way, e.g., as unitary points, so to say, their only difference would be with respect to position. So two alternatives arise: either the units in the soul differ from points or not; and these alternatives are examined.

(a) If they differ, each unit will occupy the place of a point of the body. (This is necessary, if the body is full and so without empty spaces; and it appears to be necessary even if there are empty spaces, for the unit has to be in contact with a point to cause motion). And nothing prevents many units of the soul from occupying the same point, for many units or points cannot make up a magnitude. Other absurdities arise. To take examples, the body has an infinite number of points, but the soul as a number has a finite number of units; so only a finite number of points of the body will be animate; and if only one unit can be a mover, as shown in the previous commentary, only one point will be alive. (b) If the units of the soul do not differ from the points in the body, then any body (water, a rock, etc.), having points, will have a soul; in fact, every physical body will have — nay, it will be — a soul; and the distinction between animate and inanimate bodies will disappear and so a dead body will have a soul. Again, a body will have an infinite number of souls; for a body has an infinity of points, but a soul, being a number of points, has a finite number of them. Other absurdities may be added.

32. For Aristotle, neither is a line made out of points as matter, nor a surface out of lines, nor a body out of surfaces. How can one take a surface out of a body and exhibit it as something separate, and how can the remaining part — a body without a surface — exist? A point is a limit of a line or a division of it, and it is related to it as an attribute to a subject; and the same applies to the others. Consequently, if the soul consists of a number of points, these points and so the soul cannot depart from the body, and this is contrary to fact. 231a21-9, 298b33-299a11, 1002a15-20, 1090b5-10.

5

1. 408b32-409a30.

2. Diogenes and Heraclitus, and even Democritus, are included. 405a21-9.

3. The additional absurdities appear to arise, not by the fact that Xenocratis and his followers just agree with Democritus in regarding the soul as causing motion, but by attaching self-motion to the soul as a number. The text which follows appears to bring out this fact. Self-motion of the small spheres of Democritus does not lead to two bodies being in the same place, but self-motion of a number or a unit or a point does. Accordingly, Torstrik and Hicks are mistaken in regarding the last three words in line 409b1 as spurious.

4. It is not clear whether the sentence up to here is an additional criticism. It is worse to say that a number is self-moving than to say that a body is self-moving; for a body can be in motion and cause motion, but a number, being an attribute, can never be in motion.

5. As a definition, "a self-moving number" is impossible, for a number can neither move another thing nor be moved. As an attribute, it is impossible for the same reason. Further, such *attributes* as judgments, sensations, pleasures, and the like cannot follow from the definition "self-moving number". For the terms "cause of motion" and "being in motion" belong to physics universally taken, and the term "number" belongs to mathematics, but the terms "sensation" and "pain" and the like are less general and require additional differentiae, which are principles; and principles cannot be defined in terms of or be demonstrated from other principles. It follows, then, that the definition of soul as a self-moving number is dialectical and empty (403a1-2).

6. 405b10-2.

7. The soul may consist of elements by being a blend or a juxtaposition

of them or by having them as parts in some other way. The expression "to consist of elements" is a special case of "to be from something", whose meanings are given in 1023a26-b11. See also 1092a21-b8.

8. Empedocles, 404b9-15; Plato, 404b16-18; Diogenes, 405a21-5; Heraclitus, 405a25-7; others, 405b12-5.

9. Their argument is this: like is known by like; so if all things are made up of one or more elements, the soul is made up of one or more elements of the same kind, respectively.

10. If like is known by like, then bone, which is not an element, will be known by bone, and similarly for all things which are not elements but are composites or forms of them. Hence the soul or part of it will be a bone and a man and each of the others, which is impossible. 431b28-9.

11. 1b25-7, 1017a22-7.

12. No two categories have anything in common; e.g., no quantity is a substance (1029a15), and similarly for the others. This is true whether the elements are elements of the thing itself or of its definition.

First, a quantity qua quantity is not a substance, and conversely; and neither a substance as a separate form is a quantity, nor the principles or elements of a physical substance (matter and form) are quantities. We may add, quantity as such is a principle and an element. Second, the differentiae as terms under one category cannot be differentiae as terms under another category (1b16-20). Consequently, no part which is an element in the definition of a quantity is an element in the definition of a substance; and similarly for any two categories.

It follows from the above that knowledge of things of a species or genus under quantity cannot be reduced to a corresponding knowledge of things under substance; and similarly for corresponding knowledge under any two categories. As for the axioms (or common principles), they are used analogously for different categories, and such analogy is not identity. 75a38-b20, 76a37-b2, 88a31-b3.

13. If the soul consists of elements of substances, it cannot know the elements of other categories, and so it cannot have any knowledge of those categories or of a thing under any of those categories.

14. This hypothesis is Aristotle's own position. 76a37-b2.

15. If the soul knows a quantity and a substance, then, since like is known by like according to these thinkers, the soul will be both a quantity and a substance; and this is impossible.

16. Sensation (as a process) for these thinkers is an affection, and hence an alteration and a motion, and similarly for thinking and knowing; and Aristotle agrees (415b24). But the expressions "like knows like" and "like is not affected by like" contradict each other; for "like is affected by like" follows from "like knows like". The contradiction can be avoided if the verb "knows" means "possesses knowledge" but excludes "comes to know from

ignorance". But this is impossible, for babies do not possess knowledge; and if they possess knowledge at a later age, they acquired it earlier.

17. 404b13-5.

18. For example, since earth is an element, and since like is known only by like, earth will know only earth. We may add, even this is not possible; for, as stated in the previous sentence, such earthy things as bones and hair are thought to be incapable of sensing anything.

19. The argument is as follows. Since God is an element and indestructible and has no *Strife*, He cannot know *Strife* or anything which has *Strife;* for like is known only by like. Now *Strife* is the cause of destruction and is an element of all destructible things (1000a24-9), which are composites. Hence God cannot know these things. But each mortal thing, being one, destructible, and a composite of elements, will know *Friendship*, *Strife*, and composites of elements as well as elements, respectively. Hence God is the least intelligent of all mortal or knowing things.

20. If like is known by like and A and B are alike, then A and B, whether elements or composites, know each other and have soul. So the thing sensed or thought, too, must have knowledge, whether of one or some or all of the elements, and so all things must have soul.

21. If we speak of something as being one, as of a man or a house or a tree, what is it that gives it unity or causes it to be one? Flesh and bones as such are not the animal or one animal but only the matter of it; but the cause or principle which makes them one animal is the soul, and this is the form of an animal. Since a thing's form gives the thing its unity, whereas its matter without the form has no unity but is potentially an indefinite number of things, the form is the dominant principle in the thing and, in the animals at least, the ruling or directing principle. Further, these thinkers themselves posit the intellect, whether this be *Intelligence* or the *Intellect* or some other such principle, to be simple and dominant and to rule. But how can it unify other things if, being an element, it can know only itself? 1041a6-b33, 1254a34-6.

22. Since some animals appear to be stationary, the definition of the soul (or a part of it) as "that which can cause motion" cannot be applied to them and is therefore inadequate. Besides, the definition is inadequate even for animals to which it is applicable, for the term "motion" includes many kinds of motion, whereas the soul of those animals is thought to move them only with respect to place.

23. Since plants appear to have life (and hence a soul) but do not partake of locomotion or sensation, the doctrine which regards the soul as consisting of elements so that it may think or sense is inapplicable to plants. And since plants consist of the same kind of elements, a further difficulty arises: they should be capable of thinking or sensing, but they are not. Again, only men can *think;* but those who speak of the soul as capable of *thinking* (402b3-5)

make the soul inapplicable even to animals. It may be added that those who have the power of *thinking* are able to make general statements, but such power is not possessed by cats and dogs and the like.

24. These thinkers are faced with a further difficulty. If the soul is that which can cause motion, or that which can sense or know or both sense and know, or that which has two or all of these powers, then the nutritive power is left out. If so, then (a) not every soul or part of a soul is included, (b) not the whole soul of some things (e.g., animals) is included, and (c) no soul can exist since the nutritive soul is necessary for both plants and animals.

25. Similarly, the statement concerning the soul in the so-called "Orphic poems" fails to apply to the soul of certain living things. If the soul enters certain things when or while these inhale, plants and some animals (those which do not breathe) which are regarded as having soul would be without soul.

26. If we posit that the soul consists of elements, that the elements are contraries (405b23, 1004b29-33, 1087a29-31), that like is known by like, and that the soul knows the elements, it follows that the soul consists of contraries. But this is contrary to fact. It is often the same science that knows both contraries (427b5-6, 1029a13-23). For example, it is by the mean that we judge both the mean and the extremes, as in sensation (424a2-10). Likewise, it is the virtuous man who knows and judges both virtuous and vicious actions, whether the latter be excesses or deficiencies, and he does so by virtue, which is a mean; but a virtuous man has no vice. Again, it is by the straight that we measure and know the curved, whether the latter be convex or concave. A curved ruler may be more or less curved; hence, it may be curved in an infinite number of ways. So either all of them may be posited as principles of knowledge or none of them. All straight rulers, on the other hand, are alike straight, and the straight is the mean between the convex and the concave. So, the modern mathematician uses the straight to measure both straight and curved lines. For, in finding the length of a curved line, he uses the limit of the sum of $\sqrt{(\triangle x)^2 + (\triangle y)^2}$, where both $\triangle x$ and $\triangle y$ are straight segments and not curved.

27. If the soul were in air or fire, (a) it would know things or perform the same functions as it does when it is in animals, and (b) it would know things or perform those functions even better when blended in air or fire than when blended in animals. But we observe in air or fire no knowledge or functions which are attributed to the soul when present in animals.

It is not clear whether the hypothesis in (b) was stated by these thinkers or was implied by what they said. Anyway, if the soul is the least corporeal of things (409b20-1), it would be in a better state if blended with the less than with the more corporeal things. But animals, consisting also of earth and water, would be more corporeal than air or fire. Hence the soul would be in a better state if blended with air or fire than with more corporeal elements.

28. What is the difference between "absurd" and "unreasonable". Since fire and air do not think or perform the functions of an animal, it is unreasonable to say that they are animals; and if these thinkers say that they have soul, it is absurd not to call them "animals". In the first case, the facts contradict what they say; in the second, if they say something (that air and fire have soul), they must also say something else which is absurd (that air and fire are animals), but they refuse to do so. Is this the difference?

29. Perhaps the soul of an animal is meant here.

30. Perhaps the meaning of lines 411a16-24 is as follows. These thinkers posit that the whole is homogeneous with its parts, that the soul exists likewise in a homogeneous manner in air (or fire), and that animals become or continue to be animate by taking in air, in which there is soul. The soul of all animals, then, would have to be homogeneous; for it is homogeneous in air. But the soul of man or of animals is not homogeneous, for the faculties of seeing, hearing, nutrition, reasoning, etc. differ; we cannot see with our ears, nor hear with our eyes. So only one kind or part of man's soul will be in air, let us say the sense of hearing, but the other kinds or parts will not. But (a) either soul in air is homogeneous, which leads to the absurd conclusion that all kinds of animals have the same kind of soul, or (b) some kinds or parts of the soul will not be in air, a conclusion which is contrary to the doctrine that soul comes to the animals when they breathe in air.

Perhaps the term "whole" at the end of the paragraph was used by these thinkers and meant air or fire, in which soul was posited to be.

31. The doctrine that the soul is essentially in motion and a self-mover is not true. Nor is it well-expressed, for not all of the soul can cause motion, and it can be moved, if at all, only accidentally or indirectly; so the appropriate qualifications are not stated.

32. They belong, of course, not to every kind of soul but to certain souls. The desire not mentioned is temper (414b2).

33. The nutritive soul is meant; and this soul is the only principle and cause as form in plants but is just a part of the soul in animals or men. At present, only problems are raised as to whether various functions of living things belong to the whole soul or to parts of it. Whether the body too participates in those functions is another problem.

34. Perhaps the terms "the whole soul" and "every soul" differ in meaning, the first signifying the soul as a whole or as a unit, the second signifying each soul participating in thinking and sensing and the like. Evidently, the nutritive soul neither thinks nor senses, so there is a division of labor, so to say.

35. There seems to be a difficulty with the meaning of the term "life" or "living". Lines 412a14-5, 413a32-b2, and 415a23-5 appear to say that life is that through which the thing which has it takes in food and grows and deteriorates, so life, according to some commentators, would seem to be the

nutritive soul; and lines 414a4-14, which are concerned with the distinction between matter and form in a living thing, seem to favor this meaning if the word "primary" in line 414a13 refers to that form or part of the form of a living thing which is prior in existence to the other parts of the form. Lines 413a22-5, on the other hand, appear to say that the term "living" is used in many senses; but they may be interpreted as saying that living is primarily attributed to the nutritive soul but secondarily to the other parts. For the sentient soul cannot exist without the nutritive part and so the animal lives primarily through its nutritive soul but secondarily by having the sentient soul. One may wonder, however, why Aristotle uses the Greek term for "living" if the Greek term for "nutritive soul" means the same thing. Is there some difference? Does living belong to the living thing, which is a composite of matter and form, but the nutritive soul to the form or part of the form of that thing? Perhaps so. Then it is the composite that lives, not the form or part of it.

36. Whether the word "it" refers to the soul or to the living thing as a *composite* is not clear. Perhaps the reference is to Plato.

37. A man is one thing and not many. So, if his soul is divisible into parts, there is something which holds those parts together. Now this cannot be the body, which is the matter of the composite of body and soul, as others seem to think. Further, it is when the soul departs that the bodily parts begin to rot and fall apart. It appears, then, that what unifies the parts is the soul or something in the soul; and if it is something in the soul, this would be the principle of unification and so prior to the soul, and this should be regarded as the soul in the highest sense, for this makes a man be one.

38. The type of difficulty in 411b10-4 is often raised; generically stated, it is as follows. Let X, A, B, C, D, . . . be an infinite series in which X necessitates some term in the series according to some principle. The principle in the example is the unification of the parts of the first of two terms. Now either all the terms of the series are similar (e.g., each term has parts to be unified) or some one of the terms after X is not similar to the preceding terms (e.g., has no parts). If all the terms are similar, we are faced with an infinite series without the possibility of arriving at a final principle of unification; but if there is a first term which is not similar to the preceding terms, is this A or B or which? 425b12-7, 994a1-11, 1006a8-9, 1094a18-22.

39. The previous problem was concerned with the unity of the parts of the soul, which is the form of the *composite,* with the assumption that it is the soul that holds together the body, which is the matter of the *composite.* The problem now is whether each part of the soul holds together some part of the body, just as the soul holds together the body. For example, it appears that vision holds the eye together. On the other hand, there is a difficulty in the case of the intellect; for what part of the body will it hold together? A further difficulty arises in the case of plants and some insects; for, when

divided in certain ways, their parts have the same kind of soul. So it appears that each part of the soul is in every part of the body. In the case of plants, after division, the nutritive and reproductive powers in each part are the same in species as those in the whole prior to the division; and in the case of earthworms and some others, the same may be said of the powers of nutrition, locomotion, sensation, and desire.

40. In other words, although the parts of the soul are not so separable that each of them exists only in a certain part of the body, the soul as a whole is actually one in the *composite* but potentially many in each part after division of the *composite*, and it is the same in species both in the *composite* and in each part after the division. 413b10-24.

41. A living thing may have the nutritive soul without the sentient soul, but it cannot have the sentient soul without the nutritive soul; so the nutritive soul is prior in existence to the sentient soul. This is given as a statement of fact, but it suggests the problem of whether there are other such priorities among the various faculties of soul. We shall see, for example, that vision cannot exist without the sense of touch, but not conversely.

BOOK B

1

1. In Book A Aristotle raises the main problems concerning the soul and discusses the difficulties faced by the various doctrines of his predecessors concerning the soul. In this Book he proceeds to state his own doctrine. As to the soul's nature, he raises the problem of whether it is matter or form and whether it exists as actuality or as potentiality. If it exists as actuality, what is it; and is it the same for all or is its formula generic and not specific? The two problems are stated in lines 402a22-b1 and perhaps the two terms "nature" and "*substance*" in 402a7-8 apply to them, as suggested in Comm. 7 of Book A.

Since the most common formula is sought, the soul as a whole will be considered before the parts; for the whole is prior in existence and in formula to the parts, for the part is referred to and is defined in terms of the whole, but not conversely, and the soul may exist if a part is lost, but not conversely. This takes care of the problem in lines 402b9-10.

2. An alternative to "and" is "or". It is not clear whether "*shape*" and "form" here have the same meaning, and if not, whether they imply each other, as in the case of "triangular" and "trilateral", which imply each other but differ in meaning. The two terms often appear together in other contexts.

3. The term "a *this*" here means an individual thing which is a composite of matter and form and exists separately and so is not an attribute; e.g., President Reagan or someone's dog.

4. The things which were generally considered to be substances are enumerated in the *Metaphysics*, 1017b10-26, 1028b8-9a5 and 1042a6-16; but those which Aristotle accepted as being substances in discussing the soul are the three kinds given here.

5. In a change, matter exists as potentiality, i.e., it underlies the change and can take on various or different forms. Form, on the other hand, does not underlie any change; it is that by which a *composite*, whether by nature or art, is known and named, like the shape of what we call "a cup". In *composite* things, form is actuality, which amounts to saying that form is that principle by which the thing exists and has a unity.

6. Just as a mathematician may be using the knowledge he possesses or may possess it without using it, so a man may be using his vision when he actually sees or may not when his eyes are closed; and vision is a part of a man's form. Further, the exercise of vision is to vision by itself (whether a man is actually seeing or not) as the exercise of a man's knowledge is to his knowledge by itself (whether a man is using his knowledge or not).

7. The statement is in some sense dialectical. 1028b9-15, 1017b10-5, 1040b5-10. Perhaps by "all the rest" he means those which are caused by art, e.g., houses and chairs and baseball bats; for a baseball bat has wood as its matter, and this wood comes from a tree, which is a natural body and hence a principle from which the bat is made.

8. Rocks, water, and inanimate bodies in general are meant.

9. It appears that a natural body with life is or is defined as a natural body which takes in food and grows and deteriorates. Thus, life in such a body appears to be attributed not to the body's matter or to its form, but to the body itself, which is a *composite;* and this seems to be confirmed by the text which follows immediately.

10. The term "body" for Aristotle has more than one sense. Here, it is not clear whether it means a composite of matter and form, as in the case of a natural body, such as a rock or a tree, or just the matter of a *composite,* which exists as potentiality (413a2). Perhaps the phrase "as a subject or as matter" at the end of the sentence allows the term to be used in either way, for the argument is not disturbed by either of the two meanings.

11. Things which belong to or are predicated of other things are attributes, e.g., qualities and quantities and, in general, things present in other things, or else universals which belong to or are predicated of many, as explained in 1a20-b9 and in 82b37-3a23. But a body as a composite or as the matter of a composite is not something which belongs to or is predicated of something else; it is either matter, which is receptive of a form, or a *composite* substance, in which attributes are present (1038b4-6).

12. Is the word "potentially" in the formula necessary? If the natural body considered here is taken as a *composite,* it has soul as its form when it actually has life; but if that body is regarded as the matter of the *composite* (and perhaps it does here), it has life potentially in the sense that it exists potentially or as potentiality, and if it is regarded together with a certain form, which is the soul, there is life in the *composite.*

Is the formula given here for the soul a definition or just a true statement, perhaps metaphysical, enabling us to know the nature of the soul as form rather than as matter or a *composite* (412a7-8)? Further, is the formula proved demonstratively or dialectically? Perhaps dialectically.

Some commentators object to the formula given for the soul here, for they think that it does not apply to plants, which are not asleep or awake and have no knowledge or the exercise of it. But they are mistaken. The nutritive soul has contraries similar to those of being asleep and being awake; for the nutritive soul need not be in activity, as when a man goes without food for days; and Aristotle's remark in 1102b3-5 applies to those who have food in the stomach, for digestion and growth proceed best when, as doctors say, the blood is used mostly for the nutritive soul and least for other activities.

13. Here, again, it is not clear whether "body" means (a) the *composite,*

of which the soul is the form or actuality, or (b) matter, which along with the form constitutes the *composite*.

14. Three things must be distinguished: (a) *knowledge* when it is being exercised, (b) *knowledge* when possessed but not being exercised, and (c) *knowledge* as existing without reference to whether it is being exercised or not. The soul is analogous to knowledge in sense (c); for we say that a man has soul whether he is awake or asleep. Further, being asleep and being awake are contraries which presuppose the soul, and one of these contraries must be in the soul, like oddness or evenness in a number (12b27-9).

15. A man cannot exercise his *knowledge* unless he has acquired it first; so, the possession of *knowledge* is prior in time to its exercise. Further, *knowledge* is prior in existence even to *knowledge* with one contrary or with the other; for if *knowledge* in activity exists, so does *knowledge*, but not conversely, and if *knowledge* when dormant exists, so does *knowledge*, but not conversely (i.e., dormant *knowledge* in an individual does not exist when he is exercising his *knowledge*).

16. Soul as the first actuality corresponds to soul as being possessed or being with body as matter, regardless of whether it is in activity or not; and it is analogous to *knowledge* in sense (c), as explained in the preceding commentary. The term "first" means prior in time and in existence; so the soul is prior in this sense to the soul when active or to the soul when dormant.

17. Vision requires an eye for its function, the nutritive soul requires a stomach and the like, and so on. A difficulty with respect to the intellect may be raised, and it will be considered later.

18. This formula of the soul is common to the form of all things which are said to possess life; it is not a definition of any given kind of soul. The term "organs" is used in a limited sense here; it applies to material parts of things possessing life and having a function.

19. Does "that of which" refer to the form or to the composite of matter and form? The sentence indicates an analogy. Thus, body : soul :: wax : its shape :: matter of a thing : that of which it is the matter; so "that of which" appears to signify the form. Perhaps "that with which" would be better, as in 1044a10-1, for the genitive "that of which" seems to signify a whole of which matter is a part; and to say "the matter and that of which it is the matter" is like saying "the matter of the form".

20. The matter itself is indefinite (209b9, 778a6-7, 1007b28-9) and has no unity. It is the form which is the dominant cause of the unity and existence in the composite. As for the composite, it is one in another sense, namely, numerically, and matter and form in it are distinguishable but inseparable principles (209b22-3). So one should not inquire whether the soul and body are one; he should rather start with the living thing and analyze it into its principles.

21. An alternative translation is: "it is a substance with respect to formu-

la"; and "with respect to formula" would make the soul a substance in sense (2) in 412a8, and this would be a *substance*.

22. That is, a natural body with life.

23. The use of the examples which follow illustrates Aristotle's method of getting to know things which are less familiar and more difficult by proceeding from things which are more familiar and less difficult. 71b33-72a5, 184a16-23, 1095a31-b3.

24. An axe is caused by art, so "natural" here is used in opposition to "artificial".

25. This is substance in sense (2).

26. The essence of an axe is its ability to cut, and if the axe were deprived of that ability, the result would be like a dead man who no longer has a soul. And just as a dead man is equivocally called "a man", so what results when an axe is deprived of its ability or has no such ability (like a wooden axe, which is an imitation) will be equivocally called "an axe". 21a21-4, 390a10-13, 726b22-4, 1036b30-2.

27. The term "such a body" here signifies a work of art; and such is an axe. But an axe has motion arising from art; its ability to be in motion or produce motion comes from its being a natural body, i.e., iron, prior to becoming an axe.

28. All living things are included; for all of them can grow and stop growing, and growth is a motion. Locomotion, too, is a motion, but it is limited to certain animals.

29. Just as an animal is a composite of matter and form, so is an eye. Here, however, Aristotle uses "eye" for the matter of the eye is a composite. Perhaps the "pupil" would be better; for he uses this term in 413a2-3 for the matter of the eye taken as a composite.

30. The eye of a statue or a painting or a man's eye whose vision is lost is equivocally called "an eye". For in the first two cases it cannot have vision, and in the third it is no longer an eye, whether as a composite of matter and form or as the matter of that composite; for in the third case what one calls "eye" has lost its vision and is a dead eye, and a dead eye is not an eye in the usual sense.

31. One may form two proportions. (a) vision: pupil :: sensation : sentient body, and (b) vision : eye :: sensation : sentient animal. In (a), the first ratio is that of form to matter in the case of the eye, and so is the second in the case of an animal whose soul is sensation. In (b), each ratio is that of form to the *composite*. Perhaps the proportion meant is that in (a); and in that case the sentient body would be the matter of a sentient animal. Both proportions are, however, true.

32. That which is potentially living is the body, this being the matter of a living thing, which is a composite of matter and form; but if it is not with the soul, it is no longer a potentially living body.

33. The seed or the fruit is not yet a potentially living body in the sense indicated above, for it has no soul yet or it is not with a soul yet. But it can become such a body under certain circumstances, e.g., after it is planted or is deposited in an animal; so its potentiality for such a body is like the potentiality of a boy to become a mathematician and not like the potentiality of a mathematician who has mathematical knowledge but is not using it. 1048b37-9a18.

34. Actuality as a power is distinct from actuality as the exercise of that power; and the soul, which Aristotle calls "the first actuality", is an actuality like the power of an axe to cut and the power of an eye to see, whether or not there is actual cutting or actual seeing.

35. The eye is a part of an animal, and it is a composite of matter and form, the pupil being the matter, and vision being the form of that composite.

36. For example, in animals with eyes, vision is the actuality of the eye.

37. The active intellect is meant, for this alone is separable and is not an actuality of any living body or a part of it. 413b24-7, 429b3-5, 430a10-25. The problem of whether there are activities of the soul which are independent of body was raised in 403a3-12.

38. Why raise this problem? Commentators are perplexed. The soul is a form and an actuality, but a sailor is a *composite*; and it was already stated that the soul rules the body, but not conversely. Is there some relation between the soul and the body, similar to a relation between the sailor and the boat, which has not yet been considered or discussed?

Perhaps there is. Just as the same sailor, qua a sailor and a ruler, may rule now one kind of boat and now another, so one might think that the same soul might rule now one kind of body and now another kind, as if by transmigration. Thus if a man is vicious, one might think that his soul would enter a body of a lower animal, as Plato suggests. Is a soul restricted to being the form and actuality of a certain kind of body? Perhaps this is the problem raised here. It was hinted in lines 407b20-26, and lines 414a21-28 assert the restriction of the soul, taken generically, to certain kind of bodies, i.e., those which partake of life, as stated in 412a13-15. Specific souls require bodies with further specifications; for vision necessitates an eye or the material principle of it, and the intellect necessitates a body capable of intellectual functioning, whether theoretically or practically or productively. A cat cannot produce works of art.

2

1. An alternative to "formula" is "definition". The object now is not to state just a fact about the soul, i.e., that it is a form and an actuality, but to include also the cause or causes; for, as stated in the *Posterior Analytics*, the aim in a science is knowledge through the cause, and the soul should be known scientifically. 71b9-12.

2. The things which are first known to us are acquired through sensation (980a27-1a3), and they are known either partially or confusedly. Thus a baby recognizes its mother by certain familiar attributes or accidents without knowing the nature of a mother, for such knowledge requires abstraction, etc.; and an ordinary man may know the fact that the Moon goes around the Earth without knowing the reasons, which require demonstration. 71b33-72a5, 184a16-b14, 1029b4-12. Concerning the soul, from Chapter 1 of Book B we know the fact that it is a form and an actuality, but the full formula of it requires knowledge of the cause; and it is this cause that we now seek.

3. To define the squaring of an oblong rectangle as the construction of a square with area equal to that of the oblong rectangle is not sufficient for two reasons: (a) This definition is nominal, for it is not known as a fact that such construction is possible; and if it turns out to be impossible, such a definition will be a formula of a nonbeing, like the formula of a square with unequal diagonals, and science excludes nonbeing (71b25-6). (b) Even if such construction is known as a fact or is possible, still the cause of how this is possible is not included in the definition. But if the manner of that construction, which is the drawing of the mean M between the sides A and B of the oblong rectangle, is stated, then the cause is indicated. From geometry, the line M as drawn in the semicircle with center O is the mean sought, for the product of A and B is equal to M^2; hence the area of the square is equal to that of the rectangle.

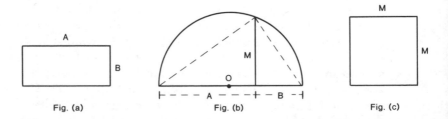

Fig. (a) Fig. (b) Fig. (c)

Aristotle raises the same objection against the definition of the circle as given at his time (92b19-25), and he would object to many of Euclid's definitions, e.g., those numbered 10, 11, 12, 20, and 22 in Book I of the *Elements*.

4. Are the terms "living thing" and "thing with life" synonymous? The meaning of "life" for natural substances is given in 412a13-6; but the term is applicable to other substances also, e.g., to God (286a9, 1072b26-8), who is not a natural substance. Here it is stated that "living" has many senses. If "living thing" and "thing with life" are used synonymously, then only one of the senses of "life", the wide sense, is given in 412a13-6. Now all natural substances which are animate have life as stated in 412a13-6; and

if any such substance has intellect, or sensation, or power to produce motion
and to rest, it too has life as stated in 412a13-6, but this has yet to be shown.
So perhaps Aristotle uses "living" here in a dialectical sense (the generally
accepted sense), in which case to have the power of sensation is to have life
in one sense only, regardless of the relations among the powers, and similarly for any other power. In the case of God, there is no power other than the
intellect, but He is not a natural substance; and since *On the Soul* comes
under physics and heavenly bodies have already been considered, only the
soul of natural substances on Earth is treated here. The relations of priority
in existence among the powers in the list are discussed beginning with the
next paragraph.

5. It appears that "mortal beings" applies to all kinds of animals which
are *composite,* and only to them.

6. This is nowadays disputed; for algae are regarded as plants, and these
are not stationary. Did Aristotle use the term "plant" in a narrower sense?
Better yet, is the locomotion of algae produced by the algae or by external
causes?

7. Perhaps the meaning is the following. First, all things which are said
to live, regardless of their powers in their soul and their special manner of
living, have one and only one power in common, and this is the power of
nutrition. Generically taken, then, all of them live because of the nutritive
power, so this power is the cause of living for all of them. Since cause and
effect are coextensive, and since here the nutritive power is the cause and
living is the effect, "living" for animate things, taken generically, must be
taken in the wide sense.

Second, just as living in the wide sense belongs to all living things because
of the nutritive power, so living in a less wide sense belongs to all animals
because of the power of sensation; and living in this sense would be sensing.
Further, the term "primarily" indicates living in that less wide sense; for
living through nutrition, too, belongs to all animals, but this sense of "living"
is not primary but secondary and generic.

The term "living things" means things which live in the wide sense; and
the term "sensation" is to be taken generically, for there are species of
sensation.

8. The word "primary" here means prior in existence to all other powers
of sensation. Thus if, in an animal, vision exists, so does the power of
touching, but the converse is not necessarily true.

9. Perhaps this is the final cause in living things, and it is discussed in
434a22-5a10.

10. An alternative to "defined" is "determined".

11. The intellect, the appetitive part, and imagination are not mentioned,
yet they seem to be parts of the soul. On the other hand, lines 413b21-4 state
that sensation implies imagination and *desire;* and the power to *think*

requires the intellect, for *thinking* is the combining of concepts acquired through the intellect (1027b25-8). The division of the soul into the four powers given here, then, appears to include all possible powers, but the principle of such division is not stated and may be dialectical.

12. What does "a part of a soul" here mean? In one sense, the power of nutrition may be part of a soul, as in animals, for these have also the power of touching; in another, it is not a part but the whole soul, so to say, as in plants. Again, since living belongs to an animal primarily because of the power of sensation (413b2), if one defines an animal in terms of the power of sensation, he somehow includes the power of nutrition. Does the power of sensation, then, include the power of nutrition as a part or does it merely imply it, as stated in 413b21-4?

13. The meaning of "separable in definition" is clear. For example, a triangle is a trilateral, and conversely; and it is the same thing which is both a triangle and a trilateral. But a triangle is defined as a plane figure with three angles, whereas a trilateral is defined as a plane figure with three sides (let these be their definitions). So a triangle and a trilateral are separable in definition but not in existence. The expression "separable in place", on the other hand, is not clear. At least three alternatives may be indicated. (a) P and Q are separable in place if as material substances they exist in the same place but can exist also in different places, as in the case of two men who are in the same room but can be also in different rooms. (b) A power, which is not a body, is separable or separate in place if it can exist only in one part of a body. Vision, for example, exists in the eye, but cannot exist in the nose or foot. (c) A power is separable in place if a thing having that power can be so divided that each of the divided parts possesses the same kind of power. The nutritive soul in plants and the sentient soul in some insects, mentioned in lines 413b16-22, are examples of things separable in place in sense (c).

When raising problems, Aristotle does not always distinguish the possible senses of terms; but he does so when he proceeds to solve the problems.

14. These are the powers of sensation, of imagination, of desire, and of motion, as stated in what follows.

15. In lines 415a6-11, 428a9-11, and elsewhere, Aristotle appears to say or imply, but with some hesitation, that not all animals have imagination. So perhaps it would be more accurate to say here that some animals have imagination also; but all of them must have desire, or better, *desire*, for wish, which is a desire, requires thought.

16. The intellect seems to differ from the other kinds of soul in genus and not in species; for it is indestructible, which differs generically from what is destructible (1058b26-9a10). The word "seems" in the text indicates that the problem has not yet been solved. Lines 430a10-25 give an answer.

17. They are not separable in existence; for the nutritive or sentient power

cannot exist by itself as a substance but must be with a body, and similarly for the others.

18. The soul is not an atom, and those who say that like is known by like make the soul a nonbeing; for what is known may be separable or inseparable in existence, but if the soul were to know both a separable and an inseparable thing, it would be both separable and inseparable — a contradiction.

19. The method used is from what is more known to us to what is more known by nature. Sensing and forming opinions are known to us before we infer the corresponding faculties. So since sensing differs in definition from forming opinions (for the first is directed to particulars as sensibles, but the second to things which may or may not be, which are not necessarily sensible or sensed when opined), the faculty of sensing, too, must differ in essence or definition from the faculty of forming opinions.

20. The statement "and it is from this fact . . . arise" is one alternative translation, and let it be (a); but there are two others: (b) "it is this fact which differentiates animals from animals", and (c) "it is this fact which differentiates animals [from plants]".

In any case, problems arise. All plants have only one power, that of nutrition, and so they would appear to come under one species; and since the number of different combinations of powers is small but the kinds of animals are much greater, some animals which are regarded as differing in species would really come under one species. So animals which have memory, imagination, little experience, and the same kinds of sensation (e.g., perhaps cats and dogs) would really come under one species. We notice, too, that in the *Treatise on Animals*, 487a11-2, Aristotle speaks of differences or differentiae of animals, not with respect to their essence, but with respect to their way of life and actions and character and parts.

21. If the cause meant is the final cause, perhaps the reference is to 434a22-5b25 and to *On Parts of Animals*. The material cause, in the sense that if A is posited then B must be as a material cause (94a21-2), is in a way included; for if A is to exist as a final cause, B must also exist. Thus if there is to be sensation, there must be nutrition; and if one is to acquire science, he must have the powers of sensation and nutrition (100a3-b5, 432a3-10, 980a27-981a2).

22. If the word "that" means the soul, one uses not the proper part by which we *know* but a whole or a composite; but although the linguistic usage is correct, it is in fact only by a part of that whole or composite that we *know*, by *knowledge* or the part which can *know*, which is in the soul as in a subject. So *knowledge* would be the cause and not the soul as a whole or as a composite; and if we are to speak scientifically, we should have "that" mean *knowledge*. The case is similar to that of the isosceles triangle, whose medians are concurrent. Its medians are concurrent not qua isosceles trian-

gle but qua just triangle; and the equality of the two sides of that triangle is not a part of the cause of that concurrence, just as the nutritive power of the soul is not a part of the cause in *knowing*. 73b25-74a3. Similarly, in what follows, a man (a composite of matter and form) is healthy not because of his body or the composite of his body and his health, but because of his health, and health is to the body of a healthy man or to the healthy man himself as attribute (or form) is to matter or subject, respectively.

23. How does *actuality* differ from actuality? Perhaps actuality is contrasted with potentiality or matter, which can be or become many things depending on the form it assumes, but *actuality* with inactivity. Thus, in a wooden table, the shape is the actuality; and it is the shape which gives that composite existence and makes us call it "a table" and know it to be a table. As for the wood as matter, it may assume other forms, for we can cut it to pieces and make something else with it. *Actuality* contrasted with inactivity, on the other hand, is like being awake contrasted with being asleep in the case of a soul, or the exercise of *knowledge* contrasted with that *knowledge* when possessed but not necessarily in use. In the case of forms which are not with matter but are in activity and exist as separate beings, like the prime mover (i.e., God), there is no contrast. The prime mover is just *actuality* (1072b27-30).

Perhaps the expression "as it were" may be indicated by the analogy *knowledge:* soul :: *actuality* : its receptive subject, for *knowledge* is to the soul which may or may not have *knowledge* as *actuality* is to that which may or may not be in activity; and the examples given of what may or may not be in activity are the *knowing* power or part and the part which causes one to be healthy. We may add, it is false to say that activity is to inactivity as *knowing* is to *knowledge;* for the activity of something denies the inactivity of it, whereas *knowing* is to *knowledge* as a thing in activity is to the same thing *with or without* its activity. Also, the *actuality* of that which can act belongs to the subject which is disposed to be or not to be in that *actuality*, as in the case of being awake, which belongs to the soul.

24. The expression "primarily that" means the first actuality, as stated in 412a27; and that actuality may or may not be an (or in) *actuality*, and it is prior in existence to its *actuality*, for a man must have a soul if he is in activity, but he need not be in activity when he has a soul, as when he is asleep. Sleeping and being awake, one may add, are contraries belonging to the soul as first actuality.

What does "living" mean? Perhaps it means all our actions and passions, whether we are awake or asleep, and these may vary and are of a certain kind but are not the soul itself. Living, then, is not the soul; but it is impossible without the soul.

25. Perhaps the syllogism which shows the cause sought is as follows. The soul is that by which such and such a thing is living; that by which that thing

is living is its form; that form is the actuality of a certain matter or body, hence the soul is the actuality of a certain body, i.e., a body with organs, as stated in 412a28-b1. If so, then, the form is the cause of that actuality.

26. An alternative to "of" is "relative to".

27. This argument proceeds from facts. We do not observe a cat or a horse or a plant having the soul of a man.

28. This argument proceeds from reason. The matter and the form of a thing must be appropriate to each other. The form cannot function without a certain kind of matter. An axe cannot cut if the material used to make it is not hard; and an animal whose food is at a distance from it cannot survive without a body capable of locomotion.

29. Does "such and such a thing" mean a natural body with the potentiality of having life, as stated in 412a27-8, or an animate body, as some commentators think, or something else?

There is also a problem with the definition. Perhaps matter and form are correlatives to be understood together as causes of a thing. If so, a body having organs may be defined as the potentiality relative to a soul; and, specifically, a body having such and such organs may be similarly defined relative to such and such a soul.

3

1. 413b10-3.

2. 413b32-3.

3. 413a31-b1.

4. 413b2. Certain animals have only the nutrient and the sentient soul.

5. Is the appetitive power distinct from the sentient power or a part of it, or is it implied by it? The same problem may be raised in the case of imagination.

6. The appetitive power is the power in virtue of which all animals desire something. The species of desire are *desire*, temper, and wish. *Desire* is a desire for pleasure; wish is a desire for that which is good and arises from reason (or else, a desire for what is thought to be a good); temper is a desire to inflict pain because of pain inflicted or about to be inflicted. *Desire* and temper belong to all animals; wish belongs only to animals which can reason. 146b11-2.

7. Pleasure and pain belong to animals and only to these; pleasurable and painful things are things which can cause pleasure or pain.

8. It is better to say, as in 146b11-2, that *desire* is a desire for pleasure; for one desires the pleasurable for the sake of pleasure, and pleasure is the cause of desiring the pleasurable.

9. In order to live, animals must avoid danger or destruction and also take in food. In the previous argument, perhaps pain and pleasure, which accompany touch, are given as sensations for the sake of avoiding danger or

destruction; in this argument, pain and pleasure which accompany flavor, a species of touch, are given as sensations for the sake of nourishment. Both kinds are needed for the preservation of an animal.

10. Vision sees only color; and when one says that the object which he sees is sugar or sweet, he senses it indirectly, and his statement is an inference; for he does not see sugar as a substance or sweetness as a flavor but only the color of the object before him. Similarly, when one says that the object which he tastes is white or sugar, he senses it indirectly, for taste is of flavors only.

11. 440b28-442b26.

12. 427a17-429a9, 433b31-434a7.

13. These two faculties belong to the rational part of the soul. The intellect is concerned with principles, but *thinking* with what is true or false; for in *thinking* one combines or divides in thought what is combined or divided in fact. *Thinking* presupposes the intellect; for indivisible or indefinable concepts are ultimately required for *thinking*, and these are intuited by the intellect.

14. A rectilinear figure is meant.

15. 413b10-3.

16. Such a formula would be as follows: "a figure is a plane bounded by straight lines". This formula is predicable of triangles, quadrilaterals, pentagons, and the rest, but it is not proper to any one of them, for it is not the definition of, say, a triangle. Consequently, the properties of a triangle cannot be demonstrated from that formula, for scientific knowledge of a thing is knowledge of its properties, which show the cause (71b9-12), and a property of a thing cannot be demonstrated without the use of the differentia of that thing. The general formula of the soul does not include the differentiae in the various species of soul; and that formula, given in 414a27-8, is like the formula for a figure given above.

17. Do "proper to each thing" and "appropriate to each species" mean the same thing, as it is thought by some commentators? Perhaps not. Definitions, which are proper formulas of things, are not limited to species. Thunder, for example, which is defined in 94a5-9, is not a species but an attribute proper to a thing, namely, to clouds; so perhaps "proper to a thing" is more general than "appropriate to a species". In the case before us, of course, the things of interest are the species of soul.

18. One may raise a problem as to the meaning of "exists potentially". Now it is evident that the nutritive power is prior in existence to the sentient power, for plants have no power of sensation but animals have the nutritive power. But are animals which have only the powers of nutrition and of sensation defined in terms of both those powers as form, or only in terms of the power of sensation? In other words, is the power of nutrition potentially included in the power of sensation and in its definition, or is it

demonstrated from the power of sensation? In the case of a quadrilateral, the triangle is included potentially in that figure, but the definition of a triangle is not included in the definition of a quadrilateral. Is this true in the kinds of soul also?

19. What kind of *reason*? Perhaps the final cause, as indicated in 434a22-5b25. If the sentient power is to be, the nutritive power must exist, but not conversely; and, in general, if A is to exist, B must exist potentially and as a material cause, but not conversely. 199b34-200b8.

20. In other words, the sense of touch can exist without each of the other senses, and so it is prior in existence to each of them; and the sentient power is similarly related to the power of locomotion.

21. Perhaps by "mortal beings" he means living things, whether plants or animals.

22. If they live only by imagination, they can sense also, for imagination is not possible without sensation.

23. 429a10-432a14.

4

1. These are mainly properties, whether of each soul or the composite of each soul and its body, and they should follow the investigation of the whatness of each soul, which is a subject. In geometry, for example, we first define a triangle, which is a subject, and then prove properties of it. 402a7-10.

2. *Actuality* is prior in formula to the corresponding potentiality, for the latter is defined in terms of what it can be, and what it can be is that *actuality*. 1049b10-17. For example, vision is a power and seeing is the corresponding actuality, and vision is the ability to see; so vision is defined in terms of seeing and not conversely. Accordingly, seeing must be *known* before vision is to be *known*. Again, seeing is directed to an object, the visible, and this is a color, which is the subject seen; for one sees color. So color is prior in *knowledge* to seeing, and *knowledge* is our aim here.

3. There are two *reasons* why food should be discussed first: (a) It is prior to the act of taking in food and to the nutritive soul, as stated in the previous commentary, and (b) it is the object of the prior and most common soul, the nutritive soul.

4. The term "living" has many senses (413a22-5), but here it is used in its most common and prior sense, which is given in 412a14-5.

5. A living thing is complete (or perfect) in its nature if it has all the parts of its soul and body; it is defective if, for some reason, it cannot have some of those parts (see Comm. 19 of Section 9, Book Γ); and it is generated by chance if it is generated not by its own kind, as it is in the case of man (for man begets man), but by causes which act in the same way as its own kind would. Aristotle believed in spontaneous generation, in spite of his general

hypothesis that like reproduces like. Microscopes and other instruments were not available at the time. 1021b12-2a2, 724b31-2, 539a18-25, 1034a9-b6.

6. Why does a doctor act qua a doctor? One may say (a) for the sake of producing health, which is a work of art, or (b) for the sake of making the patient healthy, or (c) because he enjoys it. Thus in art there seem to be three final causes. But it appears that (a) and (b) are related or are somehow one, for one might say that the doctor acts for the sake of health in the patient (for the health produced is for the sake of a healthy person), or for the sake of producing a healthy person. In *actions* there is no production of a work of art, and we may say that a man acts for the sake of someone, or because he enjoys it. For example, he performs a generous *act* for the sake of the man who needs the money, or because that *act* contributes to his own happiness. Perhaps the two senses just stated are the ones which Aristotle has in mind; and (a) and (b) taken together in the case of art may be considered as one of the senses which is analogous to the man who receives the money. In reproduction, living things act by nature, and the two senses appear in animals but not in plants. Animals appear to enjoy reproducing their kind, and the things reproduced are also a final cause. Plants, on the other hand, have no sensation and so no enjoyment; but one may say that their natural act of reproducing is analogous to the conscious act of reproducing in the case of animals.

The two senses of "that for the sake of which", listed also in 194a35-6, 1072b1-2, and 1245b15, are mentioned in 415b20-1 as having been discussed in *On Philosophy*, a lost work.

7. For example, Socrates is numerically one and is mortal; and when he dies he leaves behind his children, each of which is not Socrates but the same in species as Socrates. So Socrates partakes of the eternal and the divine as far as he can, i.e., through his descendants.

8. 198a24-7.

9. For example, a man's soul is his *substance*, and this is the cause of his existence, which is his life.

10. What is the point of this statement? According to Hicks, the soul is the actuality of what exists potentially in living things, that actuality is a formula, hence the soul is a formula. Does this conclusion suggest that to acquire *knowledge* of living things we must start from the soul's formula or definition as a principle and a cause? If so, the previous sentence speaks of the soul as a cause qua a thing, this sentence speaks of the soul as a cause qua *known*.

11. Nature, taken as a process (1014b16-7), has an end, which is a final cause, and that end in the generation of living things is the soul of that which exists potentially and is in the process of becoming. The embryo in an animal finally acquires a form, and this is the soul of the animal at birth;

so that soul is the end and final cause of nature as generation. Further, the body is an instrument of the soul, and the material parts or organs of it exist and are used for the sake of the soul or its *actuality*, whether this be its preservation or pleasure or happiness. So a man uses his material organs for the sake of his nature as form, which is his soul, and he does so according to that nature, which again is his soul.

12. See Comm. 6.

13. Trees cannot move from place to place, but they are caused by their soul to move in other ways. For they grow and deteriorate and are altered, and growth and deterioration and alteration are motions, and these in trees are caused by their nutritive soul. Sensations in animals are alterations. See Comm. 6, Section 2.

14. For Aristotle, down is the center of the Earth and also of the universe, up is the boundary of the universe, which is spherical. So travelling downwards is travelling towards the center, and travelling upwards is travelling away from the center. From the surface of the Earth, fire by its nature travels upwards, but earth downwards. So the roots of trees travel downwards not because of their weight but for a certain function, i.e., for food. 208b8-22, 308a13-33, 468a1-12.

15. What is it that holds the various bodily elements in a living thing from going their ways and so causing the disintegration of that thing? This problem differs from that in 411b6-14, in which the elements were parts of the soul and not bodily parts. Since the departure and absence of the soul, which is a form, causes the bodily elements to go their ways, the presence of the soul would cause those elements to be together, and since the presence of the soul causes the elements to be together, the absence of the soul would cause them to go their ways. 78b16-21, 1013b11-16. Similarly, the fact that growing and food-taking exist when the soul, which is a form, exists, but do not exist when the soul departs, indicates that it is the soul that causes growth and food-taking in a living thing which has that soul.

16. Perhaps Heraclitus and Hippasus among them.

17. The expression "to the formula rather than to the matter" contrasts form with matter. In a living thing, fire is to soul as a part of matter is to form; and just as the body or its organs, being the matter of a living thing, are instruments of and necessary for the soul and its functions, so is fire. Thus fire is a cause or joint-cause as matter and not as that which, as form, rules and acts and sets the limits and proportions of food-taking and growing as functions. It is the soul that decides to stop eating and not fire, which may keep on growing indefinitely; and the soul uses fire only as far as is necessary and not indefinitely. 1015a20-6.

18. The expression "it is thought" indicates that this statement or definition is not Aristotle's but one which is generally accepted. So if A and B are contraries and A is food, B is thought to be generated from A and increased by A.

19. A change from one contrary to another may be with respect to quantity or quality or place or substance. That which increases by food is changed in volume, a sick man who becomes healthy changes in quality (for sickness and health are qualities), and a man who walks changes with respect to place.

20. These contraries are (a) food and (b) that which is generated and is increased by food.

21. Whether υδωρ should be translated as "water" or as "liquid", which is a more general term, is not clear. Perhaps "water" here means oil, which is a liquid and becomes fire when ignited. Anyway, if food is regarded as stated in Comm. 18, that is, dialectically, then oil is food for fire but fire is not food for oil.

22. Since water becomes air (i.e., steam), whose volume is greater than that of water, water as defined by these thinkers is food for air. So we have another clear case of food between elements; for these are water, air, fire, and earth.

23. Perhaps these thinkers form a minority. Among them are Democritus, 323b10-5, Empedocles, 410a23-6, and Anaxagoras, 405b19-23.

24. Aristotle, too, takes this position.

25. This is one of Aristotle's own arguments, and the analogy is as follows. The carpenter is a man with a certain power, which is the art of carpentry; and when he acts on certain materials and changes them, his art changes only from inactivity to activity. Similarly, a man is a substance having a certain power, which is the nutritive power; and when he acts on food and changes it, his nutritive power changes only from inactivity to activity.

26. When distinctions are not made, contrary positions taken may be verbal because a term may be used in different senses. Aristotle's method of settling the issue is to point out the distinctions and state in what sense a position taken is right and in what sense wrong. For example, an apple initially taken into the body is in the stomach and has not been digested, and a man may call it "food"; and when it becomes flesh or blood or bone after having been digested, another man may still call it "food". Contrary positions may then arise because of the two senses, but these will be only verbal.

27. Food is now further specified; for it is taken as being relative to that which is fed, this being an animate being which takes in certain things into its body. In this sense of the term "food", oil is not food for fire, nor water for steam. Further, food so taken does not merely increase the animate being with respect to its quantity, which is an attribute; it increases it qua animate, that is, after digestion, food becomes flesh or blood or bones, which are animate parts of the animate being.

28. 322a20-33.

29. 726b1-11. Part of food is used by a living thing to reproduce another living thing of the same species.

30. Perhaps the word "that" refers to the animate thing already existing, or else to the animate body of that thing. In either case, if one of them is preserved, the other too is preserved.

31. Does "it" refer to the soul or to the principle, which is the nutritive power? In plants, it makes no difference, for the soul is just that power. In animals, if the nutritive power is not preserved, neither is the whole soul, and conversely.

32. The word "it" here refers to "that" in Comm. 30.

33. The expression "qua such" is synonymous to "qua that", where "that" has the same meaning as in Comm. 30.

34. The primary soul is the nutritive power, for this power is first and so prior to all others in existence.

35. The end here is a final cause, the others are means to an end; so it is just that the means, as relatives, should be named after the ends. Thus we use the term "healthy", for the healthy is a means to health, which is an end.

36. One might raise an objection. If the nutritive power is a power of both preserving a living thing and reproducing another such thing, it would seem that reproduction is for the sake of living and not living for the sake of reproduction, at least in animals. If so, the nutritive power would be for the sake of living and named after the term "life".

37. There are two variants in the Greek text. According to one of them, the translation in line 26 would be "that which nourishes", according to the other, the translation in line 27 would be "only in motion" and not "only a mover". Various interpretations have been given by commentators.

If the text as we have translated it is correct, perhaps the analogy is as follows. Just as the hand moves the rudder, which is moved and in turn moves the water and so the ship, so the nutritive power moves heat, which is moved and in turn acts on food; or else, if heat be taken as the mover, then food is moved by heat and is a mover — a mover by increasing the body's quantity. If the variant "only in motion" is taken, perhaps the analogy is as follows. Just as the hand, moved by the practical good or by desire, moves the rudder, which is only moved, so heat, moved by the nutritive power, moves or digests the food, which is only moved. These analogies are only interpretations. See also 433b13-30, 652b7-16, 740b25-34.

38. Probably a treatise on food, which is lost. It is mentioned in 456b5-6.

5

1. An alternative to "all the kinds of sensation" is "all the powers of sensation"; for "sensation" has two meanings, as stated later in 417a9-14.

2. Since sensation is an alteration, it is a motion, and since it is caused by an external object, it exists in the sensing being. Consequently, sensation in a sensing being depends on being moved and, by being altered, on being affected, for that which is altered is affected. 410a25-6, 415b24, 417a2-4.

3. Democritus, Empedocles, and others. 404b11-5, 405b10-21, 410a23-9.

4. 323b1-328b22.

5. If a power of sensation has an organ or exists in an organ, which consists of material elements and is therefore sensible, why does that power not sense its organ? The other part of the problem does not seem to have the same force; for if a sensation is to be sensed, it has to be sensible, but there is a problem as to whether a sensation, being mental, is sensible. Anyway, a discussion of sensible objects is required.

Perhaps the phrase "directly or indirectly through their attributes" is mentioned because at present it is not yet clear whether a sensible object is a substance or an attribute of a substance. This problem will be settled later when sensible objects qua sensible are considered, 418a7-25.

6. The sentient soul qua a power is not in activity, i.e., it is not actually acting or acted upon, although it may be acted upon when something acts on it.

7. We usually indicate these distinctions in the translation by using "power of sensation" or "potential sensation" in sense (1) and "sensation" in sense (2).

8. There seems to be a redundancy, for the senses of "to sense" have already been considered. Is there corruption in the text? Alexander mentions the term "sensible object" instead of "to sense", and Torstrik proposes this term; and this seems reasonable, for what is sensible may exist potentially or may exist in activity when it is producing a sensation.

9. They are the same generically, for they are all *actualities,* whether complete or incomplete. In another sense, of course, they are numerically one if viewed as related; for, in a motion, there is that which acts and that which is acted upon, and they must all be simultaneous. 202a13-21, 1066a27-34.

10. 201a9-11, b31-2.

11. 416a29-b9.

12. Things which are like are in the same genus, and so are things which are unlike, as in the case of black and red, which are colors or qualities. The same or similar remarks apply to that which can act and that which is capable of being acted upon. Fuel is actually unlike fire, for it is cold or not hot, but it is like fire when it is set on fire by fire. More will be said of this later.

13. The statement "a man is a *knower*" here means that a man has the potentiality of acquiring *knowledge* when he has no *knowledge* yet.

An alternative to "his kind and his matter" is "his kind or his matter". If our translation is correct, perhaps it means that the composite of matter and form in a man is such that the man, because of these two principles, is able to acquire *knowledge.* If the alternative is correct, perhaps it means that a man's form or matter is such that he can acquire *knowledge;* for his form and his matter correspond to each other, i.e., his matter is proper to his form, and his form is proper to his matter. Alternatives to "kind" as the translation of γένος are "race", "species", and "genus", the last being the usual translation of the Greek term.

14. When a man has learned geometry, which is *knowledge* and hence a quality, he has changed with respect to that quality; and that change is an alteration. When the change is from a contrary habit, the alteration is from what Aristotle calls positive ignorance, i.e., what we usually call "mistaken knowledge" or "mistaken thought", to its contrary, i.e., to *knowledge*. For example, if a man has the mistaken knowledge that tangents to a circle may be unequal but later changes through a demonstration to the *knowledge* that they must be equal, he changes from positive ignorance to *knowledge*.

15. Both grammar and sense (or power of sensation) are similar as potentialities. The first is *knowledge* already acquired and ready for immediate use, the second is a power present at birth, and it too is ready for immediate use.

16. When one changes from the inactive possession of grammar to the exercise of grammar, he is not altering, for grammar as *knowledge* and a quality remains with him both before and during the exercise. So the change from a potentiality already possessed or acquired to the exercise of that potentiality is not the same as the change from the absence to the presence of a quality. The latter change is an alteration, the former is a change from inactive possession to the exercise of that possession, and what is possessed, e.g., *knowledge* or any such quality, does not change as a quality.

17. When a cold object is acted upon by fire, the coldness of that object is destroyed. Similarly, when food is acted upon by the nutritive power, it is changed to flesh or bones or the like. But when that which possesses a power is so acted upon as to be changed to that which is exercising that power, as when a man with *knowledge* already acquired begins to use that *knowledge*, that *knowledge* is not destroyed by any contrary but is rather reinforced or becomes more stable. So the change of *knowledge* as possessed to *knowledge* as exercised is not an alteration of that *knowledge*; or else the term "to alter" will have two meanings: (a) to change from a contrary to a contrary, as from cold to hot, and (b) to change from inactivity to activity and so help to preserve by reinforcing or strengthening or stabilizing that which is changed. For example, one makes a habit more stable by using it repeatedly.

18. A prudent man has prudence, and he changes not from prudence to a contrary but from inactive prudence to prudence when in use; and such change is not an alteration from a contrary to a contrary but a change from inactivity to activity. The same remarks apply to a builder with respect to his art of building, for when he builds he does not lose his art but strengthens it.

19. Perhaps the point is as follows. To learn is to acquire knowledge not yet possessed, knowledge being a quality. Once acquired, that knowledge, actually existing, may be activated and put to use for certain things. In the first case, the learner starts without any knowledge and the change is one from ignorance (or no knowledge) to knowledge; in the second, the change is from dormant knowledge, which is a quality possessed but not in use, to *actual* knowledge, which is knowledge in activity. The two changes differ, and if one calls them "alterations", then he is using the term "alteration" in two different senses. Since that which alters is acted upon, the term "to be acted upon" as applied to the two changes just given will likewise have two meanings. Now just as acquiring and using knowledge differ, so do acquiring and using prudence, acquiring and using judgment, and so on. And since one man may be changed either from not possessing to acquiring or from inactivity to activity of something possessed, an agent, too, may produce changes which, if called "alterations", will be equivocally so called.

20. The first change of the sentient power is from nonbeing or potential being to actual being, that is, the sentient power comes into existence when a man or an animal is born. Thus that power is neither learned, like a science, nor acquired through habituation, like a virtue; and it is ready to be used, just as *knowledge* already acquired and possessed is ready to be exercised. Animals just born can see by opening their eyes.

21. That which as a mover causes sensation is color or sound or flavor or some other sensible object external to the sentient being. This fact will be discussed in detail later. 418a7 sq.

22. By "these" he means objects of thought, and these are of a universal nature and exist in the thinking part of the soul, e.g., "the concurrence of the medians of a triangle", along with a demonstration of it. A mathematician possesses such objects and can use them to demonstrate other such objects without recourse to external objects. He may draw a diagram; but this is an individual, whereas his thought signifies an object universally taken. So diagrams may help but are not necessary. 76b39-77a3.

23. A scientist may initiate thinking without using any of his senses, but he cannot have a sensation without the corresponding sensible object.

24. This is not *knowledge* of sensibles universally taken, like knowledge of the fact that white is contrary to black or that sounds cause hearing, but *knowledge as used* in, say, the production of an individual, e.g., a particular chair or a particular house. A science may be theoretical or productive or practical. The last two kinds are not for the sake of just *knowledge* but for the sake of the use of that *knowledge*. Medical science is a productive science (or an art), and as possessed it is universal; but its purpose is its use on particulars. So a physician must cure Socrates or Plato or someone else and not man universally taken. 993b20-3, 1140a10-6.

25. The thinking soul will be considered in Book Γ, 429a10-432a14.

26. Aristotle's main concern is to point out the various senses in which a term has been used or may be used in order to avoid confusion. Once this is done, he usually does not bother to introduce new terms; instead, he leaves it to the reader to pick the right sense of an equivocal term, and this gives rise to interpretations. Book Δ of the *Metaphysics* lists various senses of a number of philosophical terms. Each of the terms "to be acted upon" and "to be altered", then, will be used in one of the two senses, depending on the particular occasion.

Perhaps Aristotle was writing for mature thinkers.

27. Perhaps he is referring to lines 417b17-8, "Once born, . . . *knowledge*;", or to lines 417b31-2, which states that the sentient soul exists like the actual power of a general who can lead an army. The sensible object qua sensible, too, exists in actuality like the sentient soul or the power of a general, and this actuality is like the first actuality of the soul, as explained in lines 412a19-28. When the sensible object is acting on the sense organ or the sentient soul, then its actuality is like the second actuality of the soul; and it is only then that the sentient soul is being acted upon by the sensible object.

28. The expressions "a likeness of that object" and "in a way like that object" need clarification. We can only interpret.

To become a likeness of that object here is to become not that object or even the essence of that object but, to use a phrase, the sense impression of that object; and the sense impression is to that object when it has been sensed as a relative is to its correlative. And just as a master and a slave qua correlatives are different, so are a sensible object when sensed and the sense impression of it. So to say that a man has the essence of redness in the sentient soul is to say not that he has the essence which exists as such in an instance of redness but that he has the sense impression which corresponds in a proper way to that essence; for "essence" has two senses, (a) as it exists in a thing, and (b) as it exists not as essence in that thing but as a thought or an object of thought or as a sense impression of that essence in the soul.

The sentient soul, then, while being acted upon by the sensible object, is in the process of receiving the sense impression of the form of that object (without the matter); and the sense impression of that form, when received, is not the form of the sensible object but in a way like that form. To use a rough analogy, the sense impression of a sensible form is to that sensible form as a picture of a tree is to that tree.

There are other interpretations.

6

1. As stated in 415a16-22, the powers of the soul are posterior in definition to their activities; and the activities, too, are similarly related to the corresponding sensible objects. So the study should begin with those objects.

Besides, the objects are more evident than the corresponding activities or powers, and one should begin with what is more evident.

2. Later in 442b4-7 Aristotle shows some hesitation in using the word "all". Anyway, each common sensible is sensed by more than one sense; but all common sensibles are sensed by vision and the sense of touch. More of this later.

3. The same thing is stated in 428a11, 430b29, 442b8-10, and 1010b1-2; but in 428b18-9 Aristotle says "the sensation of proper sensible objects is true or has the least possible falsity", perhaps because sometimes the sense organ may be ailing or defective. 1009b3-6.

4. For example, when seeing something white, one may take it to be sugar; but it may be flour or something else which is white.

5. Can motion be sensed by the other senses? If a sound changes pitch, the sense of hearing can sense this change, which is an alteration and so a motion. Similarly, a change in flavor may be sensed by the sense of taste, and a change in odor may be sensed by the sense of smell. Similar remarks may be made concerning rest, which is the privation of motion, and concerning number.

6. Vision can be affected only by color, which is its proper object; and it is affected or even destroyed by the Sun not insofar as the Sun is a substance but by the extreme color of the Sun, for it is the Sun's color that acts on the eye and so on vision.

7. Direct sensibles are either proper or common; and it appears that common sensibles are known partly through the proper senses. So perhaps sensibles in the basic sense are sensibles upon which common sensibles partly depend in order to be sensed or known but which do not depend upon common sensibles in order to be sensed or known.

7

1. A color is a visible object, and conversely; but to be a color and to be a visible object differ. To be visible is to be related to something else, to vision, and "visible object" is a relative term; but to be a color is to be a certain quality, and a quality is not a relation. As Aristotle expresses it, a color and a visible object are numerically the same but different in definition, like an equilateral triangle and an equiangular triangle.

2. This is what we may call phosphorescence; and it is like color but is seen in darkness. Phosphorescence, too, is a quality.

3. But the visible object may be phosphorescence and not color. Is Aristotle inconsistent, as Hicks thinks? Inconsistency is very rarely found in Aristotle's works; there are variants. We may point out three alternatives.

(a) Essen places a period after προελθοῦσι. The translation, then, becomes: "This will become clear as we proceed. Now the object which is especially visible is color, and color ..." This interpretation is reasonable; for the discussion which follows is concerned with color, which is visible in light; and as for phosphorescence, Aristotle says later in 419a2-7 that its discussion is another matter. No such discussion appears in the extant works.

(b) The term "visible" in line 418a26 is used as a genus to include color and phosphorescence. Here it is perhaps used as a species and thus limited to color. This is a common practice for Aristotle; he does this with the term ἕξις (= "habit" and also "disposition", 8b25-9a13), with the term αὐτόματον (= *"chance"* and also "chance" (195b31-7b37), and some other terms.

(c) The terms ὁρατόν and χρῶμα may be interchanged, and then the translation becomes "Now color is a visible object, and this exists . . .".

Perhaps the first alternative is correct; but the others, too, avoid the inconsistency.

4. The expression "that which is visible in virtue of itself" may have two or more senses. Here, it means the surface of a physical body, and that surface is visible because it has color, which is the cause of the visibility of that surface. But the formula or definition of a surface as a quantity alone does not have the term "color". The phrase "in virtue of itself", then, has the second of the various meanings given in the *Metaphysics*, 1022a14-36; it means: a body's surface is visible because of its color, but color is not the essence or a part of the essence of a surface as a quantity — it is merely present in the surface of a physical body.

5. A transparent medium in activity is a transparent medium which is being acted upon by some fiery object; it is like the day, when air is acted upon by the Sun, or like the lighted air in a room, when the air is acted upon by a lighted bulb. The medium is a body and not a void — Aristotle denies the existence of a void. Colors are seen only in a transparent medium in activity.

6. In other words, one does not see the transparent medium; what he sees is color through a lighted medium, which is transparent. One may say, then, that the transparent medium is visible, if at all, indirectly because of the visible color acting on that medium which, in turn, acts on the sense organ and the corresponding faculty.

7. Transparency as a nature is a certain quality present in air, water, glass, ether, and other such objects, and it is a necessary attribute of a medium through which, when lighted, colors are seen. The term "transparent" is derived from "transparency" and is therefore posterior in formula or definition to "transparency". A transparent medium is a medium in which transparency is present, just as a virtuous man is one who has virtue, which is a quality. There is no vicious circularity here.

The eternal body of the uppermost region of the universe was called αἰθήρ (= "ether").

8. As an activity, light is not a substance. In a sense, it is like motion, which

is inseparable from a moving body; and it can be an attribute, if at all, only of a transparent medium. Aristotle's view of light, then, is in one respect the same as, but in another respect different from the view that light is a motion of a sort, whether longitudinal or transverse; for motion is a qualified activity — an incomplete activity — but light for Aristotle is a complete activity.

Would light travel according to Aristotle? If he had known that light takes time to reach a distant object, he would have said something like the following: "The transparent medium is actualized by light in the direction away from the fiery source at such and such a rate per second". Thus the medium itself would not travel but would be actualized; and light itself would not travel (except metaphorically), for it is not a body — only bodies travel, by definition.

A transparent medium is either dark or lighted (or in a state between the two); and light and darkness are in that medium as possession and privation in it.

9. The phrase "as it were the color" does not mean color but something analogous. The analogy may be as follows; whiteness : body :: light : transparent medium, or, blackness : body :: darkness : transparent medium. One might use "surface of a body" instead of "body".

10. Something which is of one and the same nature in both fire and stars causes light in a transparent medium.

11. The Greek word for "the transparent" may mean either the transparent medium, which is a substance, or transparency, which is a quality of such a medium.

12. Plato spoke of light as being something like fire coming out from the eyes. Timeaus, 45B-46B.

13. The verb "to emanate" means to come out as a bodily part from another body. Empedocles believed that light emanates from that which sees or from that which is seen. 437b23-8a5.

14. The term "something" here does not necessarily mean a body; in fact, it is something present in a body, i.e., an attribute, and in this case it is light.

15. If light were a body, since a transparent medium, when lighted, is lighted throughout every part, two bodies would exist in the same place. But this is impossible.

16. There seems to be some difference between the expressions "contraries" and "privation and presence". The Greek term translated as "presence" is infrequently used; the term commonly used is translated as "possession". Anyway, contraries are defined as being furthest apart within a genus (1018a25-31), but presence and privation are, within the same genus, like a thing possessed and the same thing not possessed by a subject (1022b22-36). However, contraries are opposites, and so are presence and privation. 11b15-23.

17. Perhaps the truth from argument arises from the impossibility of two bodies to be in the same place, and the truth from observation arises from what has just been said. For other details concerning the position of Empedocles and Aristotle's objections, see 324b26-35, 437b26-8a5, 446a26-7all.

18 . In the case of colors, this is the transparent medium taken without reference to its being dark or lighted. The expression "can receive color", then, appears to mean: can be activated by color in accordance with that color's nature; for colors qua colors can exist only in colored objects, and different colors activate the medium in different ways.

It is not clear to me whether the statement is put forward as a nature or part of the nature of the transparent or as a statement of fact. See also 429a15-26, where statements concerning facts are made.

There is another problem. Is the transparent medium to be understood, when taken potentially, as being a subject without reference to its being dark or as being a subject when dark?

19. There seems to be a difficulty. Light is thought to belong to the transparent medium as an attribute or an activity to a subject; and similarly for darkness. If so, then it would seem more reasonable to say "the same nature which is at one time dark and at another time lighted". If we use "transparency" and not "transparent medium" (for the Greek term has two senses), then, again, light appears to be related to transparency as an attribute or an activity to a subject.

One may raise this problem: is darkness the contrary of light or is it related to light as potentiality to actuality? For one thing, it is the privation of light, but not the kind of privation which cannot, like blindness, become its contrary.

20. It does not appear in the extant works.

21. Lines 418a31-b2 state that color has the power of setting in motion a transparent medium in activity, and that this is the nature of color. One of the senses of "nature" is the *substance* or form of a thing existing by nature (192b8-3a2, 1014b16-5a19). Here the definition of color is explicitly stated, for a definition of a thing signifies what it is to be a thing (or, the essence of a thing). Hence color is a quality, for a power is a quality, and as a quality it is present in a substance.

22. If a color is to act on the eye (i.e., to be seen) and hence on vision, it has to do so in accordance with its definition. But if a colored object is in contact with the eyes, its color cannot act on a transparent medium; hence it cannot be seen.

23. If the intervening space were to become void, there would be no intervening medium which could be affected by color and in turn affect the eye and vision; so seeing an object through a void would be impossible. Further, if the colored object were transmitting corpuscles or emanations, it would do so in all directions and continuously, and so the surrounding

space would not be void but full of these emanations. But then, many bodies would be in the same place, for the same space would be filled with emanations issuing from a great many colored objects in space. Again, Democritus would find it difficult to explain why a colored object, when in contact with the eyes, is not seen through its emanations.

24. Perhaps the meaning here is that, given a dark medium or space, like air at night, if fire is placed in it, it acts like the Sun and activates that medium as the Sun does, at least to the extent that fire becomes visible. So it would not be true to say that the medium which surrounds fire is completely dark.

25. 422a8-424a16.

26. The argument is as follows. Since odors affect both air and water, these media have something in common, like the transparency which exists in air, water, and some solid bodies, like glass.

27. 421b13-422a6.

8

1. Is sound according to Aristotle analogous to light, or to color? But color is present in a colored object, whereas sound seems to be presented sometimes as a certain motion of the air (420a7-9, 21-3, b11), as if it were analogous to light (419b28-9, 420a27-9), sometimes as present in the sounding object (418a13, 419a21-30, 425b29), as if it were analogous to color, and sometimes as a collision of two objects or a blow (419b14, 420b27-9, see Comm. 3), as if it were analogous to the action by the light-producing object on a colored object. Two senses of "sound" are mentioned here, but from the way they are stated it is not clear to what they apply. We may consider the following analysis of sound and light.

First, let the term "sound" in "P makes sound" mean the sound as an attribute of P, in which case sound is the activity of P, now known as P's vibration; let "sound" in "P produces sound" mean the sound as an attribute not of P but of the air which is acted upon by the vibrating P; and let "a sounding object" mean an object when making this kind of sound. Further, since hearing is an attribute of that which hears and not of sounding air or of sounding hard and smooth objects, let the expression "a sounding object produces hearing" be used for consistency, whether that object is air or a hard and smooth object.

In the case of sound, there is (A) the power — a quality — of a smooth and hard object P to make sound when struck, (B) the activity (now known as a vibration, e.g., of a tuning fork) of P corresponding to that power when P is struck, (C) the power of the air to be activated by P when P is sounding, and (D) the activity or motion of air (now known as longitudinal waves of air molecules) or of a medium produced by P when sounding. Let the term "sound" in the main sense, when applied to air, mean not a scattered activity of air but one which is unified and can be heard. In the case of light, there is (a) the power — color, which is a quality — of an object Q to be seen when there is light, (b) the activity of Q corresponding to that power when there is light, (c) the medium's power — transparency, which is a quality — to be activated by Q when there is light, and (d) the medium's activity (now known as transverse waves) produced by Q (the colored object) when there is light. We may add, P has the power of making sound, whether it is *actually* making it or not, and similarly for air; and the same remarks apply to the power (i.e., the color) of Q and the power of the transparent medium.

From the text of this and the preceding chapter it appears that Aristotle is aware of the distinctions made in the above analysis. If our analysis is correct, then (a) corresponds to (A), (b) to (B), (c) to (C), and (d) to (D). As for sound in the sense of a collision or a blow, perhaps this is an additional sense, or else it is sound in sense (B), since both P and the object that strikes it may be sounding after a collision; and if the text is corrupt (see Comm. 3), there is no problem. The distinction between a power and the corresponding activity, then, seems to imply that sound in sense (1) may be sound in sense (B) or sound in sense (D), and that sound in sense (2) may be sound in sense (A) or in sense (C). Similar remarks apply to light. Accordingly, it is true to say, as in the text, that smooth and hard objects have sound, whether in sense (A) or in sense (B), and that they can make sound, in sense (A), and also produce sound, in sense (B). Further, just as a red surface, when the Sun shines upon it, activates the transparent medium in such a way that the medium produces the sensation of redness when it reaches the eye, so a particular smooth and hard surface, when struck by another object, activates the air in such a way that the air produces the sensation of the pitch corresponding to that surface. Finally, *actual* sound in a hard and smooth surface is analogous to the color of a colored object in daylight, potential sound is analogous to the same color in darkness; and *actual* sound in air is analogous to light in a lighted medium, and potential sound in air is analogous to the transparency of that medium in darkness — by "potential" we mean the state of the sound or the color when it is not in *actuality*.

2. In other words, since locomotion is necessary for a collision, a medium is required.

3. The Greek text, perhaps corrupt, translates into "sound is not the collision of any chance things"; but if $\pi\lambda\eta\gamma\dot\eta$ is changed to $\pi\lambda\eta\gamma\hat\eta$, the part "[produced by]" is needed. It seems to me that the reading with the change is literally more correct, for the sounding object is not the collision itself but the result of that collision.

4. Perhaps "sound" means the sound in air, and this is the motion or activity of air caused by the sounding hard and smooth object. However, it appears that the object struck may be the air itself, as in the case of a guitar

string or a whip. In either case, the sound in air is produced by the sounding hard and smooth object, which has sound in sense (2), and not conversely, and this sound is produced by the collision of this and another object.

5. Perhaps "this" refers to the sound in air when collision takes place.

6. As in the case of light rays, which are reflected when striking a mirror perpendicularly, so sound in air which is enclosed rebounds, so to say, like a ball when the motion of that air strikes an object in its course perpendicularly.

7. By analogy, just as light rays are reflected when striking a colored object, so does sounding air when striking a hard object. And just as some of the Sun's rays reach our eyes when they strike a colored object, so does some of the sounding air when it strikes an object. In the first case, the colored object is usually seen, for vision is our best sense and reveals most distinctly differences in things (437a3-9, 980a26-7); in the second, an echo is hardly heard, unless the object struck by the sounding air has a surface which is smooth and oriented in such a way as to reflect in the direction of the ear much or most of the activated air.

8. An alternative to "be everywhere" is "proceed in all directions". Thus a colored object in daylight is seen regardless of the position of a man relative to the object, as long as the medium between the man and the object is transparent and lighted.

9. If there is no object in a given direction, light in that direction cannot give rise to any sensation of color, and one sees darkness, so to say; so one sees color only in the direction of colored objects.

10. I am not sure of the meaning of this part, and hence of my translation of it. I may venture an interpretation. In view of the rough surfaces of the objects on the Earth, light from the Sun striking them are reflected repeatedly in all directions and so do not produce shadows as they would from the weak light of, say, a candle or even the Moon at night.

11. Perhaps the word "basic" here refers to the sounding air as both necessary for hearing and the proximate or nearest moving cause of hearing. The sounding object is a moving cause, too, but a distant cause, and so is that which strikes a hard and smooth surface. If the air within the ear is regarded as a part of the organ of hearing, then it is the air which is external to the ear that is basic to hearing.

Some thinkers (perhaps few, or else a popular view, 656b15) regarded air to be void, or void to be air. In so doing, they were right in saying that void is basic to hearing.

12. Apparently, the air external to the ear is meant, and its motion is that which is caused by the hard and smooth object which is sounding.

13. Perhaps "motionless" here means without any of the kinds of motion which might be caused from the external sounding air and which produces hearing of a sound; for if any such motion were in the air within the ear,

hearing would result, and this motion along with a different motion caused by the external sounding air would prevent the latter motion (or sound) from being heard distinctly or as coming from outside.

14. If sound can be heard when a man is in water, it should follow that sounding air affects water, and water so affected affects the air within the ear. Perhaps this is Aristotle's position and is implied in 419b18 where he says "Further, sound can be heard both in air and in water".

15. If the palm is lightly pressed on the ear, a continuous murmur is heard as if issuing from the air within the ear.

16. What is thought to be a void is the enclosed air within the ear; and this air is resonant, that is, it has its own proper motion — a murmur of some sort.

17. For example, a ball rebounds when it strikes a smooth surface. Similarly, one thing striking another rebounds, so to say, and then it is sounding and has sound in sense (2), as stated in Comm. 1.

18. The kind of sound (i.e., its pitch, loudness, etc.) of the air, which is sound in sense (1), is caused by the kind of vibration or activity of the sounding smooth and hard object, which has sound in sense (2). In modern terms, the number of vibrations and the amplitude of a vibrating tuning fork cause in the air struck corresponding differences in its sound, and this sound causes corresponding sensations when heard. The sensation of pitch and loudness corresponds to the sound (in sense (1)) in air and also the sound (in sense (2)) in the tuning fork.

The analogy between colors and sounds is as follows. Just as differences in colors cause corresponding differences in a lighted medium, so differences in smooth and hard objects struck cause corresponding differences in the sounds in air; and just as those differences in a lighted medium cause corresponding differences in the sensation of color, so those differences in the sounds in air cause corresponding differences in the hearing of sounds as sounds in air.

19. In other words, high and low notes as sounds do not travel in air with different speeds. 448a19 sqq. When they reach the sense of hearing, however, higher notes act more quickly and with greater intensity in reaching that sense than lower notes do; but the difference in time is very small, for the time interval from the moment each note arrives at the ear till the moment it is heard is very small, and so the two notes appear to be heard simultaneously.

It is evident, then, that Aristotle is not contradicting himself in lines 420a32-3. In the first case, he is speaking of speeds of differing sounds (which are motions) in air as being equal, in the second, he is speaking of speeds of different sensations (which are motions) as being unequal because they are caused by different kinds of sounds as movers.

20. If our translation is correct, then the acute sound in air is fast indirect-

ly, i.e., not by travelling faster in air but by imparting a quicker motion to the sense organ from the moment it reaches it. There are other interpretations, and hence alternative translations.

21. Just as "sound" may mean either the activated hard and smooth object or the motion of air caused by that object, so "voice" may mean either the activated larynx or the motion of the air caused by the activated larynx.

22. This is not a syllogism. What is stated is that people speak of the flute or the lyre as having voice because they notice traits common to these and to the voice in humans. The conclusion, of course, is that the term is equivocally used for animate and inanimate objects, in spite of the similarities. A term univocally used for those objects would be "sound".

23. 535b14-26.

24. So far, the genus and differentia of voice are given, and these correspond to matter and form. The genus is sound, the differentia restricts the sound to a certain kind, namely, that of an animal which takes in air. The final cause or purpose and the moving cause are considered next.

25. According to Aristotle, breath is used not to furnish warmth to an animal but to cool excessive warmth in it; and it is also used for the sake of a good life, for communication by voice contributes to a good life, and nature does nothing in vain. 476a7-15, 668b33-9b12, 291b13-4, 658a8-9.

26. Here we are given a part of the soul as the moving cause of voice, and also the manner in which voice is produced.

27. 474b25-31, 476a1-2, 669a2-5.

9

1. The sense of smell in man is inferior also to his other senses. 440b31-441a3.

2. Concerning hard-eyed animals, see 444b25-8, 657b29-8a3.

3. Since the cause of smelling poorly lies in the sense of smell itself, it is not true to say that the odors are not accurate or definite. Just as hard-eyed animals discriminate colors poorly because of their vision, whereas man does so clearly, so we distinguish odors poorly because of our inferior sense of smell, whereas dogs do so far better because of their superior sense of smell. But the ability of hard-eyed animals to see what is dangerous and what is not is sufficient for their safety, and the same applies to man's ability to smell. 436b18-7a1.

4. For this analogy, see also 420a26-b3, 443b12 sqq., 445a29-b1.

5. The abbreviated syllogism, limited to men's senses, is as follows. The sense of taste is a sense of touch, the sense of touch is more accurate then the sense of smell, hence the sense of taste is more accurate than the sense of smell; and the sense of touch is the cause. It is like the syllogism: an isosceles is a triangle, a triangle has two right angles, hence an isosceles has two right angles; and the cause is the triangle. Thus the two equal sides of

the isosceles do not contribute to the fact that the isosceles has angles whose sum is two right angles; and similarly, the differentiae of the sense of taste do not contribute to its being more accurate.

6. Why is touch so related to prudence? One might argue thus: The most prudent is that which has the greatest virtue; such virtue can belong to that which has the most accurate basic sense; such sense, which is touch, belongs to man; hence man can be the most prudent of all animals.

7. Since the names "sweet", "pungent", and the others are analogously predicable of the corresponding qualities of odors and of flavors, they are not univocally predicable of them.

8. How does a slight odor differ from a poor odor. Perhaps "slight" indicates a small quantity of odor, regardless of the species of odor, whereas "poor" indicates the quality of odor, whose quantity is small.

9. See also 443a2-8, 444b7-5a4.

10. Aristotle is mistaken, for some other animals sense odors only when inhaling. According to Aristotle, then, it appears that animals which are not men and which smell and depend on air do so in a manner different from that of men.

11. The argument is as follows. The sense of smell is defined as a sense which can sense odors. So since, as a matter of fact, it is odors that fish and bloodless animals sense and since it is by odors that they too can be destroyed, it follows by definition that they have a sense of smell and not a sixth sense. And since they do not smell by inhaling, they do so in some other manner. So all odors are sensed by the sense of smell, but the manner in which they are sensed may differ.

12. Are odors substances according to Aristotle? Colors and sounds and flavors are not substances but qualities, or else motions. So if odors are analogous to flavors (443a7-8) and sounds and colors (for all of them are sensible objects), it would follow by analogy that odors, too, are not substances. Does the odor in a substance, then, produce a motion in the air in a manner analogous to that in which the sound of a struck hard and smooth object produces a motion in the air or the color in an object produces an activity in a lighted medium? If not, do odorous substances emit dry emanations, which are themselves odorous substances causing smell when in contact with nostrils during inhaling? What is Aristotle's position?

Second, if "the organ of smell is potentially of such a kind" means that the organ is dry, it would appear that the word "potentially" is misleading, for the nostrils exist actually and not potentially. Perhaps it means that the organ, or the power in it, is potentially the sensible object or potentially in a way like the sensible object (418a3-6), which belongs to what is dry, just as vision is potentially the visible objects qua visible and the intellect is in a certain sense potentially the intelligible objects (429b30-1). Is there another alternative?

10

1. Since the object tasted is also touched, and since what is touched is sensed directly and not through an external medium, the object tasted is sensed directly.

2. Perhaps "object of taste" here refers to flavor, which has no matter but exists in a material object.

3. If flavor, which is a quality, exists in a liquid, then flavor qua sensible is to the liquid in which it exists as form is to matter, or else, flavor is present in the liquid as in a subject; for the liquid as a medium is as such without flavor and is not sensed qua an object of taste. 441a3-4.

4. The word "this" refers to the liquid which has flavor.

5. The surface of the solution or of a drink (like a coke) which is in contact with the tongue has flavor, and this flavor is sensed directly, as already stated.

6. The color seen through the transparent medium does not exist in that medium. Instead, the medium is activated by the color in a manner appropriate to that color, and it is this activated medium which affects the eye and produces the sensation of that color.

7. Dry salt does not produce a salty sensation, except potentially, for it must be dissolved first.

8. An excessive object of sense damages or destroys the sense or makes it incapable of sensing temporarily. 424a29.

9. The term "invisible" in sense (a) is the contradictory, but not the contrary, of the term "visible". In this sense, a number and a relation and a sound are invisible, for they are not at all objects which can be seen by vision.

10. We do not speak of a number or of water as being footless, but of a man or a cow and the like; for these usually have feet, and feet can be parts only of animals. Certain animals by their nature have feet; but when they do not have them, they are said to be deprived of them. But no one speaks of water as being deprived of feet.

11. The term "tasteless" corresponding to sense (a) of "invisible" is left aside without mention, and only the term in the sense corresponding to (b) is used, for it is this sense which is of importance here.

12. It is not clear whether the words "slight" and "poor" differ in meaning. A weak sound may or may not be pure in pitch, and so one may specify it when it is pure but fail to do so when it is a mixture of a sort. Similarly, one may detect the quality of a weak flavor if it is pure but fail to do so when it is not pure; and perhaps the terms "slight" and "poor" are used for this difference in weak flavors.

Assuming that "weak" as applied to flavor may be pure or mixed, then "weak" by itself is like a genus relative to "weak and pure" and "weak and mixed." But Aristotle often uses only two terms, one of which is given two meanings, one as a genus (e.g., "weak"), and the other as a species (e.g., "weak and pure"). He uses διάθεσις and αὐτόματον in such a manner. So since he uses only φαύλη (= "poor") in line 422a33 and elsewhere, perhaps it is this term which has two meanings; for if it is used alone, it must be used generically if it is to include both species.

13. In what sense are the drinkable and undrinkable objects starting-points? For one thing, Aristotle starts with the objects of sense, then he proceeds to their activities and those of the senses, and then he ends with the senses. Further, it is the objects of sense that are movers and cause the medium to be in activity; then the activated medium causes the sensations as affections or as motions. So the objects of sense are starting points or principles as movers and also prior in knowledge to that of the corresponding activities and sensations and the senses themselves.

14. Perhaps the Greek term should be ἀμφωτέρων in line 422a32.

15. The sense of taste exists by nature for tasting flavors, and tasting objects which are not destructive of the sense of taste is sensing them according to nature and for the best, for nature does nothing in vain. 192b35-3a1, 291b13-4.

16. The tongue senses the drinkable qua drinkable and also qua tangible, for in tasting one also touches the object tasted, and the flesh as the organ of touch senses the drinkable qua tangible. So it is only qua tangible that the drinkable is sensed by both senses and is thus common to both.

17. If the organ of taste is a liquid, will it be affected by the object of taste, which is a solution and also a liquid? Like is not affected by like, or if it is affected, the liquid qua liquid will not preserve its nature.

18. If the tongue is very moist, it is still in contact with the moisture of the previous drinkable object, at least to some extent; so it is prevented from sensing only or purely the drinkable object just entering the mouth, for the two kinds of moistures form a blend consisting of both drinkable objects.

19. Contraries are principles; and these principles, not being composed of other principles, are elements and hence simple. Things between contraries, on the other hand, are mixtures or solutions of contraries, and so they are not simple. 442a12-3.

20. By "each of these" he means each of the species of flavor. But, "potentially such as each of these" does not mean, for example, that the faculty of taste itself tastes bitter when it has the sensation of bitterness; for having the sensation of bitterness does not imply tasting bitter or being bitter, just as having the idea of a circle does not imply being circular. This fact is brought out more clearly in lines 418a4-6, where it is stated that a sense, when acted upon, is a *likeness* of the sensible object and exists *in a way like* that object.

11

1. If the sense of touch is presupposed by the other senses (for without it none of the others can exist, 415a3-6), why is it not discussed first? Perhaps its discussion is the most difficult, in view of the problems which follow.

2. One might be tempted to regard the skin or outer flesh as the organ or part of the organ of touch. But if that flesh or skin is to the organ of touch as the transparent medium is to the eye, it is not a part of the organ of touch, unless the expression "organ of touch" includes also the medium. The word "primary" is used here in the main sense, and in that sense it excludes the medium 653b19-30.

3. The term "contrariety" here includes the contraries as well as whatever lies between them. Thus vision is of black and white as contraries and of the other colors between them.

4. Contraries are present in a subject. So if, in the case of hearing, sound is the subject in which high and low pitch, loudness and softness, and the others are present, then, in the case of touch, one should inquire first what the subject is and then attend to the contrarieties which are present in that subject. If the subject admits many contrarieties, one may still raise the problem as to their relation with respect to priority; perhaps there is a primary among them. In sound, perhaps the contraries in pitch are prior to those in volume, just as quality is prior to quantity. 1069a20-1.

5. One variant is "motions and sensations". Of course, a sensation is an alteration, and hence a motion. In line 423a16 the term is "sensations". Anyway, corresponding to a given sensation there is a motion or activity of a medium and also of the sensible object which caused the motion or activity of that medium.

6. Air is a medium for the organs of sight, smell, and hearing, and the hypothesis that the outer flesh, like air, is a medium for touch raises the problem whether there may be more than one organ in the case of touch and, correspondingly, that there may be not one sense of touch but many. Air as a medium is separate from animals, and it is evident that vision and the senses of smell and hearing require three organs; but flesh is grown on to us, and in view of this it is not clear whether there is just one organ and so one sense of touch or many. The problem was raised at the start of this Section.

7. This is more fully considered in 435a11-b25.

8. One senses tangible objects and also flavors with the same part of the tongue; but not every fleshy part in contact with flavorous things senses flavors. So it appears that the fleshy part which may be in contact with tangible and flavorous objects is a medium like air, which is not an organ but through which colors and sounds are sensed.

9. That which is moist differs from that which is wet. Water is moist, i.e., every part of it is moist or has moisture by its nature, but if an object has water on its surface, it is said to be wet, like a wet glass or skin. 330a12-24.

10. The extremeties here are surfaces.

11. Since the surfaces of, say, two equal wooden cubes in water are always wet, they cannot coincide as dry surfaces when one tries to make a square surface of one of them coincide with a square surface of the other; for, since each of those surfaces is always everywhere wet, there will always be a thin film of water between the two surfaces when they are thought to be in contact. One of the surfaces, then, will be in contact with the film of water, and this film will be in contact with the other surface.

12. An argument similar to the preceding leads to the conclusion that the two square surfaces of the two cubes in air cannot touch each other, for a film of air will lie between those surfaces.

13. 423a2-11.

14. The outer flesh is meant.

15. Perhaps in the region of the heart. 469a10-27.

16. For example, when a colored object is placed on the eye, it is not seen; for the object can be seen only through an activated medium, such as air.

17. These two are the primary contrarieties yielding four primary attributes of bodies as objects of touch and six possible pairs of attributes. Since a bodily element cannot be at the same time hot and cold, or dry and wet, there remain four pairs each of which determines one of the four bodily elements. 329b7-331a6.

18. To be potentially such as the tangible object is not to be potentially the tangible object itself or its form but to be capable of receiving the form of that object in the sense of sensing it, otherwise the organ of touch (or the sense of touch) could become cold when sensing a cold object or dry, whether earthy or fiery, when sensing a dry object. See also Comm. 28 of Section 5, Comm. 12 of Section 9, Comm. 20 of Section 10, and 435a19-b2.

19. For example, if the tangible object were of the same temperature as the hand which touches it, it would not act on it so as to raise or lower its temperature and communicate the difference to the sense of touch, and hence there would be no sensation of that object's differing temperature. If there is to be a sensation of a differing temperature, then, the tangible object must be colder or hotter than the hand and so act on it; and if so, the organ of touch and the sense of touch in it senses and discriminates the difference in temperature and so functions as a mean between objects which are colder and hotter than the hand. A sense relative to its objects which are contrary is a kind of a mean, like a virtue relative to the corresponding contrary vices, as in the case of boldness relative to rashness and cowardice. 1108b11-23.

20. 422a20-31.

21. The term "intangible" here is the contrary of "tangible". The contradictory of "tangible" would be "not tangible", and numbers and virtues are examples of things which are not tangible. Some contradictories of tangible objects, of course, are contraries; for contraries are also contradictories, like

the black, which is not white, but contradictories are not necessarily contraries.

12

1. Perhaps οἷον (= "in a sort of way") indicates a similarity of the form of a sensible object as received by the corresponding sense to the impression of the signet-ring as received by the wax. For clarity, let us use a golden hemisphere, whose curved surface is convex. The impression of this surface in the wax is not quite the form of the original surface, for it is concave and not convex; but there is one-to-one correspondence, so to say. The same kind of correspondence exists between the picture of a tree and the tree. Similarly, there is an analogous correspondence between the form of a sensible object as received in sense and the same form as existing in that object. Literally, then, the essence of a sensible object, say of color, as existing in a colored object is not the same as it is when existing in the corresponding sense, but the two essences are correlatives; for a sensation is of a sensible object as sensed and is relative to that object as that object, whereas that object exists in sensation not as that object but as sensed and is relative to that sensation.

2. An alternative to "qua gold or qua bronze" is "qua golden or qua bronze", in which "bronze" is used as an adjective. In either case, just as the impression in the wax is the same regardless of the kind of material used, as long as the form in that material is the same, so the sensation of a white object is the same, regardless of whether that object is sugar or flour or some other thing which is white.

3. If sugar and saccharin are both alike sweet, one who senses each has the same sensation regardless of whether one calls the one "sugar" but the other "saccharin"; for what one senses is the same sweet flavor, and the formula or essence of that flavor is the same in both cases.

4. By "that" he means the organ, and that organ is or has magnitude. It is not clear whether the term "organ" here signifies the composite of matter and form or just the matter, as in the case of an organic body as matter relative to the soul as form. If it signifies the matter, then the sense as a power and the organ are related as form to matter in a single thing. So the two are numerically the same, for they are inseparable; but they are distinguishable, just as the surface and the bronze in a bronze sphere are distinguishable. If it signifies the *composite*, then again they are distinguishable, for a *composite* is not the same as one of its two principles, except numerically. The sense power, of course, being a quality and not a body, is not or has not a magnitude.

5. Sense, being a power and a quality, is not a magnitude; and sensation, if regarded as an alteration and a motion, is accidentally a magnitude and not essentially. 1020a26-32.

6. 421a23-5, 422a29-33, 424a14-5, 426a30-b3.

7. This is the nutritive soul through which food is taken from the soil. 411b27-30, 414a32-3.

8. Food is tangible and affects plants; in turn, it is affected by plants and becomes a part of them. 324a2-9, 328a19-21, 768b15-25.

9. Unlike the sentient soul, which is so affected by the sensible object that it is in a certain way receptive of its form without its matter, the nutritive soul is not so affected, for it is acted upon by food as a composite of matter and form and acts upon it likewise.

10. The air's thunderbolt is not a substance but an attribute. It is a certain activity of the air, a violent or excessive disturbance of it. And whereas such activity affects the sense of hearing by causing hearing, it is the air along with that activity—i.e., the activated air—which may affect inanimate things and animate things which have no sense of hearing.

11. Universally, tangible objects cannot be affected or altered unless they are in contact with things which act upon them. 327a1-6.

12. The argument appears to be as follows. Inanimate objects are altered or affected by tangible objects; e.g., a cold body in contact with warm water cools that water. If so, one may claim that objects with flavors or sounds or light should likewise affect inanimate as well as animate bodies.

13. Aristotle appears to agree, but with a qualification. Air is affected by an odorous object; but it is affected by becoming itself an odorous object or an object which transmits odor and not an object which smells the odor, for smelling an odor is distinct from becoming odorous or transmitting odor. Further, not all inanimate objects are affected by odor or light or sound, e.g., perhaps gold or stones are not always affected by odors or sounds or light (one may question Aristotle's position here). Again, inanimate objects soon lose the affection they acquire, as in the case of air which loses its odor; but when a man hears a sound, he retains its sense impression for some time—perhaps a long time.

BOOK Γ

1

1. The discussion in Sections 1 and 2 is still about sensibles and the senses, and one may raise the problem whether these Sections belong to this or to the preceding Book, or even whether the division of this work into Books and Sections was Aristotle's. The discussion concerning thinking begins with Section 3, and perhaps Book Γ should begin there, if there is to be a division into parts at all.

2. Sensing requires a power of sensing, i.e., a sense, and a sense requires an organ; and since (a) we possess the sense of touch along with the corresponding organ and (b) we sense all the tangible *attributes* (these are listed in 329b18-34, along with their priorities), these assumptions take care of things which we sense directly and not through a medium which is not part of us (for we touch tangibles by our flesh as a medium, which is a part of us).

3. The elements for Aristotle are four: air, water, fire, and earth. It is not clear here whether earth and fire are considered as intervening elements through which things may be sensed indirectly. Some solid materials are listed as transparent (418b6-7), and perhaps these are regarded as being earthy or mostly so.

4. Sensibles sensed through a medium which is not a part of us are now considered. Why should such a medium be limited to simple elements?

5. Colors and sounds, for example, differ in genus; and similarly with the others. But high and low notes on the scale do not differ in genus, for all of them come under the genus of sound.

6. Perhaps in the case of land animals the organ of smell is regarded as being made of air, but in the case of water animals, as being made of water (421b8-13).

The organ of smell is taken here as made of air or water, but in lines 438b16-27 it appears to be regarded as made of fire or as being potentially fiery, for odor is regarded as being of a dry (422a6) and smoky nature. Has Aristotle changed his position? If so, which is his later position? What is potentially fire, of course, may not be fire or fiery, just as what is potentially air may be water, which becomes air when heated. Various interpretations have been given.

7. Since tangibles may be liquid or earthy or even gaseous, if the sense of touch is to be a mean in order to discriminate the various tangibles, the organ of touch must be partly earthy. 435a17-24.

8. No organ is made of fire alone or earth alone, although these elements may exist partly in an organ. But animals do possess organs made of air or

water. So since the five organs are receptive through their corresponding senses of the various forms or *attributes* of the four elements and of their composites, all animals which are complete must possess these five senses. The mole is considered as being maimed. 532b31-3a12.

9. The final assumption is that there are no other kinds of bodies and hence no corresponding attributes in the part of the universe where there is generation and destruction, i.e., where animals exist. Ether, which is an element, and the celestial bodies exist outside of this part of the universe. The argument on the whole paragraph appears to be dialectical.

10. The unit is not mentioned in 418a17-8. Perhaps it comes under number, which is composed of units; for a unit is a principle of a number, and a number cannot be known unless a unit is known. 1016b17-25, 1021a12-3. In one of the manuscripts, the Greek word for "unit" does not appear.

11. According to 418a7-25, we sense the common sensibles directly by the proper senses. Is there a contradiction here or a corruption of the text?

Torstrik follows an old Latin version which inserts "not" before "indirect-ly", and the result appears consistent with 418a7-25 and also with 425a27-8. Hicks supports the text here as it is by using arguments which seem to me artificial, forced, and contrary to Aristotle's assumptions. Others think that Aristotle, in using "indirectly" here, states not his own view but a hypothetical view which would follow if a sense organ with a sixth sense were posited as proper to the so-called "common sensibles", for each of the other five senses would then sense the common sensibles indirectly, as stated in 425a30-1. The text, if one uses the word αἰσθανοίμεθα in 425a15, would read: "Further, neither is there an organ ... unity, which we would then sense indirectly by every sense; ..." The first alternative fits in with Aristotle's thought, and so does the third, which I am inclined to adopt. But I do not accept Hick's position, which will be considered at length in Comm. 20.

12. By what motion? Perhaps by the motion (other than proper sensing) of the sense organ. The eye moves when it senses a number of objects or the motion of an object, the hand or a part of it moves when it senses a magnitude or a number of objects, etc. Torstrik thinks that the term should be κοινῇ (= "commonly [by each sense]") and not κινήσει (= "by motion"); and, as Hicks points out, this emendation appears to be a reasonable antithesis of "proper sense" in line 425a21.

13. Is shape a magnitude? According to 10a11-2, shape is a quality; but according to 1020a9, it is a quantity. Perhaps "shape" has two meanings; for if it is taken as a differentia (we speak of the shape of an object as being triangular), it is a quality, since a differentia is a quality (1020a33-b1), but if it is taken as a composite of genus and differentia, it is a quantity, for a triangle is a quantity and not a quality, just as a man is a substance and not rationality.

14. A privation is a species of negation and is known and often defined by the use of the corresponding possession. Accordingly, rest is the absence of motion in that which by its nature can be in motion. Similarly, a unit is a principle of number and is known by the privation or negation of continuity; so a number, being a plurality of units, is known by the privation or negation of continuity. 143b33-5, 430b20-3, 1022b22-3a7, 1055a33-b11.

15. We can number marbles by seeing or touching them, we can number notes by hearing them, we can number different kinds of odors by smelling them, etc; and a number is a negation or privation of continuity.

16. For example, in sensing redness, vision senses some unity or unit, namely, one color; and since colors are many in species (and even in number), vision may sense a number of them. Further, redness is not continuous, and half a color cannot exist.

17. If there were a proper sense for motion, we would sense motion by each of the other senses only indirectly, just as we sense a sweet object by vision. But motion and each of the other common sensibles is sensed directly by each of the five senses. 418a8-20.

18. We sense an object's yellowness by vision, we taste its bitter flavor by our sense of taste, and we judge that the two are together. Later, if we sense the color of that or a similar object, we recognize or judge that the object tastes bitter; but vision senses the object's flavor indirectly. One might raise a problem here. What faculty judges that the color and the flavor belong to one object? It must be one faculty, and it cannot be either vision or the sense of taste. The problem will be considered in Comm. 20.

19. A thing which is sensed indirectly may be (a) a sensible object or (b) a substance. Bitterness is indirectly sensed by vision (425a30-1), but it is directly sensed by the sense of taste. A substance, too, is indirectly sensed by vision, but it cannot be directly sensed as a substance by any of the five senses; so a substance qua a substance cannot be sensed by those senses at all. 418a20-4.

20. The English translations of αἴσθησις κοινή posit for the common sensibles a faculty distinct from the proper senses and call it by such names as "general sensibility", "common faculty", "common perception", and "common sense". But some difficulties appear to arise.

No such faculty is mentioned in 418a7-25, and the common sensibles are stated there as being directly sensed by the five proper senses. Further, if such faculty is posited, each common sensible will have to be sensed directly by at least two distinct faculties (which is impossible), i.e., by the so-called "common faculty" and by at least one of the five senses as stated in 418a8-11, or else, indirectly by the common faculty—and this too is impossible—and directly by some proper sense. Hicks thinks that a common sensible is sensed indirectly by a proper sense, and he supports his position by misreading the text and making improbable assumptions in it. But the text states clearly that the common sensibles are directly—even if not in the basic sense—sensed by the proper senses (418a24-5). Finally, if there were a faculty which senses the common sensibles directly, it would be proper and not common to them, and it would require a proper organ (impossible according to 425a13-4), just as vision requires the eye and hearing requires the ear.

I translate αἴσθησις κοινή here as "common sensation", and there is a sense in which "a common faculty of sensation", too, would be correct. The translation as "common sensation" merely repeats what has been already stated, namely, the fact that a common sensible may be directly—although not basically—sensed by more than one of the proper senses. The translation as "a common faculty of sensation" would be correct if Aristotle's position on the senses in general is taken into account.

Now each proper sense along with its organ is not totally independent of all other faculties, otherwise a man's soul would have no unity and would be a plurality, and different senses would perform different functions without any communication with a central faculty. Evidently, there is a common faculty which asserts that the sweet is not white (426b12-22), so vision and the sense of taste must be accompanied by or communicate with or be related in some close way to this faculty, or else, this faculty must discriminate the sweet from the white by using as parts of itself, so to say, vision and the sense of taste; and it is by this same faculty that we sense that we see, we sense that we hear, etc. (455a15-20). Further, this basic faculty or sense has an organ, one which is basic and common to all the proper senses and sensations (455a19-21) and at which all *actual* sensations must reside or terminate (467b28-9), and this organ is the heart or in the heart, which is the principle of motion and of this faculty, (456a4-6, 469a5-7, b3-6, 656a27-9, 666a11-3). So there is a common faculty, called also "sentient soul" or "primary sentient part" or "sentient part". 449a7, 450a11, 451a16-7, 741a11.

The sentient soul is in one sense one but in another sense many. As a power, it is one numerically (449a8-20); but as an *actuality* with respect to its function, it is many in essence and definition, for sensing sweetness and sensing whiteness differ when the sentient soul receives sensations of sweet and white objects through the corresponding organs, and each of these two *actualities* differs from sensing that the sweet is not white or that the sentient soul senses that it sees. Thus, the *actualities* of the sentient soul may differ either specifically or generically, for sensing a sweet object differs specifically from sensing a bitter object but generically from sensing a white object or sensing that the sweet is not white. Accordingly, "sensation" is not limited in its meaning to each of the five sensibles when these are sensed separately, and the same applies to "sense". In a way, the sentient soul is like a substance, which is one numerically but has many kinds of inseparable attributes each of which differs in essence and in definition from the others. In a similar way, the sentient part or power of the soul is one numerically; but its *actualities* are many specifically or generically and hence in essence and in definition, and they are inseparable from the sentient part, just as the attributes are inseparable from the substance to which they belong. 449a8-10.

One may raise the further problem of whether the *knowing* soul and the sentient soul are numerically one or not. It appears that they are, according to 431b26-7, if ταῦτα is the correct variant there, or if the knowing soul in general is to be numerically one or a part of the whole soul, which is numerically one. If so, the same knowing soul senses and *knows* and judges, and it senses qua sentient, whether specifically or generically, *knows* qua *knowing*, etc.

One may say, then, that the common faculty of sensation (or the sentient faculty) senses a proper sensible directly through the corresponding proper sense (which requires its proper organ) and is not mistaken; it senses each common sensible directly by a proper sense, but it may be mistaken; it senses a substance indirectly by a proper sense, and it may be mistaken; and it senses a proper sensible (whiteness or sweetness) indirectly by a sense which is not proper to it, and it may be mistaken. Further, just as we say that that which heals is the doctor, or his art, or the doctor through his art, so we may say that that which senses whiteness is the sentient soul, or vision, or the sentient soul through vision. It follows, too, that it is false to say that the sentient soul senses a common sensible directly in the same way as a proper sense senses its object; for, if it did, it could sense it without the need of the five senses. But it is true to say that it senses it directly through some one of the five senses.

21. Perhaps "otherwise" is synonymous with "if we could not sense them by some one of the proper senses". If so, then there would be no proper faculty to sense a common sensible, and such sensible would be like Cleon's son, which is a substance and which cannot be sensed by any of the senses, except indirectly.

22. If vision sees something yellow, then it is not vision which senses that the yellow is bitter nor the sense of taste (for the latter sense is not even functioning); it is the common faculty of sensation, and it senses or asserts that the yellow is bitter by way of vision and not through the sense of taste. So, since the sentient soul does not sense bitterness directly through the sense of taste, it may be mistaken.

23. An alternative to "simultaneously" is "together". The sentient soul senses different sensibles simultaneously or as being together, but not in the same way. In the example given, it senses yellowness directly through vision and is not mistaken, but it senses that yellow object as being bile or as being bitter indirectly, and it may be mistaken in so sensing it.

24. Further discussion of this fact starts at 426b12.

25. If we had only vision, and if vision were limited to white objects without any differences in shade or brilliance or any other attributes of whiteness, we would be sensing an expanse of whiteness, so to say, without being aware of motion or number or shape or any of the rest of the common sensibles. But if our vision could discriminate the species of color, we would sense red and green and other colored objects along with their different figures and motions, etc., but these common sensibles might be thought to be necessary attributes of colors. As it is, we sense these common sensibles together with other proper sensibles also, and in view of this we conclude that they do not depend on any one genus of proper sensibles for their existence but are independent and distinct from any genus of sensible objects. To be complete, then, man needs all the proper senses if he is to be able to have knowledge of things which are distinct from each other.

2

1. That which is sensed is either a proper sensible or a common sensible or the fact that one senses a sensible object or the fact that, for example, a green object is different from a red object or from a sensible object coming under another genus, e.g., sound. Thus "to sense" appears to have many meanings. We usually say "we are aware that we see" or "we are conscious that we see" and not "we sense that we see"; but regardless of terminology, the kinds of objects we are aware of or sense are different, so the problem of whether those objects are made known to us by one or two faculties is not one of language or semantics but of psychology.

2. Seeing is relative to the object seen; so the faculty which senses seeing, be it vision or some other, must be sensing the object seen also, just as knowing a certain thing as a double must include knowing that of which it is the double. But a problem arises. Does one sense vision when he senses that he sees? Vision is a power, seeing is the activity of that power, and a power differs from its *actuality*. The assumption implied is that sensing that one sees is sensing vision as seeing a visible object — a color. Anyway, the subject in this paragraph is treated dialectically.

3. If the faculty which senses that one sees is not vision, then both that faculty and vision would be sensing a color; but if that faculty is vision, it would be sensing itself. In the first case, there will be two faculties which sense color and not just one, and two sense organs are needed; in the second, both the faculty and the object sensed will be identical. It is hard to believe either the first or the second alternative.

4. If one posits this alternative, he assumes the principle that every sense can be sensed by another sense. Such assumption would lead to an infinity of senses or faculties in a man and is therefore unacceptable.

5. If an infinity of faculties is to be avoided, one of the faculties must be

sensing itself. Each of the faculties other than vision has the same reason for being the candidate which senses itself, but vision is the first and is prior to all of them. Hence vision must be taken. The argument is dialectical and is often used by Aristotle.

6. The primary object of vision is color, which is seen directly. That which has color, on the other hand, is seen indirectly as a substance, e.g., as Cleon's son; for it is its color that is directly seen.

7. The expression "that which is seeing" has two senses: (a) the eye, which has vision, and (b) vision. The eye sees through its power, which is vision. Accordingly, that which primarily sees is vision, which is a power. But that power is neither colored nor has color, for it is not a body. So we are faced with a dilemma; for we ruled out an infinity of faculties and accepted vision as the faculty which senses vision, but this alternative too is unacceptable.

8. Since both an infinite regress of faculties and vision as a faculty which senses itself are impossible, it follows that the expression "to sense by vision" has two meanings.

9. By "that which sees" he means not that which primarily sees, which would be vision, but vision along with the organ — a composite of matter and form. The qualification "in a certain sense" is necessary. When the eye or organ of vision sees yellow, it is affected and so altered by receiving the form of the yellow object, so to say, but it does not become yellow when it receives that form without the matter. It is so affected as *to see yellow*; and to see yellow is not to become yellow, just as to know a square is not to become a square. Thus the term "to receive" must be taken in a metaphorical way and not in the sense in which one receives a book. In general, then, the form of a thing as it exists in the thing is not the same as that thing's form as it exists in our knowledge; it differs just as, in the case of vision, the color of a colored object differs from the activity (in modern terms, certain transverse waves) it produces in the transparent medium or from the sensation produced by that medium in a man. There is a correspondence, but not an identity in essence. A dog's form is the form of a substance, man's knowledge of that form is a quality.

10. A sign that the organ of vision is being affected when seeing yellow and retains the affection after seeing yellow is the fact that, when the yellow seen is no longer present, we have an image of the object seen and can activate it, whereas before seeing we have no such image or sensation. 459a24-8.

11. When there is an *actual* sensation, it is a sensation of a sensible object, and both the sensation and the sensible object become at the same time inseparable parts of a single relation which exists between the sensible object in activity and the *actual* sensation of that object. Each part of that relation, then, cannot exist or be understood without the other part, for the sensible object and the sensation of it are taken when both exist in *actuality* and not

when one or both exist only potentially (6b28-8a12). But the two parts can be distinguished, for the *actual* sensation of the sensible object is not the sensible object when it is being sensed. Consequently, there is a difference in their essence or definition, just as there is a difference between the ratio 2:1 and the ratio 1:2 and a difference of length AB when viewed from A and when viewed from B.

12. The term "to have hearing" has two senses: (a) *actual* hearing and (b) the power to hear or potential hearing without the actuality; and the same applies to "a sounding object", e.g., whether predicable of the bell or of the air. In (b) there is no unity of hearing and the sounding object, for each of these may exist when the other does not exist.

13. If the motion of a mover is in that which is moved, then the mover, if primary, is unmoved; but the change of that mover is one from potentiality to *actuality*, as in the case of a man's art, which changes from potentiality to *actuality* when a work of art is being produced. Hence, just as the motion of such a mover is in that which is moved, so similarly the action of an agent is in that which is acted upon (for acting is a species of producing motion, 323a15-20). Corresponding to mover, motion, and moved, then, we should have agent, action, and acted upon. There are two Greek terms for "acted upon", and these correspond to the terms "acted upon" and "affected"; and perhaps those two terms are synonyms due to language, just as the two English terms are synonyms.

One may raise a problem. It is evident that *actual* hearing is in that which can hear when it hears; but how can *actual* sound be in that which can hear? We grant that the two *actualities* are numerically one and inseparable; but they are distinct in essence. Perhaps *actual* sound is in that which can hear in the sense in which *actual* color is in that which can see. If so, then just as that which sees has the sensation of color and not the color itself (except metaphorically), so that which hears has the sensation of sound and not the sound itself. Again, if *actual* sound is regarded as an *actual* mover, then just as motion is in that which is moved, so sounding (but not sound) is in that which hears. Again, one of the meanings of "to be in" is to depend on. This is just an interpretation.

14. An ultimate (or first) mover is unmoved, whether it be God or art or the practical good or something else; but an intermediate mover is movable. Thus art when active moves the hand or the instruments used by it without being itself moved, but the hand and the instruments are in motion when an object is being moved by them. So it is not necessary for a mover to be moved.

15. The term "sound" may mean actual sound or potential sound. So to say that the activity of that which can sound is to say that that activity is *actual* sound, and this sound is the same as *sounding*, as stated in 426a1. The same applies to *hearing,* which is hearing as an activity.

16. What is the meaning of "in" in the expression "the activity of the sensible object is in that which can sense"? It seems that that activity (a) belongs to the sensible object and not to that which can sense, (b) is related to the activity of that which is sensing, and (c) is producing an affection not in the sensible object but in that which can sense; for the sensible object changes only to its *actuality*, which is complete, but that which can sense changes by the process of acquiring an affection, and this process is a motion, which is an incomplete *actuality*. So it appears that, if "activity" in this sentence means incomplete activity, then this activity is in that which can sense and is an affection in process of being acquired, but if it is a complete activity, it exists as an *actuality* in the sensible object but not in that which can sense. Further, if it is the affection just mentioned, then "action" and "affection" signify a motion which is numerically one but is named in two different ways; for an action would be a motion as produced by an agent but an affection would be a motion as belonging to a thing in motion, and so the action and the affection would be numerically one but in essence or definition distinct. Thus *sounding* and *hearing* would be numerically one but in definition distinct. But if *sounding* is the agent's complete actuality, it cannot be numerically the same as the *actuality* of hearing. Perhaps there are other interpretations.

17. Vision and seeing are distinct, for vision is a power but seeing is the power's activity. But "color" appears to have one meaning, the capability of being seen or the power to produce seeing, and there is no name for color when it is *actually* producing seeing. One might say that we use the term "color" whether we see the color or not. In either case, no other term is used for color when it is producing seeing. Similar remarks may be made about flavor and the other sensibles.

18. 1046b29-7a20.

19. Voice and hearing are numerically one when both are *actual*, voice being to the hearing of it as a sensible object when *actual* to the sensation of that object. Potentially or in definition, of course, voice and hearing are distinct.

20. Why introduce harmony, which here is a species of voice, and not the genus voice? Is it for the sake of indicating by the use of example that hearing too, like voice, is a formula which exists analogously as a formula and functions when the agent itself functions as a formula but not when the agent exceeds the limits of a formula? Logically, the argument appears to be an incomplete induction.

In harmony, the formula takes the form of a ratio or proportion, such as 1:2 in the case of a note and its octave, and similarly for a combination of a note and its third or fifth. The sensation of harmony, however, is not a ratio or proportion in a literal sense but something analogous to it; it is the hearing of such a ratio or proportion, but it is a formula proper to the sense of hearing.

21. That which can be cooled or heated is closer to the mean qua sensible than the hot or cold; hence it is more pleasurable than the hot or the cold. For the sense of touch is a formula analogous to the formula of a sensible object, whose temperature lies between certain limits. So since the excess is contrary to the mean and a sensible object in excess causes pain or destroys the sense, that object becomes more pleasurable as it gets closer to the mean. For just as the mean is contrary to the excess, so the effect of the mean is contrary to the effect of the excess; and the contrary of pain is pleasure, while the contrary of destruction is preservation.

The text is extremely abbreviated, and perhaps corrupt. So the commentary should be regarded as my interpretation.

22. A sensible object and the sensation of it are correlatives. 6b28-36.

23. The difficulty lies in the fact that two objects sensible by different senses are somehow sensed by one sense and are sensed not separately but relative to each other, i.e., as being different or distinct. Difference, of course, is a relation, and it relates things within the same genus. Otherness or distinctness is more generic or wider than difference; and both "difference" and "otherness" are metaphysical terms, for they are used by every science or discipline. They are considered in the *Metaphysics*, Book Δ, and elsewhere.

24. One might raise a problem. Does the term "sense" here have the same meaning as it does when used for each proper sensible? The things which are said to be sensed are distinct in kind; for they are qualities, if sensed as proper sensibles, but things in relation to each other, if we say that we sense them as being distinct or different from each other. In either case, however, those things are said to be sensed qua sensibles and not qua intelligibles; for one might say that, universally, redness is distinct from whiteness or bitterness, and this statement is of intelligible objects.

25. If flesh were the ultimate organ of sensing that the white and the sweet are distinct, then contact would be the means of so sensing them. But color cannot be so sensed, and white is a color. It appears, then, that this organ of sensing the distinction between the white and the sweet must somehow communicate with the organ of vision and that of taste or touch if it is to judge that distinction; and it is reasonable that this organ should be the heart or near the heart (a hypothesis now discarded).

26. Just as, among sensibles, it is the same faculty that asserts that the sweet differs from the white, so, among intelligible objects, it is the same faculty that asserts, for example, that a line differs from a plane. Thus, whether two objects which differ are sensible or intelligible, the faculty which asserts that they differ is in each case one and the same.

27. To distinguish two sensibles is to relate them in a certain way, namely, as being different, and the faculty that does this must sense both, using the verb "sense" in a wide sense here. But neither vision nor the sense of touch

can do this, for the sense of touch is limited to the tangible and vision is limited to the visible. To relate the visible and the tangible, then, another faculty is needed; and this is one faculty and not many, for it is one relation which is asserted: in the example given, this relation is the distinction between the white and the sweet. Further, to assert something is to express what is thought or sensed.

28 . In other words, if faculty P senses just A and faculty Q senses just B, neither P nor Q can judge that A is distinct from B.

29. If I assert that A differs from B, the time at which A differs from B is asserted as being one and the same; for just as it is the same relation that is signified by "A differs from B" and "B differs from A", so the time when A differs from B is the same as the time when B differs from A. If at time T one asserts that goodness differs from evil, T is accidental to the fact that it is at one and the same time that goodness differs from evil; for that difference would exist at one and the same time regardless of the time at which the assertion is made. Thus two time intervals may be considered in the assertion "A differs from B": (a) the time at which the assertion is made, and (b) the simultaneous time during which A and B differ.

30. The thought in this and the next paragraph is highly abbreviated and not spelled out, and there may be corruption in the text. There are many variants, and many interpretations — neither convincing nor clear — have been given. One more interpretation may be offered, but not with conviction.

One might argue as follows. Since a body cannot be white and black at the same time, the same organ which senses it cannot, qua undivided and at the same time, be affected by two contrary motions, the one by whiteness and the other by blackness, and hence the corresponding power — whether vision or the common faculty of sensation — cannot sense or judge the blackness and whiteness in an object or objects simultaneously. Consequently, since to sense whiteness as being different from blackness (and such sensing occurs at an undivided time, 426b23-8) necessitates sensing blackness and whiteness simultaneously, sensing that difference would necessitate contrary sensations — which are motions — by the same organ at the same time; and this is impossible. In an analogous manner, sensing that the white is different from the hot would lead to the same impossibility. But can that (i.e., the sense) which judges the white and the black be, qua sensing when it senses, at the same time both (a) inseparable and numerically indivisible and also (b) divisible in essence (for to be sensing whiteness is not to be sensing blackness)? On the other hand, there is a sense in which it is the divisible which senses divided objects, but also a sense in which it does so qua indivisible; for sensing whiteness and sensing blackness are two things, even if they occur simultaneously, but that which does this is locally and numerically one indivisible faculty. But this explanation, too, appears incomplete or unconvincing, as the next question indicates; more clarification is needed.

31. Now the same indivisible (or undivided) thing may be potentially two contraries at the same time, for at time T Socrates has both powers, that of being sick and that of being well, i.e., of becoming sick at a later time and well at some other time later; but he cannot be both sick and well at the same time, whatever that time may be. So if he is sick and well, he is so disposed at different times, and being sick differs in essence from being well. Similarly, a body B may be black and white, but at different times. Accordingly, the sensation of B as black and the sensation of B as white cannot occur simultaneously. But these two sensations may be related by the sense which judges them; and it judges them as it judges, in a line XZ, a point Y within XZ but in relation to the two parts XY and YZ. It judges Y as being the end-point of XY, which is the left part of XZ, and the same Y as being the beginning of YZ, which is the right part of XZ. Similarly, the sense judges not the black alone or the white alone or just both simultaneously, but also their relation, which is a difference that relates the black and the white, just as it judges Y relative to XY and to YZ; and just as this difference is one relation, so the judgment of that relation is one and not two. But this difference relates two things, the black and the white, and it is in this way that the sense which senses the difference is divisible, namely, into the two things — the black and the white — whose relation it judges. Thus it is one sense that makes a judgment and does so at one time, but its judgment is of two things *in relation* to each other.

It has already been stated that the sense which makes the above judgment is the common faculty of sensation; and it is the same faculty which judges sensibles differing in genus, e.g., the difference between the white and the hot. Can that faculty sense its objects simultaneously or must it sense them at different times. It may sense a white object, then sense a black object, and later judge that blackness differs from white. But it appears that it can also sense at one time an object which is partly black and partly white and then make the judgment. Would this be Aristotle's position?

There is one main faculty which senses all sensible things, and this is the common faculty of sensation or the primary sense (455a12-22). Its organ is the heart or near the heart, which is the principle of sensation (456a5-6), and the various sensations occur by or terminate at that sense (467b28-9). So one may say that we see whiteness with the eye or by vision; but we may also say that the primary sense sees whiteness through the eye or by vision, for all sensible things are ultimately sensed by one faculty, as stated before. Vision, then, appears to exist potentially in the primary sense, just as the primary sense itself exists potentially in a faculty which includes also the *knowing* faculty (431b26-8). In general, of course, a man's soul is one thing, a unity of parts, and the problems which arise are such as the nature of each part, the relations of the parts to each other and to the whole soul, and the like.

3

1. Sensation has been considered. But there is also imagination and thinking; and these are considered next. First, the views of other thinkers are stated and criticized.

2. Perhaps the term "judging" here means or includes discriminating.

3. The two cases are: (a) thinking and judging rightly, and (b) sensing.

4. Fr. 106.

5. Fr. 108.

6. *Od.* xviii. 136.

7. 404b8-18, 405b10-7, 410a27-9.

8. 404a27-9, 1009b12-25.

9. The argument is as follows. These various thinkers posited that both judging and sensing are corporeal, that in both these activities the soul knows and discriminates things, that judging is a sort of sensing or the same as sensing, and that like is known by like; but they did not discuss error. For, according to some of them at least, if thinking is judging and judging is knowing like by like, it would follow that there can be no error in thinking. But error is a fact; it exists mostly in nonrational animals, and to some extent in men. Anyway, they must admit that (a) either all appearances must be true, or (b) error must be an apprehension of what is unlike; for, since error is contrary to truth and apprehension of like is contrary to apprehension of unlike, and since truth is apprehension of like, error must be apprehension of unlike. Now (a) not all appearances are true; for there exist contrary thoughts about the same thing, and the same thing cannot have contrary traits at the same time, otherwise the principle of contradiction will be violated (1005a19-1012b31). Moreover, (b) an apprehension of what is unlike is not necessarily an error; for it is by the same science, or the same erroneous disposition, that we know two contraries (105b4-6, 251a30, 1129a13-4). For example, oddness and evenness are known by the same science, arithmetic, and black and white are sensed by the same faculty, vision; and neither arithmetic nor vision is divisible materially into elements. Hence neither (a) nor (b) is true.

10. Perhaps "sensing" here is used in the narrow sense, that is, for proper sensibles; for it is in this activity alone that all animals share. From what follows in the text, the term "judging rightly", too, appears to be used in a narrow sense (980a27-b23), not for sensing proper sensibles or for thinking, but perhaps for such things as comparing or contrasting sensibles or sensing that we sense (425b12-3, 426b12-15).

11. Thinking presupposes sensing but is not accompanied or not necessarily accompanied by sensing. It is a genus of *thinking*, which is merely

combining concepts truly or falsely, as in opinions or *knowledge*. Similarly, "right" and "wrong" are genera, respectively, of "true" and "false"; they apply also to wishes and to desires in general (433a26, 1139a24). Intuition and prudence are always true, and hence right (100b8, 11, 1140b20, 433a26, 427b9-10); but their contraries, ignorance and folly (or imprudence), are not true or right. Animals other than men, such as dogs and worms, do not combine concepts so as to form truths or falsities; hence they have no power of reasoning, whether this be *thinking* or expressing such thinking.

12. Imagination differs from thinking and from sensing; for thinking includes also *thinking* and intuition, 427b27-9, and one may imagine something when not sensing anything, and he may imagine it without thinking it as being true or false, as when he forms an image of a triangle or a tree. But imagination is thought to be a species of thinking; and some animals have imagination but not other kinds of thinking, such as *thinking*, but animals which think must imagine (427b27-9, 431a16-7). One can, however, form no image if he has no power of sensation, nor can he have a belief — a species of thought — without having combined concepts or images, which presuppose the power of sensation. 100a3-11, 980a27-981a3.

13. He who is believing is also thinking, but he who is thinking is not necessarily believing. One may imagine a circle becoming greater, or even a rock moving by itself upwards, without believing that what is imagined is either true or false; but if one believes that there is a monster in the lake, he also has an image of a monster in the lake, and imagining is thinking. (427b28-9). Why is it not up to us to form opinions? It is because an opinion is a species of a belief (427b24-6), and whenever one believes that P is Q, he must take into account a fact or its contrary which does not depend entirely on his thinking or imagining, for a belief is an affection which is related in a certain way to something else, to P as being Q, even if P is not actually Q. It is true, however, to say that a belief depends partly on us; for it is we who do the believing, even if what is believed is or is not a fact. An opinion, of course, is a belief; for it is a species of it.

14. Here we have an example of the difference between thinking and believing. When we merely think of a tiger, we are not afraid, for this thought is not followed by the belief that the tiger is near; but if the tiger is near, it is so believed. But when in a forest we hear a sound which resembles that of a tiger, we are afraid; for then we believe that a tiger is actually near.

15. The contraries of the species of belief are ignorance as a disposition, false opinion, and folly. An example of ignorance as a disposition is the belief that 15 is a prime number (79b23-29). Folly is the inability of a man to deliberate about things for his own good (1140a24-b30).

16. Since believing is a species of thinking and thinking cannot exist without images (431a16-7), and since one can form images without believ-

ing (980a27-b28), imagination is prior in existence and in definition to belief; so it should be discussed first.

17. The meaning of "that" is left open; for the category under which imagination comes is yet to be ascertained. Imagination may be a potentiality or a disposition or something else.

18. In saying "that's your imagination", meaning an unfounded belief, we use the term "imagination" metaphorically and not in the main sense. The corresponding Greek term, too, was used metaphorically. But psychology is a science; and Aristotle's concern here is the definition of imagination taken in its main sense and as an element.

19. The Greek term for "sensation" has two meanings: (a) sense as a power, and (b) the corresponding *actuality* of that power, when one is sensing a sensible object. So here we are using "sensation" with a double meaning, as is evident from what follows.

20. An objection may be raised, for it seems that one has the power of sensation even when asleep. This is true in one sense, but not in another. A man has the power of sensing when he is awake, so when asleep he has the power of sensing later when he wakes up, but not during sleep; for sleep is a temporary cessation of the primary sense organ and hence of its power to function (458a28-9). So since one may be imagining (i.e., dreaming) but not sensing during sleep, imagination is distinct from sensation; and since one may be imagining but cannot be sensing during sleep, even then the distinction stands. Thus to show that sensation as a power differs in essence from imagination, Aristotle chooses the meaning of "sensation as a power" which does bring out the difference rather than the meaning which does not. This device is often used by Aristotle.

21. Does "sensation" here mean the power or its *actuality*? Perhaps the power; for the actuality of it is taken up next. Sensation as a power (in the first sense, see Comm. 20) is always present in animals by definition, but imagination is not always present in them; and if *actual* sensation were the same as *actual* imagination, all animals would have such imagination. But bees and ants and worms have no imagination. (Is this true?).

22. Sensations of proper sensibles are always true (418a11-3, 427b11-3, 428b18-9); but most imaginations are false, i.e., they are imaginations of nonexisting objects, e.g., dreams and images we form when not sensing (428b25-30, 459b5-20, 1024b17-26).

23. This is a dialectical argument. We use the phrase "it appears" when we are not sure; but we use "it is" when we are sure; so there is an existing distinction. If the two phrases were identical in meaning, the distinction would be lost.

24. 459b5-20.

25. By definition, intuition (or intellect) is a habit, i.e., knowledge of principles, such as concepts and definitions and axioms, and these are of

what exists. For example, the principle of contradiction is necessarily true
and signifies what necessarily exists. Intuition as defined by Aristotle must
not be confused with our popular usage of the term "intuition", which may
be false. 88b35-6, 100b5-14, 1040b31-1041a8, 1042a25-6. *Knowledge* (or
science), too, is by definition of that which exists of necessity and is accompanied by conviction (71b9-12). So since imagination may be false, it cannot
be intuition or *knowledge*.

26. If a man has reason, he has the ability to combine or relate thoughts,
whether concepts or *thoughts*. As expressed, concepts and certain thoughts
take the form of terms and statements, respectively. Thus if a man thinks
that seven is odd or infers a conclusion from premises, he uses reason; and
in both these cases he forms beliefs. But brutes cannot so think, for they do
not have the power to reason.

27. The phrases "aided by sensation", "through sensation", and "combination of opinion and sensation" appear in Plato's works and indicate species or kinds of imaginations all of which, unlike Ideas, are about sensible
objects which are subject to change. Perhaps (a) an opinion aided by sensation is a *thought* which requires sensation for its formation or apprehension,
as in the case of an opinion of a man at a distance as being or as having been
Socrates, (b) an opinion through sensation is a *thought* which is outwardly
expressed, like a vocal statement, and (c) an imagination as a combination
of opinion and sensation is an appearance of a sensible object along with an
opinion about it. These distinctions are not explicitly made by Plato but
seem to be suggested in *Timaeus* 52A and *Sophist* 263-4.

According to Aristotle's own terminology, (a) opinions aided by sensation
require sensation, (b) opinions through sensation are *caused* by sensation,
and (c) combinations of opinions and sensations would make opinions independent of sensation; but he would reject imagination as (a) or (b) or (c) by
using examples which violate all three.

28. The fact that imaginations, at least some of them, cannot be or include
opinions and/or sensations is an argument against Plato's identification of
imagination with the three kinds he gave as its species. One may say that
Plato has a right to assign to the term "imagination" a meaning which he
chooses. If so, he departs from linguistic usage. And if he does this, there
is also the problem of whether he is adequate in making the distinctions
which Aristotle points out, and the problem of whether he faces contradictions.

29. The terms "to appear" and "imagination" are derived from the same
root. We might have used "to imagine" instead of "to appear"; but perhaps
it is better to retain the linguistic distinction, for the corresponding Greek
terms for "appearance" and "imagination" are not synonyms. If Plato
chooses to use the two terms synonymously, he destroys the distinction and
is faced with certain difficulties, as will be shown.

This sentence, with the qualification just made (favorable to Plato), appears to state explicitly what Plato has in mind when he says that imagination is opinion aided by sensation or a combination of opinion and sensation.

30. Here we begin with the difficulty faced by Plato. If imagination or appearance for Plato is opinion with sensation or opinion aided by sensation, then a man to whom the Sun appears to be white and a foot in diameter will be sensing the whiteness of the Sun and having the opinion that the Sun's diameter is one foot long (for his opinion is aided by his sensation of the Sun or is formed directly from the sensation of the Sun). If so, then the man cannot have at the same time the opinion that the Sun is greater than the Earth (345b1-4).

31. Plato is faced with two alternatives, (a) and (b); and both lead to difficulties. If the Sun, which does not change in magnitude, appears one foot in diameter, then, by Plato's own definition of imagination, the man has the opinion that the Sun's diameter is one foot long and so has abandoned his previous opinion; and this is not the case, for the man is still convinced of his previous opinion. But if the man retains his previous opinion and at the same time imagines the Sun as the Sun appears to him, then he has one true and one false opinion at the same time, for his opinion that the Sun is greater than the Earth is true, but his opinion according to the Sun's appearance (or imagination, in Plato's term) to him is false.

It is evident from all the arguments, then, that imagination is neither sensation, nor opinion, nor yet a combination of the two.

32. In a series of movers or things moved, there is a first mover which is not moved and a last thing moved which does not move another thing. 256a4-b24.

33. This is a dialectical premise which will be included later as a part of the definition of imagination.

34. Should the Greek term be translated as "sense" or as "sensation"? The English translations use "sensation". But a man can imagine things which he is not sensing or even which he never sensed. So it appears that "sense" should be used.

35. Here, again, it appears that (1) the term should be "sense" and not "sensation", as is usually translated, for sensation is already an activity. Besides, when a man imagines, he is not necessarily sensing but, with his sense or power of sensing, sets in motion sense impressions or images which are already present but not in activity or forms images which may be of sensible objects. Further, images may occur after and not during sensations. On the other hand, (2) one might argue that imagining can occur after sensing, e.g., when a man with eyes closed has lingering and changing images of an object just seen, in which case the sensible object is a moving cause but sensation or the organ of sensation is a subsequent and proximate moving cause of imagination or of the images formed. Does "imagination" apply to both (1) and (2) or is it limited to only one of these?

36. In what sense is imagination similar to sensation? Both are motions, and the image in imagination is somehow similar to the *actual* sense impression caused by the sensible object; but they also differ, for the moving causes are not the same or always the same, and the object imagined in imagination appears to be less vivid than the corresponding object sensed in sensation. Is the similarity due to the fact that in both cases the object appears to be similar or somehow the same, regardless of the moving cause?

37. In 418a11-2 it is stated that sensation of a proper sensible cannot be mistaken, and in 427b11-2, 430b29-30, and 1010b2-3 it is stated that such sensation is always true. Then why the use of the phrase "or has the least possible falsity"? Is the sensation of a proper sensible object sometimes in error for some *reason*, such as sickness or a diseased organ? 1010b6-7, 22-3.

38. Such objects are substances to which proper sensibles belong as attributes; and this is indicated by what follows and lines 418a20-4.

39. How can a substance be accidental to or an accident of a proper sensible and at the same time underlie that sensible? Commentators see difficulties or inconsistencies in the text; but the point is simple. By definition, if the word "is" in the statement "A is B" has its most general meaning, B is accidental to A if A may or may not be B. Now the white may or may not be Cleon, which is a substance, for Cleon does not always follow the white; so Cleon is accidental to the white. Aristotle's example in 1017a9-10 confirms this; for he uses the expression "the musical is a man", in which he considers man to be accidental to musical. For the various senses of the term "accident", see also 1025a14-34.

40. The position taken here is that a man is mistaken about the common sensibles more than about substances. Some reason for this is indicated in 425b4-11.

41. The meaning of this sentence is not spelled out. Is this motion, which is an imagination, regarded as following the sensation by a sensible object as stated in 428b10-11, or is it an imagination which arises from or by a sense but not immediately after sensation? Is there another alternative? Again, what kind of difference is alluded to, and between which things? If our translation is correct, perhaps the things which differ are imagination and sensation, and perhaps the difference is with respect to truth or falsity, or else, with respect to vividness, for imagination is a sort of weak sensation (1370a28-9). There are other interpretations.

42. When the sensible object ceases to act, there is a change in the lingering sensation, and the imagination which follows may not represent truly the original sensible object.

43. 428b11-3, and also truth and falsity.

44. The moving cause is implied by "why"; so "why it exists" amounts to "what mover causes imagination to exist".

4

1. Perhaps the term "knows" refers to the things as merely known without reference to any action with the aid of the corresponding knowledge, whereas the term "judges rightly" refers to things to be done or produced with the aid of knowledge (433a14). Thus theoretical knowledge would be of things in the first case, but practical or productive knowledge would be of things which may or may not be *acted* upon or produced, respectively. Sensing, too, is a species of knowing (731a33-4), but this is excluded here; only knowledge which results from thinking is included, and judging rightly is not sensing (427b6-7). Right judgment, of course, may be *about* theoretical things in some sense; for, when a man judges rightly that he should pursue philosophy, the pursuit of philosophy may or may not take place, and this pursuit is contingent and not theoretical like philosophy.

2. Perhaps the expressions "separable in magnitude" and "separable in place" mean the same thing (413b13-15), namely, to be capable of leaving the body or the other parts of the soul and of existing by itself as a man or a chair does. Two things are separable only in definition if they are distinguishable and differ in definition but if each cannot exist separately from the other. Convexity differs in definition from concavity, but the two always exist together in a curved line or surface.

3. The differentia refers to the specific nature of the intellect, thinking refers to the activity of it.

4. Sense and intellect are similar in some ways but dissimilar in other ways. Since their activities as affections are similar, their natures should be likewise similar; and just as sense, prior to any sensing, exists as a potentiality without any affection and is affected by proceeding from potentiality to nature and actuality and not from a contrary to a contrary (417b3-7), so in the case of the intellect prior to thinking. Further, just as sense is receptive of the form of a sensible object and is potentially such as that form but is not the form itself, so in the case of the intellect with respect to the intelligible object. And just as a sense, prior to receiving any form of its objects, is a mere potentiality and has none of the forms of those objects (for vision as such potentiality has no color, since any color which it might have would prevent it from seeing the true nature of a different color, as it would in the case of seeing a white object through red glasses, which change the whiteness of that object to a red color), so the intellect which can think all objects is a mere potentiality and is none of (or, is not mixed with any of) the objects or their forms which it can think. So this kind of intellect (for, there is another kind, 430a10-25) is mere potentiality for its objects.

Why the phrase "or be some other thing as this" in line 429a15? Perhaps because of some difference between the manners in which a sense and the intellect are affected. For a sense is affected by a sensible object, which is an agent external to a sentient being; but the potential intellect is affected by an internal agent, the active intellect. Would the reference be to the two kinds of affections discussed in Book B, Section 5?

5. The term "intellect" in this Section is used in a wide sense, perhaps a sense in which other thinkers used it. For Aristotle, the specific meaning is: the power for, or possession of, first principles; here, any thought or belief is included, but sense faculties are excluded. 100b5-17, 1140b31-1141a8.

6. By Aristotle's definition, a blend is a union of bodies, readily adaptable in shape, which have acted upon and so altered each other (327a30-328b32); for example, a union of coffee and cream, not of pepper and salt. But the intellect, being a part of the soul, which is a form, is not a body, and so it cannot be blended with any body. And, not being a body, it cannot become cold or hot, and this is also evident from facts. If "blend" is used in a popular and wider sense which includes, for example, a union of body and form, even then the intellect could not be a part of such union; for, unlike a sentient power which requires an organ, the intellect has no organ and hence cannot be blended in this manner with a body.

7. The metaphorical expression "the soul is a place of forms", perhaps used by Platonists, has some truth in it; and if "soul" is replaced by "thinking soul" and "place of forms" is replaced by "potentially the forms", the result is Aristotle's literal position. For only the thinking part of man's soul can receive intelligible forms, and place is something actual (a quantity), whereas the intellect is potential.

8. The similarity of the sentient part of the soul to the intellect with respect to impassivity has just been considered; the dissimilarity of the two parts will now be examined.

9. A sentient soul is a power of an organ, which is a body or a bodily part of a body, and so its function when in activity depends on the proper state of that part; for when that part is disturbed excessively or permanently injured by the sensible object, its form or formula, which is the corresponding sense, loses its power partly or totally of discriminating its objects. This is what happens when, for example, the organ of hearing is affected by an external sound which is excessively strong; for one cannot hear afterwards either temporarily, or permanently if the organ is permanently damaged. But in the case of the intellect the situation is different; for there is no organ for it, and so there can be no disturbance or injury of an organ. And when the intellect thinks a highly intelligible object, it can think a corresponding object which is less intelligible not less but even more.

But it is not spelled out as to what is meant by a highly intelligible object, or by a less intelligible object, or by being able to think a less intelligible object even more than a more intelligible object. Let us assume that a genus is more intelligible than a species of it, and, in general, that the more universal is more intelligible than the less universal. Then, one who thinks or knows a genus clearly or highly — i.e., scientifically — may now know more clearly a species of that genus, for he may now know the differentia of that species. On the other hand, one who comes to know a genus scientifically finds no difficulty at all in knowing that a given species of it comes under that genus; for, having abstracted that genus from the species of varying differentiae, he can easily think it — or detect it, if you wish — in any one of those species. Popularly stated, one who really understands mathematics — i.e., in terms of causes — can easily apply it to instances. This is just one interpretation. Anyway, when the intellect thinks something very strongly, it seems that it does not cease to function temporarily or permanently as a sentient power does, for its activity does not depend on a body which is subject to damage. Is this Aristotle's position? One may add, if thinking requires an image, which is an attribute of a body, it would appear that the intellect depends on the body. Again, is it the passive or the active intellect here? What is separable is the active intellect, but thinking and thoughts require the passive intellect also.

10. When a man *knows* mathematics by his intellect, having acquired his *knowledge* either through a teacher or by himself through research, he may not be using it, as when he is asleep or attending to other things; and then, although he possesses that science, he is not exercising it but has the potentiality of exercising it. Now that science, being a quality, is actual and not potential like that of a child which has not yet acquired it; but it is potential relative to its exercise when the mathematician is using it, whether by applying it or for further research.

There is an analogy between the two potentialities or actualities in the case of *knowledge* and those in the case of the soul. The soul as first actuality, when one is not awake, is to the soul as second actuality, when one is awake, as mathematics when actually possessed but not in use is to mathematics when in use. A similar analogy exists in the corresponding potentialities. The sperm and the egg are potentially a being with a soul not in a state of awareness, and this being in this state is potentially a being when awake; likewise, a child is potentially a mathematician before learning mathematics, and a mathematician, when not using mathematics, is potentially a mathematician as one who is using mathematics.

11. An interpretation may be given. Just as the common faculty of sensation can sense that it senses sensible objects but does so after sensible objects have been sensed, so the intellect can think that it thinks intelligible objects after intelligible objects have been thought. Evidently, one senses that he has sensations after having sensations of objects, and the latter sensations are, so to say, materials and are presupposed when one senses that he senses. Similarly, one acquires thoughts first by abstraction from images of things, and these thoughts are, so to say, materials and are presupposed when the intellect attends to them. It is in this manner that the intellect can think of itself, whether as actual or potential, and also of its own operations. Logic

is a science of certain operations or thoughts of the intellect; but some of the objects of psychology are concerned with the intellect whereas other objects of it are external to the soul (402b14-16).

12. This is not a magnitude universally taken but some one individual magnitude along with its accidents, and the same applies to water; and these are considered here as sensible objects, whether sensed by a proper sense or in some other way.

13. Examples of things being the same as their essences would be things without accidents, as in the case of separate forms; for the prime mover has no accidents.

14. The term "them" refers, for example, to a given instance of flesh and the essence of flesh.

An example of a power which is differently disposed in discriminating two objects would be the faculty of common sensation; for it discriminates color through vision but sounds through the sense of hearing.

15. Does "flesh" here mean flesh universally taken or an instance of flesh? The same applies to "matter". The phrase "*this* snubness in *this* [nose]" which follows appears to suggest an instance of flesh; and the two powers — the sentient, and another and different power — which are mentioned in the next sentence appear to confirm this position. Further, the essence of flesh must mention matter, universally taken; for the definition of flesh — and a definition is an expression of the essence of a thing, 1031a12-3 — must include matter, since flesh is a physical object.

16. Does "separate" here mean separate in existence or in some other way? Only the active intellect would be separable in existence; but when it exists separately after one's death there can be no thinking (430a23-5), for thinking without the potential intellect, which ends in concepts and knowledge universally taken, is impossible. If "separate" means distinct in definition but not separate in existence, as in the case of convexity and concavity which, in a curved line, are one numerically, then one may raise the problem of how the two powers are related.

17. The simile here appears to suggest a certain relation between the thinking power and the sentient power. An interpretation may be given. The thinking power is to the sentient power as a straight line is to a bent line. Now one and the same straight line may assume an indefinite number of forms when bent, yet it is the measure of them all; and so it has a one-many relation to those forms. Similarly, the thinking power, when actualized in knowing flesh, becomes a single thought of the essence of flesh, regardless of the number and variety of instances in which that essence may exist; but the sentient power, when directed to those instances, senses them in a variety of ways because each instance has varying accidents. So here, too, when directed to many instances, the thinking power when actualized in a thought has a one-many relation to the sentient power when actualized.

An alternative translation starting with "or related" is "or related to it as a bent line is to itself when straightened out,". The Greek text allows both translations; and this alternative favors those commentators who liken the thinking power to the bent line and the sentient power to the straight line, for they regard sensing as directed straight to the object sensed but thinking as directed reflectively to the essence of that object. I do not agree with this alternative or these commentators.

18. It is not clear whether "the straight" here means straightness or a straight line; and for linguistic consistency, we use "the snub" which follows.

Perhaps the two powers which are mentioned as being either distinct or else the same but differently disposed are still the sentient and the thinking powers. If so, then "the straight" here means a given instance of the straight, which is a common sensible and is sensed as such, as stated in 418a17-20; and what we have in such a case is an individual straight line. Now that line has accidents also, for it is in a specific place at a specific time, etc., and these vary in different instances, whereas the essence of the straight as such is known by being abstracted from those accidents and is unique.

One may object to what has just been said, for it is stated in 412b6-11, 1043b1-4, and elsewhere that the essence of a composite is its form alone, like the soul in a man. On the other hand, the essence may be also that which exists in the soul as the form or species of a thing or as the knowledge of it universally taken (1032b11-4), and that form exists without the matter of the thing, like the sensation of a sensible object; for when the sentient power is affected, what it becomes — and this is a sensation or sense impression — is not the form as it exists in the sensible object but a likeness of that form (418a3-6), and the same may be said in the case of the thinking power. If so, then the essence as existing in the soul, although without matter, may be of a composite but universally taken, like the idea of man; for man, being a physical substance, cannot be defined without matter, and a definition signifies the essence of a thing (101b39, 154a31-2, 1031a12-14).

What is the truth of the matter?

19. What are those concerning the intellect? The powers or the objects of the intellect, or something else? They cannot be the sensible objects, nor their sensations or sense impressions. So, since the common sensibles as such (e.g., lines and figures and the rest) are abstracted from sensible matter and are thus distinct from those with sensible matter (e.g., flesh, the snub, etc.), perhaps their corresponding essences, too, are discriminated by the intellect as being of objects without sensible matter in the one case, but of objects with sensible matter in the other case. It appears, then, that there are two distinctions: (a) the objects discriminated by the sentient power differ from their corresponding essences discriminated by the thinking power; (b) the essences themselves differ, for those of the common sensibles differ from those of the objects which include sensible matter.

20. If, as Anaxagoras says, the intellect is simple, and this means always simple, then it cannot think; for to think is to be affected, to be affected is to be changed, and that which changes cannot keep its simplicity. Besides, if one thing acts and the other is acted upon, they have contraries and also have matter which is capable of acquiring or losing each of the two contraries. For example, a hot body makes a cold body warmer. So if the intellect is to be affected, it cannot be simple but have also matter, 323b29-4a9. The argument is dialectical.

21. Again, if the intellect is intelligible, then it is intelligible either (a) in virtue of its essence or (b) in virtue of possessing an attribute, which is not an element of its essence. If (a) in virtue of its essence (and in this case it will be *because* of its essence, for the intellect is simple and hence intelligibility of it cannot be in virtue of a part of its essence), then the other things, too, will be intelligible because of the essence of intellect, for "intelligibility" has a single meaning for all things qua being intelligible. Consequently, those things, too, will be intelligible qua possessing an intellect or the essence of intellect; and this is impossible. And (b) if the intellect is intelligible in virtue of possessing an attribute (for, in this way other things besides the intellect can become intelligible by possessing the same attribute), then the intellect will not be simple. And this alternative, too, is impossible.

22. Since the potential intellect is nothing prior to becoming actually its intelligible objects, in changing to actuality it is not affected as one contrary is affected by another; for that which acts and that which is affected are actually contraries and have common matter, but the potential intellect has no matter or is not matter, 323b29-324a14. Thus, in changing from potentiality to actuality, the intellect is not altered like cold water which becomes hot but its change is from mere potentiality to actuality.

One may raise the problem whether such a change is like the change of a scientist from having science without exercising it to exercising that science; for science when not in use, though potentially a science when in use, is a quality, which is actual, like the soul of a man as first actuality. But the potential intellect is not an actuality at all.

23. But is it possible for the intellect to be likened to a tablet? Unlike the potential intellect, a tablet is actual even if it has no writing at all. In view of this, some commentators liken the intellect not to the tablet itself but to its potentiality of having writing on it.

The abbreviated text gave rise to various interpretations and translations. The translation I give adds in brackets what was stated in the preceding sentence but is not repeated here, for Aristotle often does not repeat phrases. I take the simile as helping the reader to understand the phrase "in a certain way potentially". Then "potentially as in a tablet which has no actual writing" certainly does not liken the potential intellect to the tablet. What it suggests is something like the following: Just as in a tablet, there is a change from no writing to writing, so in a man or in his soul there is a change from potential to actual intellect. In this manner, the tablet without any writing would be like the soul with the potential intellect or without any actual intellect, and just as no writing is nothing at all prior to writing, so the potential intellect is nothing at all prior to becoming actual.

24. The manner in which the intellect can be intelligible has been considered in Comm. 11. As intelligible object, then, the intellect — whether as potential or as actual — exists potentially or actually in the same way as the other objects.

25. In what way are they the same? Perhaps numerically; for to be a thinking object and to be an object thought differ in essence or in definition. When we think universally that nine is a square number, the object thought has no external existence; for what exists externally is an individual (or individuals), not one of which we think but one to which our thought may apply, so to say. A man's thought, or better, the object thought is universal and exists potentially with respect to individual instances, for it has the potentiality of being applied to every such instance, whether present or past or future. Further, if thought is moved by the object of thought (1072a30), thought and the object of thought must differ in essence or definition. 86a22-30. See also Comm. 3 of Section 2 under *Categories* in my *Aristotle's Categories and Propositions*.

Do the objects in the phrase "in the case of objects without matter" refer to essences as existing in things with matter or as existing in thought, or to some other objects?

26. Theoretical knowledge when in actuality is a species of that which thinks, and another species is an intuition when in actuality. The same applies to the theoretically *known* and to the object intuited.

27. Since to think is to be affected in a certain way (429b24-6), thinking would be a motion in which there is that which acts and that which is acted upon. Now the Intellect (the prime mover) is always in *actuality* and so always thinking, for there is no matter in Him, and so He cannot be affected; but a man is a composite of physical matter and form, and as such he can be affected and so change. Perhaps the answer to this problem is given in the next section.

28. A thing which has matter is sensible qua an individual, and it is intelligible not qua an individual but qua coming under a universal; for what is intelligible is, as stated in Comm. 25, a universal which is (numerically) one with the intellect and is potentially, so to say, each of the individuals coming under it. So what is intelligible in a *composite* is its form or essence without the matter.

5

To many and perhaps most commentators, this Section in this treatise

appears to be the most difficult to understand. The interpretations are
diverse, and each of them seems to give rise to problems. Perhaps the main
difficulty lies in one's lack of understanding of the text and the meaning of
the terms. If so, one can only resort to dialectical thinking and arguments.
I can only point out various problems as I perceive them, with some indica-
tion as to my position.

1. Perhaps the argument, proceeding from what is more familiar to us
to what is less familiar to us, may be stated as follows. In every case in which
there is a change from something to something else, there is that which exists
as potentiality and can become something else and also that which, as a
maker or a mover, can cause that becoming. In things by nature, this
potentiality is physical matter which can be caused to become something
else when taking on another form, like that which is caused by a father (for
Aristotle) to become a baby; in things by art, it is the materials which are
caused by art to become a work of art, like bronze which is caused to
become a statue by the art in an artist. Both the potentiality and the moving
cause of becoming are principles, but they differ in the way stated. Since
in the thinking soul there can be a change from, say, pure ignorance of
something to the knowledge of it, these two differing principles must exist
in the soul also, and one of them exists as a potentiality but the other as a
maker or a mover of that change.

Art is to its material as an agent which is not affected when acting to the
patient which is affected when acted upon. It will be shown later that the
active intellect is likewise related to the passive intellect; hence art is chosen
as something more familiar to us for the sake of coming to know the active
intellect, which is less familiar to us.

2. This is the intellect as potentiality, which in English is often called
"passive intellect". This intellect, prior to being affected, was described in
the last Section as (a) being unmixed with anything, (b) without affection,
(c) not requiring an organ, and (d) not an *actual* thing prior to thinking but
like the unwritten letters on a blank page of paper. The term "all things"
means intelligible things, i.e., things as they exist not externally but in the
soul universally or an universal knowledge; and it does not mean that all
things taken together can ever become intelligible by the intellect of a single
individual, but rather that *any one* thing can by its nature become intelligible.

When the passive intellect becomes actual, is the result, whether thinking
or a thought, a composite of matter and form? If so, perhaps it is a composite
of actuality and passive intellect, and so perhaps thinking or a thought will
have passive intellect as matter. But the passive intellect is nothing prior to
its *actualization*, and it can become not only one but many thoughts; and
being nothing, it cannot be divisible so as to become many thoughts. Perhaps
the result of the *actualization*, whether it be *actual* thinking or a thought,

does not have any passive intellect as an element or a principle but is (a) thinking, when one is *actually* thinking, but (b) a thought, when one has the thought but is not *actually* thinking. As a thought which is dormant, then, it is a potency, for it has the potentiality of becoming *actual* thinking; and perhaps thinking in this sense can be regarded as a composite of potentiality and *actuality*, but this potentiality is a dormant thought and not the passive intellect. If this be so, then thinking is to thought as the soul when awake is to the soul when asleep (412a21-8).

If the passive intellect is nothing prior to *actualization*, one may raise the problem whether the expressions "unmixed with anything", "without affection", and "not requiring an organ" as applied to it are negations or privations. It would appear that they are negations, for privations are applied to beings and not to nonbeings, but negations are applied to both beings and nonbeings. So one may raise the problem whether the terms "unmixed", "unaffected", and the like are univocally or equivocally applicable to the passive and to the active intellect.

3. A disposition is something actual in a thing, and it may be a habit (which is a stable or permanent quality) or a nature as form or just a form (324b17-8, 417b16, 1070a11-2), but not a potentiality or a privation or a composite of matter and form; and perhaps the phrase "like a sort of disposition" is used to suggest what kind of thing this intellect is and not to define it, for certain things are (a) either impossible to define but made clear by analogy (1048a25-b9) or (b), if definable, made clear by example or induction or analogy and not by a definition. Translators and commentators use the term "active intellect" for this intellect, for it is a cause as that which makes or acts on something, like light which is a cause as the *actuality* of a medium and which, as such, makes colors visible. Unlike light, however, the active intellect does not exist with matter or with an organ, for it is an *actuality* separate or separable from matter.

4. In what sense? Light seems to be necessary but not sufficient for a color to be seen; for color, too, seems to be a mover, but in the presence of light. Light seems to be a joint cause, whether as a mover or in some other way; for the organ of vision is affected by a lighted medium, but the lighted medium itself is affected by a color as a mover (419a13-15). If so, what is it, when one is thinking an intelligible object, that corresponds to a color? Now colors are external to the medium and to vision, but in the case of an intelligible object there is no external mover. So if the intelligible objects are in the forms of the sensible objects (432a3-6), do they become intelligible by the active intellect alone as a mover? Again, if the change from the passive intellect to what it becomes is an affection not from a contrary to a contrary but from potentiality to *actuality*, and if the active intellect alone is the mover, is that change the abstraction by the active intellect of the intelligible forms from the sensible forms? If it is, the active intellect will

be changing, for sometimes it will be acting and at other times it will not. And if that which thinks and the intelligible object are one, not in definition but numerically, is the thought which results from the abstraction the intelligible form or *of* the intelligible form? If of the intelligible form, it would be like a tree's picture, which is not a tree but *of* a tree. Other problems may be raised.

5. The medium in the case of seeing is the transparent. What is the medium, if any, in the case of thinking?

According to Thomas Aquinas, just as light *actualizes* the transparent medium, so the active intellect *actualizes* the intelligible notions themselves by abstracting them from matter, i.e., by bringing them from potentiality to actual intelligibility. If so, then the active intellect would be to the intelligible notions as light is to the transparent medium. But are those notions a medium, or like a medium, or neither of the two but something else? As existing in the sensible forms, they are to those forms as color is to the colored object and not to a medium, but as existing when *actualized* from the potential intellect (and thought and the intelligible object in this case are numerically one), they are to thinking or thoughts as colors seen are to seeing or sights. To say that the intelligible notions are like the transparent medium, then, does not appear to be correct. It would be better to say something like this: just as light *actualizes* the transparent medium so that colors can be seen by vision, so the active intellect *actualizes* the sensible forms (or some medium, if such exists) so that the intelligible objects in those forms can be understood when the passive intellect is affected.

The expression "by abstracting them for matter", too, does not appear to be appropriate; for to abstract is to perceive or attend to one element in a composite, but matter is not a composite from which an element can be abstracted, unless "matter" is taken to mean a composite of matter and form, which in this case would be a sensible form. The equivalent expression "by bringing them from potentiality to actual intelligibility", on the other hand, appears to have some plausibility, yet the medium is not mentioned, and an intelligible notion cannot be a medium.

Another problem arises. Since the definition of man is the same for all men, it appears that all active intellects are the same in essence; and since those intellects are just forms, they cannot admit of degree. If so, why is it that they do not all act in the same way in individuals who have the same sensations? For example, all (or most) men have sensible forms in which quantity as an intelligible object exists, yet not all of them have formed or can form by abstraction the idea of quantity. Is this due, if at all, to the difference in their sensible forms or to the differences in their passive intellects or to some other formal but destructive part which differs in ability from man to man?

6. One might think that the active intellect, while acting, is at the same

time being affected; but this is not the case, for it is like art, which acts in producing a work of art but is not being affected while doing so. There is, however, a difference between the active intellect and art. Art is inseparable from a man and is destructible, and it is sometimes dormant and a potency, which is a quality, but at other times in activity. The active intellect, on the other hand, is both separable from a man and indestructible, and it is just *actuality* and not a potency like art when the latter is dormant. Further, since there is no potency or potentiality in this intellect, there can be no change in it, and so the active intellect, if thinking at all, would be thinking always of the same thing or things if its *actuality*, like that of the prime mover, is thinking. This argument seems to help those (e.g., Simplicius, Zabaraella, Hicks) who regard the active intellect as always thinking. But if this intellect is of this sort, problems arise.

A man is not thinking always; and, when thinking, he is not thinking always of the same thing. If the active intellect is thinking always, then when a man is thinking he will not be doing so just with his active intellect, otherwise he, too, will be thinking always. It appears, then, that a man is thinking with the passive intellect (whether with or without the active intellect as a joint cause) during its *actualization* or after it has been *actualized*. It appears also that, since the passive intellect, when being *actualized* or in *actuality*, thinks but not always, the active intellect will sometimes act on the passive intellect but sometimes not, and hence that, when it is not so acting, it will have the potency or potentiality of so doing. But the active intellect has no potentiality at all. Further, the active intellect, being impassible, will not be thinking now of one thing and now of another, otherwise it will be changing. So either it will be thinking always of one thing or always of all things; we say "always", for, since the passive intellect can become all things, why should the active intellect as the cause of the *actualization* of the passive intellect be thinking of some things but not of the other things also? If it is thinking of one thing always, how can it help a man think of some other thing; and if it is thinking of all things always, how is it possible for it to be acting on the passive intellect in different ways (this would be a change for it) when the latter intellect is thinking now one thing and now another? Again, if in a man both the passive and the active intellect are thinking, there will be two thinkings at the same time. Perhaps this is possible; for thinking for the active intellect will be acting or just *actuality*, whereas thinking for the passive intellect will be a species of being affected (410a25-6, 411b1-2, 429b22-30a2), and so "thinking" will have two senses in a man. Again, while we are thinking — and this is when we are being affected — we are aware of that fact during the thinking or after we thought, but we are not aware of any thinking by the active intellect, whether this intellect be regarded as thinking of one, or of some, or of all things. Again, if the active intellect is thinking, whether one or some or all things, what need is there of the sensible forms of phantasms if it already has the intelligible form or forms? Certainly it cannot acquire a form from them, otherwise it will have changed after the acquisition; but it cannot change. Perhaps the intelligible objects of the active intellect differ from those of the passive intellect when *actualized*. If they do, the active intellect may be thinking of itself, or of the prime mover, or of the other intelligences; for what else can it be thinking? If so, how can it help the passive intellect think its own objects?

But to regard the active intellect as not thinking at all leads to other problems. If it is more honorable than the passive intellect (430a18-9), it is better than the latter with respect to some good which is an *actuality* and not a potentiality; and since this good is primarily Thinking in the prime mover and primarily thinking in a man (1177a12-7, b30-1), it must be primarily thinking in the active intellect also. Perhaps the active intellect is more honorable than the passive intellect taken as just potentiality prior to its *actualization*, for the *actuality* of a good thing is better and hence more honorable than the potentiality of it (1051a4-15). So perhaps the active intellect, by acting on the passive intellect, imparts to it the intelligible object. If so, it is reasonable to assume that, as a cause, it is itself thinking that object. But if it does, we are faced with the difficulties in the preceding paragraph. Again, the active intellect is immortal (430a23), and to deny this intellect of any thinking is to deny it of immortality; for immortality and mortality are contraries, and in their primary sense they belong only to things which have life (286a9, 479a29-b7), and the only kind of life in the active intellect would be thinking. So, again, we will be faced with the same difficulties as before.

Perhaps the active intellect is like light (430a15), whose nature is an *actuality* of a certain kind (418b9-10); and just as the sensation of a color cannot be acquired without the presence of light, so perhaps the thought of an intelligible object cannot be acquired without the presence of the active intellect. Light, of course, is an inseparable *actuality* of a composite whose matter or subject is a transparent medium, but the active intellect is an *actuality* without a medium; it exists separately from matter, and it is separable from a man. Now the intelligible objects exist in phantasms or sensible forms (432a3-6); so there is no necessity for them to exist in the active intellect. We may then form an analogy suggested by the term "light" in the text. Intelligible objects : colors :: the active intellect : light :: passive intellect : vision :: knowledge of intelligible objects : sensation of colors; and just as light makes colors known to vision by causing vision to become sensation of colors, so the active intellect makes intelligible objects known to the passive intellect by causing it to become knowledge of intelligible objects. Now the active intellect of a man while alive does not exist outside of the man; and although it exists separately from matter and has no organ, it is somehow in the man or is a part of the man while he is alive. Yet it is separable from the man; for, when the man dies, this intellect is not destroyed but is immortal and eternal (430a23). How it can exist in a man in the manner stated, however, is a problem.

The interpretation just indicated seems to lead to certain difficulties or problems. We stated that both color and light are causes, light making the transparent medium *actual* and color acting on such medium as a moving cause. Now color in a colored object is a moving cause of the sensation of color, but the intelligible object in the sensible form can hardly be taken to be a moving cause when the passive intellect becomes that object after abstraction. Further, is the abstraction of intelligible objects caused by the active intellect, or by some other agent, or by both as joint causes? Again, if the active intellect is not itself thinking but only acting like light as described above, and if thinking as an affection in a man results when the passive intellect becomes *actualized*, whether this affection as such be an activity or a dormant thought, is it reasonable to regard the *actuality* of the active intellect as more honorable than this affection? One may grant that thinking as an affection is impossible without the active intellect, whether this intellect be a mover as the cause or as a joint cause, and that the active intellect is eternal while the passive intellect is destructible, but one may not be easily convinced that the activity of such a mover, without being accompanied by thinking, is more honorable than thinking as an affection, even if the latter is not eternal and is somehow caused by that mover. This problem does not arise in the prime mover. Again, if the passive intellect becomes *actualized* intermittently and not continuously by the active intellect, it would seem that the active intellect sometimes acts but sometimes not, and hence that it changes, and this is impossible. But if this intellect is compared with light, perhaps it need not change. Light in daylight, if we assume the Sun to be fixed, stays the same as the *actuality* of the medium, whatever this medium may be, but the different sensations in a lighted medium are caused by the differences in the colors acting as moving causes. If so, then while the active intellect remains impassible and continuously in *actuality*, perhaps the intermittence of the *actualization* of the passive intellect is caused by other movers acting as joint causes, so to say.

According to Thomas Aquinas, what makes the active intellect be in act with respect to intelligible objects is the fact that it is an active immaterial force which can assimilate or immaterialize other things to itself, and that this force is a kind of participation in the intellectual light of separated substances. Such participation seems to make the active intellect more honorable than the passive intellect, but I am not sure that this would be Aristotle's position; for it appears that by immaterializing or assimiliating other things to itself, the active intellect will be changing, for it will be doing this intermittently and not continuously or eternally. But it cannot change, for it is impassible (430a17-18). The phrase "can assimilate", too, indicates a potency, but the active intellect is an *actuality* without potency. The term "assimilates" would be more appropriate if it signifies an eternal activity, but it will not eliminate some other difficulties.

7. Among things which are or can be good, and thinking is good, that which acts or makes something, being a cause, is better and hence more honorable than that which is affected or is made; and that which is the first that acts or makes is a principle as form, but that which is affected or is made is or has potentiality or matter. Hence the active intellect, being a principle as form and also eternal, is better and hence more honorable than the passive intellect, which is potentiality or matter and becomes something and is destructible. 265a22-4, 430a22-5, 1051a4-31.

8. Why limit the statement to *actual knowledge* and the object *known*? A more general statement would seem to be "thinking in *actuality* and the object being thought are the same", and this would include intuition in *actuality* and the object which is being intuited. A still more general statement would include also thoughts acquired but dormant and the corresponding intelligible objects; for such thoughts are qualities and actual and of intelligible objects, although in a certain sense potential to the exercise of them when one is thinking. 429b5-9.

Anyway, if *knowledge* in *actuality* is the same as the thing *known*, then there is no need for the existence of Plato's Ideas; for the thing *known*, or the manner in which *actual knowledge* exists, though related to the individuals which exist externally in a certain way (i.e., universally), still exists in the soul and not outside of it. Further, since it is the active intellect which, as the cause or a joint cause, makes or causes the passive intellect to become *actualized*, external moving causes, such as Plato's Ideas, are not needed.

Here one might raise the problem as to the meaning of the statement "universals do not exist apart from particulars", for an essence may be regarded as existing in thought as well as in particulars, although in a different manner. Perhaps it exists (a) in thought universally as knowledge or in knowledge as the object of that knowledge, but (b) in particulars primarily and as such. If so, then the term "essence" has two related meanings, a primary and a secondary. Thus, in the primary sense, an individual substance is or has an essence; in a secondary sense, a thought or object of thought is not an essence in the primary sense but is *of* an essence in that sense, but universally, i.e., of an essence of any individual under a given species or genus.

9. A baby at birth has *knowledge* potentially, i.e., it has such matter and form that it can acquire *knowledge* at a later time.

There is a problem. The literal translation of this part of the sentence is: "potential *knowledge*, however, is prior in time in the one,". But is this *knowledge* meant to be prior in time (a) to actual *knowledge*, or (b) to the thing which is *known*, or (c) to the object of *knowledge* (i.e., the thing qua *known*, which is numerically one with that *knowledge*)?

(a) In an individual man, of course, the potential *knowledge* of a thing is prior in time to the actual *knowledge* of it, for that man first has the potentiality and then comes to possess knowledge of a thing. (b) A man's potential *knowledge* of a thing cannot be prior in time to that thing; for if the thing exists always (*knowledge* is of the necessary, and what exists necessarily exists always), it is prior in time to its *knowledge*, and if it exists potentially always, it must exist *actually* always also, and hence not later than the man's *knowledge* of it. See 203b30, and Comms. 16 to 26, pgs. 129-31, in my *Aristotle's Categories and Propositions*. (c) A man's potential *knowledge* of a thing is prior in time to that thing qua *known* by him but not qua *known* in general; for, since a man's *knowledge* of a thing and that thing qua *known* are simultaneous, his potential *knowledge* of it exists before his *knowledge* of it and hence before that thing qua *known* by him, but since others may have had that *knowledge* before he did, his potential *knowledge* of the thing is not necessarily prior in time to that thing qua *known* by others. So perhaps (c) as described and as translated is meant, if "as a whole" means by everyone, or something of this sort. See next Commentary.

10. The translation "as a whole" from the Greek is literal. Alternative translations given by others are "in general", "universally", "in the universe as a whole", "absolutely", and perhaps others. What is Aristotle's meaning? Further, if the word "prior" relates potential *knowledge* to (*actual*) *knowledge*, how is the term "*knowledge*" to be taken?

A man existed before any given individual man existed, for, as stated in 1032a25 and in other places, "man begets man"; and, in general, given an individual T which is destructible and has a form, another individual of the same species as T existed prior to T. So it might appear that *knowledge* is prior in time to potential *knowledge*, for that which exists potentially and is to be must come to be from that which exists *actually* (431a3-4); and some commentators mention as an example the priority in time of a teacher's *knowledge* to that of a student who learns from the teacher. But if this were always the case with *knowledge*, everything *known* now has been *known* before, and discovery of new necessary truths would be impossible; but this is contrary to fact. So it seems that in some cases *knowledge* is prior in time to potential *knowledge* but in other cases it is not. Further, the statement "as a whole, it is not prior in time" does not necessitate the statement "as a whole, it is posterior in time".

First, it seems to me that whenever Aristotle relates potential *knowledge* to *actual knowledge* with respect to priority, he assumes that the *known* thing, whether as a thing which is *known* or as the object of *knowledge*, is the same in both cases. If so, then Thomas Aquinas, in commenting on the priority in the two kinds of knowledge in this context, appears to be in error when he says "No one comes to *know* anything *actually*, whether through his own effort or another's teaching, except in virtue of some pre-existing *knowledge*, as it is said in Book I of the *Posterior Analytics* (71a1-4)". For, in 71a1-4, the pre-existing knowledge indicated is of principles and is not of all demonstrated knowledge, which is *knowledge*, and what the student acquires from such prior knowledge is demonstrated knowledge or syllogistic knowledge and not knowledge of those principles. The term used in 71a1-4 is γνῶσις, which means knowledge but not necessarily *knowledge*, and "knowledge" is a genus of but not the same in meaning as "*knowledge*".

Second, the term ὅλως may be translated as "universally" or "as a whole" or even "in general", but not as "absolutely" or "in the universe as a whole". The term "universally" is a species of "as a whole" (1023b26-4a10). But the term for "absolutely" is ἁπλῶς, which is opposed to πως (= "qualified"), and it is not a genus of, or a species of, or opposed to, or univocal with ὅλως. As for the translation "in the universe as a whole", it is confusing or indicates a redundancy, and there is nothing in the Greek text to justify the part "in the universe". Does the expression "as a whole, it is not [prior] in time" refer to the active intellect, as the next clause seems to indicate?

11. Some commentators think that the word "not" should be omitted, and in some manuscripts "not" does not appear.

12. Let us assume that the word "not" appears in the original text. Now the passive intellect becomes *actual* intermittently, and so thinking is intermittent (430a5-6); but here it is the active intellect that is discussed. And since the latter intellect exists always and as *actuality* without matter, it cannot think intermittently, if it thinks at all. Further, the denial of "sometimes it is and sometimes it is not" is "it always is or it never is"; so the above denial does not necessitate an active intellect which is always thinking. If the active intellect is always thinking, we are faced with the difficulties raised in Comm. 5; if it is never thinking, it is strange that it should be more honorable (430a18) than the passive intellect to which, after *actualization*, thinking as an affection is attributed, as already stated.

13. When separated from the body after death, the active intellect exists as form or as mere *actuality*, like God, and it is the only part of a man which is immortal and eternal. The term "eternal" means existing always or of necessity (337a35-8a3), like the prime mover, and perhaps "immortal" means that which, having a soul above that of plants, will never die. There is a problem whether "immortality" includes eternality in its meaning. Perhaps not, but since, for Aristotle, that which will exist always in the future can be proved to have had no beginning in the past, what is immortal is also eternal (279b4-280a11, 286a9).

Thomas Aquinas states in Comm. 742 that what is separated after death and exists eternally and is immortal is the whole intellect, i.e., both the passive and the active intellect, for both of them operate without a bodily organ. Further, in Comm. 745 he seems to speak of two parts of the passive intellect, one of them depending on the passions but the other not depending on them; and he regards the former part as being destructible but the latter part as being immortal and eternal and as existing with the active intellect after death. And since, in Comms. 742-5, he does not reject any of Aristotle's beliefs or principles, it is evident that he is interpreting Aristotle's position.

First, there is no mention anywhere in Aristotle's works of two parts in the passive intellect, and the reference given by Aquinas as indicating two such parts (1102b13-3a10) is not interpreted correctly. Aristotle uses such terms as "irrational" (or "nonrational"), "contrary to reason", and "obeying reason in some sense" to describe what Aquinas regards as the destructible part of the passive intellect, and he further says that to call this part "rational" is to use "rational" in two senses; and these two senses would then be equivocal and not species under one genus. Anyway, this destructible part happens to be the *desiring* part, which is a species of the power of desire; and it is not a part of any intellect (414a31-2, 433b1-4). Second, it is stated in lines 430a24-5 that the passive intellect is destructible, and no qualification is made. Third, if the passive intellect is nothing at all prior to thinking, how can it exist at all after death, and how can it be immortal if what is immortal is also eternal according to Aristotle's principles, or of what use will it be by being with the active intellect? Fourth, if the active intellect is unblended (430a17-8), how is it possible for it to be a part of any surviving composite of a man, e.g., a composite of the active intellect and one part of the passive intellect after a man's death?

If Thomas Aquinas is not interpreting Aristotle but expressing his own position, then he must state which of Aristotle's principles he abandons and what others he adopts, for consistency requires this.

14. Does remembering as used here apply to a man's memory of his pre-existing active intellect, if this did so exist, or to a memory after he dies? (a) According to 408b24-30, there is no memory after death; for memory of a thought is an affection of a body, and since a man's body is destroyed when he dies, so are his memories. (b) It is unlikely that remembering applies to one's memory of the active intellect in a pre-existent life; for assuming that a man neither remembers nor is aware of any prior thinking of his active intellect while he is alive, then if that intellect thinks at all, it is unlikely that Aristotle would make reference to any thinking of that intellect in a pre-existent life.

15. The meaning is not spelled out, and three alternatives arise: (a) the passive intellect cannot think without the active intellect, (b) the active intellect cannot think without the passive intellect, and (c) a man cannot

think without one or the other of the intellects. Now if, as some think, the active intellect is always thinking, then (b) is ruled out; and those (e.g., Simplicius) who say that the thinking of this intellect is here restricted to things remembered (for the memory of such things requires the passive intellect, and this is destroyed) are positing an active intellect which is subject to change. How can the active intellect be impassible if at one time it remembers some things but at another time it fails to do so? Further, since (b) is ruled out, and since a man can then think only with his passive intellect when in *actuality*, (c) is reduced to (a). Finally, alternative (a) makes sense.

16. Concerning the active intellect as posited by Aristotle, certain difficulties appear to arise with respect to its existence, nature, and number. If this intellect is impassible, and if each man has such an intellect, it seems to follow that either (a) there are as many intellects as there are men, or (b) there are more intellects than there are men, or (c) there is just one intellect — whether this be God or something else — in which all men share.

It is unlikely that (c) be the case. For one thing, Aristotle would have said something about it. Further, the object of God's thinking is Himself, whereas the object of man's thinking is not just God. Moreover, if that intellect is something else and is always thinking, how is it possible for it to be in different men at the same time, and how can such intellect, being impassable, be thinking simultaneously different things in different men or be changing its thinking as men do? And if this intellect is not thinking or not always thinking, it will be or have potentiality; so it will not be just active.

If (a) there are as many intellects as men, then the number of men will remain constant; and as one man dies, another man is conceived or born. But this appears to be impossible, for the number of men is changing.

If (b) the intellects are numerically greater than men, then their number cannot be actually infinite, for no such infinity exists (202b30 8a23); and if they are potentially infinite, they must be generated or else be created out of nothing. They cannot be created, if we are to adhere to Aristotle's first principles of physics; nor can they be generated, for then they will be destructible and not impassable. It would then follow that their number is definite and also very great. But what is that number? Anyway, let a definite and great number of intellects be assumed and let there be no transmigration. But another difficulty arises. Since the intellects are immortal and eternal, their number will have to be always greater than or as great as the number of men who existed and will exist. But the number of such men is potentially infinite, and a definite number of intellects, however great, will eventually be exceeded by a potentially infinite number of past and future men. One would then have to conclude that there is a definite and great number of intellects and that there is transmigration. Would this be Aristotle's position? There is nothing in the extant works to indicate this; what we are told is that the active intellect is separate or separable from a man and also divine, and that it comes to a man from outside (736b27-9).

Are the active intellects of men the same in essence or different? A difficulty arises if we assume that they are the same in essence. We are told in 1074a33-5 that things which have the same definition and are numerically many are with matter or have matter. So if the active intellects were all the same in essence, they would have potentiality or matter. But these intellects are forms without matter and are separable in existence from men. On the other hand, if these intellects were all different, another difficulty would arise. All men come under one species and so under one definition; and a definition contains or signifies the essence of a thing (101b39, 154a31-2). So since the active intellect is a part of the essence of man and hence a necessary element in the definition of man, a difference in the active intellects would necessitate a difference in the definitions of different men.

There is another alternative, namely, the exclusion of the active intellect from the definition of man; for in this way all men would come under one definition. But this alternative would be difficult to accept. The soul is the form of a man, and all parts of that form are essential to a man and to his definition; and the active intellect is such a part. Would one regard this part as external to a man, like a father who is a mover external to a man, and exclude it? But the father is always external, whereas the active intellect, although eternal and still existing when a man dies, is a necessary part while a man is alive.

6

1. The discussion here is not about the indivisible things external to a man but about the thinking of those indivisibles; for truth and falsity are attributes only of certain thoughts. Hence the term "things" here refers to thoughts of (or as) indivisibles, and such thoughts may be activities or qualities; they are activities when one is thinking, but qualities and possessed by a man when he is not thinking.

But of what indivisibles are those thoughts? Perhaps of essences of things; for each essence is one and indivisible, and one cannot state an essence as a composite of essences. Now an essence in the primary sense is of a species but, if at all, secondarily or in a qualified way of a genus, whether intermediate or ultimate. But is not a definition, which signifies an essence, a composite each of whose terms signifies an essence? Not so; for genus and differentia are like matter and form, respectively, in a definition, and as such they are principles but not terms each of which signifies an essence of the thing defined. 1016a24-8, 1024b6-9, 1038a5-9. Further, an essence in the primary sense, i.e., of a species, is primarily of a substance but secondarily of a thing under some other category; and the examples which follow in the text seem to indicate that the indivisibles mentioned are not limited to those under the category of substance.

Can thoughts such as "a square with unequal diagonals" be of indivisibles? But this is a thought of a nonbeing; and since the terms "divisible" and "indivisible" are contraries, each of which can be an attribute or a trait only of a being, a nonbeing is neither divisible nor indivisible. One may apply the term "not divisible" to a nonbeing, but this term is the contradictory and not the contrary of "divisible".

2. Why not include truth and say "there can be no truth or falsity"? The term "truth" has two senses, and in the secondary sense of that term the thought of an indivisible is true. See Comm. 18.

3. Each of those thoughts (or concepts, if you wish) is indivisible; and truth or falsity in the primary sense applies only to certain combinations of such thoughts. For example, the combination "Socrates was black" is false, but "Aristotle was a philosopher" is true. The term "true" has a secondary meaning, but this will be considered in lines 430b27-9.

4. Fr. 20, 57. According to Empedocles, various unities or elements were the first to come into existence, then combinations of them were formed by *Friendship,* a principle posited by him as a moving cause.

5. Time may be past, present, future, possible, and eternal or necessary. These modes of time are discussed in the treatise on *Propositions* (*De Interpretatione*). The time signified in a proposition is said to be necessary if there can be no part of time in which that proprosition is false; and the contrary (not the contradictory) of "necessary" is "impossible". An example of a necessary proposition is "the diagonal of a square is incommensurable with the side of that square".

6. Perhaps the meaning is as follows. Both affirmations and denials are composites, i.e., statements in each of which a subject and a predicate appear; but in an affirmation the predicate is affirmed of (or combined with) the subject, whereas in a denial it is denied of or divided from it. For example, the statement "Socrates is not white" states that whiteness is not in or with Socrates.

7. Is it the active or the passive intellect, or both? One might think that it is the active intellect. Anyway, if such a unity is to be produced, both are necessary, each in its own way.

8. From what follows, it appears that a thing is said to be potentially indivisible if it cannot be divided; and if so, then it is also *actually* indivisible. But a thing is said to be *actually* indivisible if it is indivisible while it exists *actually* but may or may not be divisible potentially; and since the *actually* indivisible which cannot be potentially divisible is potentially indivisible, the *actually* indivisible with which Aristotle would be concerned here is the potentially divisible. Instead of "*actually* indivisible" we could have used "*actually* undivided", for the Greek term for "indivisible" has two senses; but we are keeping the term "indivisible" for consistency in translation and adding a commentary.

If terms in Greek are lacking to signify distinctions, Aristotle often uses a term in two or more senses. Thus if terms exist for each of two species, he often uses one of those terms for the genus of the two species also. For example, habits are difficult to displace, but dispositions come and go, and both these qualities exist in a man and are species of a genus; but he uses the Greek term for "disposition" as a genus also. 8b25-9a13.

9. An alternative to "indivisible" is "undivided".

In what way is time similar to a length with respect to indivisibility? Let T be the primary — i.e., least — time interval taken to think an *actual* length L as a whole. Then L is thought as *actually* undivided in an *actually* undivided time. For in a time less than T it is not possible to think L, or even a part of L, since L is thought as a whole and not in parts.

10. In other words, if the line is not *actually* divided, whether divided itself or divided in thought, it exists itself or in thought, respectively, as many only potentially.

11. If the intellect thinks each half separately, then it thinks not the line as a whole but two separate parts and at different times; and if the parts are so thought, this is as if the intellect were thinking two different whole lines in two separate time intervals and not one line.

12. We may give an interpretation of this sentence. If one thinks the two parts both separately and as being parts of the whole in time T, then again the time taken to so think the whole line is indivisible; for the line thought in this manner cannot be so thought in a part of T.

13. There seems to be a break in continuity of thought. If this sentence is shifted to line 430b20, after the word "length", it appears to make sense.

14. According to the manuscripts, the translation should be "that by which it thinks" and not "the object thought"; but I fail to see how that by which it thinks, being a thought of a line or any other indivisible concept, can be divisible qua such a thought. Two commentators suggest that the word $\tilde{\omega}$ should be $\ddot{o}$, which appears more reasonable, and which the last part of this sentence suggests; and we translate accordingly. If we are not correct, perhaps "that by which it thinks" signifies the soul, for "soul" appears in line 430b15.

15. Like the pairs "white" and "black", "with teeth" and "toothless", and others of this kind, the pair "divisible" and "indivisible" are contraries, and the second term in each case is a privation; and a privation is the absence of an attribute in a thing in whose genus that attribute belongs. Thus evil is the absence of goodness in a man or animal, blackness is the absence of a color in a physical substance. Since a point is a division or an end of a line, which is divisible and a quantity, then it comes under the genus of quantity but is indivisible; and perhaps it is in this sense that it is a privation of the divisible. The same applies to a unit in a number. 1022b22-3a7.

16. Just as blindness is known and defined in terms of vision, (for it is the absence of vision in that whose nature is to have vision), toothless in terms

of absence of teeth, and darkness in terms of light, so, in the case of a point or a unit, indivisibility is similarly known in terms of divisibility. Thus divisibility is prior in knowledge to indivisibility. The same applies to the knowledge of evil and of other privations, for they are known by the knowledge of their contraries. The phrase "that which so knows", then, refers to "vision" as knowledge in the case of blindness, and similarly for the others. 1032b2-5, 1054a20-29.

17. The reference is to the prime mover or God. He has no contrary or the potentiality of it because He never changes, and His thinking is always of a single object, Himself. 1075b20-2.

18. Perhaps the term "assertion" here means a statement, for sometimes Aristotle seems to use this term as a synonym for "statement". If so, then an assertion, being a combination of indivisible terms each of which stands for an indivisible thought, as explained in Comm. 3, may be true or false, depending on whether it signifies a being or a nonbeing. Thus one may say "five is odd" and also "five is not odd"; and one of them is true but the other false. In the case of the intellect, on the other hand, this is not always the case; for the intellect may be of indivisibles as well as of combinations of them, and truth and falsity apply to the latter, as stated. But if the intellect is a thought of an indivisible, then there is no combination; and a man either apprehends the indivisible or does not, e.g., he either knows what a line is or he does not, and this is analogous to either seeing a color or not seeing it at all. A normal man sees green when this color is present, but he who is color-blind does not. In thought, then, "truth" in the secondary sense (see Comm. 2) applies to apprehending or knowing an indivisible; but "ignorance", and not "falsity", applies to not apprehending or not knowing it. Further, although it is possible to say that the white is not white or that two contraries exist in the same thing at the same time and in the same respect, it is impossible to so think (1005b23-34); for, just as a man, when seeing an object as being all white, cannot at the same time be seeing it as black, so he cannot likewise be thinking objects as having contrary or contradictory traits, in spite of what he may say.

In answering the question "what is X?", one should give either the definition or a genus of X. In the latter case, he states an essential element of X, in the former, he states the (whole) essence; and perhaps the expression "things without matter" refers to essences, which as such are indivisible. 90a15-6, b30-1, 102a31-5.

7

1. This sentence and that in lines 430a19-22 differ only in their last part. One manuscript omits it here, but Thomas Aquinas takes it to be the last sentence of the preceding Section. There is, of course, the problem whether the sectioning of the whole work is Aristotle's or not. Anyway, if the sen-

tence belongs here, the last part of it should indicate its relevance to what follows; so one may raise the problem whether there is such relevance or not, i.e., whether what follows has any bearing on the part "for all things . . . exist actually". Now the sentence which follows relates the sensible object to the faculty of sensation as a prior cause to its effect; and the text starting with line 431a14, too, indicates a similar relation of images to thinking and thoughts. So it appears that the initial sentence of this Section is relevant to what follows.

First, we may return to the problem raised in Comm. 10, Section 5. Is potential *knowledge*, as a whole, always posterior in time to *actual knowledge*? If so, new *knowledge* would be impossible, as stated earlier, and this would be contrary to fact. But is not *knowledge* of all things eternally in God and hence prior to any *knowledge* in man? On the other hand, His thinking is always of Himself and not of any other object (1074b15-5a10), so new *knowledge* in man is possible. Now *knowledge* is of the *known* or the *knowable*, and the term *"known"* may be taken in two senses: (1) as existing in the soul, and (2) as being external to the soul. In the first sense, *knowledge* and the *known* are numerically one; and let the *known* as so existing be called "object of *knowledge*" or "the *known* thing qua *known*". In the second, the *known* is usually external to the soul but sometimes in the soul (if, for example, *knowledge* is of the concept of a triangle and not of the triangle itself), yet in both these cases it does not exist as an object of *knowledge*, which is the first sense of the *"known"*; and let it be called "the *knowable* thing" or just "the *knowable*". For example, the form of a triangle external to the soul exists in the triangle, but as an object of *knowledge* it exists in the soul and universally; and the second form is not the same as the first but is, so to speak, like the first (οἷον τὸ πρῶτον), as in the case of sensibles (418a3-5).

Evidently, since *knowledge* and the object of *knowledge* are numerically one, they are simultaneous and both reside in the soul, and they both constitute something which is, so to say, universally predicable of many; but the *knowable* is usually, if not always, prior in time to the *knowledge* of it (7b22-8a12), for things which exist of necessity are prior in time to the *knowledge* of them. See also Comm. 3 of Section 2 of the *Categories* in my *Aristotle's Categories and Propositions*.

That which is *known* in the second sense seems to give rise to a problem. If *knowledge* is of the *known*, it is relative to the *known*, but is the *known* one individual or many? If one, then the same *knowledge* in a man is prior in time to some but posterior in time to other *knowable* things, for these are generable and destructible, like a tree, which of necessity has certain attributes or properties but only while existing. Perhaps this *knowledge* is qualified, for it is not *knowledge* taken universally (i.e., not *knowledge* potentially or indeterminately taken in the sense that whenever P exists, it must have Q) but of an individual or of individuals existing at a certain time (1087a15-25). Now if unqualified *knowledge* is related to the unqualified *known* (i.e., to the *knowable*), then unqualified *knowledge* is never prior in time to this *known;* for *knowable* things exist potentially in the manner in which the *knowledge* of them does (for such *knowledge* is of whatever may exist and not of that which happens to exist), but *knowledge* may not exist if the corresponding *knowable* things exist. For example, *knowledge* of the impossibility of squaring a circle with ruler and compass did not exist among the Greeks, but the corresponding *knowable* things always exist (let us assume their existence), for it can be demonstrated that, whenever a circle exists, it cannot be squared by ruler and compass.

If the *knowable* thing is unique (for Aristotle, as in the case of the Sun, the Moon, the prime mover, etc.), it must have a continuous and eternal existence (for it must exist of necessity if it is to be *knowable*, 71b9-13), and so its necessity must be unqualified. Accordingly, it is prior in time to the *knowledge* of it. But is this *knowledge* qualified or unqualified? If it requires a demonstration, it appears to be qualified; for a demonstration requires universal premises, but the premise which includes the subject of the *knowable* here is not universal. Thus if P, the prime mover, has the property R, with Q as the cause of R, then RP follows from RQ and QP; and RQ is universal but QP is not.

In a way, then, *knowledge* of certain things is qualified in one sense but unqualified in another. If *knowledge* is of a composite whose subject P is destructible, it is qualified in the sense that it is necessary but hypothetically so. Thus "all men are mortal" is a necessary statement, and so is the corresponding *knowledge,* but the statement is necessary on the hypothesis that men exist, for men are destructible and some exist at one time but others at another. If, on the other hand, the things which can be *known* are many and always existing continuously, then their existence is unqualified, and so the *knowledge* of their properties is not hypothetical. This latter *knowledge,* then, would be unqualified in the primary or absolute sense, whereas the former would be unqualified in a secondary or hypothetical sense.

2. When one is seeing something, his power to see is not affected unless the organ of vision is injured or destroyed. Similarly, when an architect is building a house, his art as a quality remains intact, for its change is not a motion from one contrary to another but from inactivity to activity. Man's soul, too, when he wakes up, does not move but changes from inactivity to activity. In general, then, a change from a power or a form to the exercise of that power or form is not a motion but a change from potentiality to *actuality.* During such change, however, motion of some other thing occurs.

3. As stated earlier (417b2-16), the change from mere potentiality to *actuality* is not a motion; for a motion is from a contrary to a contrary, and there is no contrary in what is just potentiality. Hence that change is not

174

an affection or an alteration. A motion is an incomplete *actuality*, and it persists as such till the end. An *actual* sensation, on the other hand, is a complete *actuality*, and the same applies to thinking. As Aristotle puts it in 1048b30-5, "one thinks and has thought, sees and has seen", for the seeing or thinking of the same thing does not move, if other things remain the same; but when one builds a house, he has not yet built it, except partially.

A question may be raised. If one is syllogizing, which is thinking, it would seem that one cannot truly say "one thinks and has thought", for there is a process which is completed only at the end of thinking. Would not this process be a motion, i.e., an incomplete activity at any stage before the end? On the other hand, one might argue that the change which the text is discussing is not from the initial start of syllogizing to the end but, if at all, from the potentiality of syllogizing to the activity of syllogizing, and this potentiality does not have a beginning like the motion of a body from one place to another. Of course, if thinking of the same thing is uniform, like gazing at a picture in a changeless manner, it is not a motion but every part of it is complete. Does Aristotle mean any kind of thinking or certain types of it, or any thinking taken as a whole (e.g., that of a syllogism as a whole) which, in contrast to its potentiality, is an *actuality*?

4. Perhaps this would be thinking of indivisibles, as stated in 430a26-7.

5. The same sensible object may cause, besides a sensation of itself, either pleasure or pain; and pleasure, pain, and sensation differ in definition, regardless of whether the sensation along with the pain or pleasure which accompanies it is numerically one or not. To use an analogy, just as one affirms in thought that 9 is a square number, so he pursues a sensation which is pleasant; just as he denies the thought that 9 is an even number, so he avoids a sensation which is painful; and just as an affirmation or a denial requires two things, a subject and a predicate, so pursuit or avoidance requires two things, sensation along with pleasure or pain, respectively.

6. Three questions arise. (a) To what does "qua such" refer, (b) which sentient mean is meant, and (c) to whose good or bad is the activity directed?

The pleasure here is the good of the senses, and, in general, pleasure (in a narrow sense) is the proper end of the activity of sense; but pain is bad for the senses, for it harms or tends to destroy them. Thus the good is a genus of pleasure, and the bad is a genus of pain. Concerning the sentient mean, each proper sense has its own mean which is affected by or judges pleasure or pain of the corresponding objects. So if the activity meant is of the common faculty of sensation, at which the proper senses terminate, perhaps it arises by way of the sentient mean of the sense which senses its sensible object. Thomas Aquinas takes the activity of the mean here to be that of the common faculty of sensation. As for "qua such", if it refers to the good or the bad, then it refers to them qua pleasant or painful, for it is these species which are good and bad, respectively, for the senses, or else, to the good or bad of the soul in general; but if it refers to being pleased or being pained, one might say that being pleased or being pained, qua such, is being in activity by way of the sentient mean towards the good or bad of the corresponding sense, or else, of the common faculty of sensation (according to Thomas Aquinas).

7. Would it not be better to use the term "pursuit", if one's desire, when it is being fulfilled, is pursuit or avoidance?

8. According to a variant in some manuscripts, the translation should be "the same" and not "that". But to what does "that" or "the same" refer? Now there is a difference between *actual* desire to pursue or avoid when one desires something (and desire is accompanied by pain, at least in the case of the senses, 1119a1-5) and *actual* fulfillment of that desire (and this fulfillment is pleasant). Again, when the sentient mean is being affected, it is in activity either pleasantly or painfully; and the soul accepts or pursues the pleasant activity but tries to avoid the painful activity. Let the correct translation be "that". Then if to be pleased is to be in activity with the sentient mean towards the good, such pleasure would be *actual* fulfillment of what is desired; and pain would be *actual* aversion. But if we take "the same" as the translation, a difficulty arises. Pain and pleasure are distinct traits of the same part of the soul, the part which can pursue or avoid; and the text is concerned with those traits as such, which differ, and not with the problem whether they are traits of the same subject or not. I think the correct translation is "that".

9. Numerically, it is the same part which can desire or avoid, and, we may add, which is at one time pleased but at another time pained; and, as stated in the previous Commentary, pleasure or pain are numerically one with that part, for they are traits of it. But pain differs from pleasure in essence and in definition, and each of them differs from their subject (the part which can desire or avoid) to which they may belong. We may liken these to Socrates who remains numerically one whether sick or healthy, although Socrates, health, and sickness differ in essence and in definition.

10. Sense impressions are affections caused by sensibles and exist in the sentient part of the soul, i.e., the common faculty of sensation. Similarly, images are to the *thinking* soul as sense impressions are to the sentient soul.

Why the term "*thinking*" instead of the genus "thinking"? But we are concerned with judgments, each of which requires two things, as in the case of statements, and it is *thinking*, and not thinking in general, which judges that whiteness is not blackness or sweetness. Intuition, which is a species of thinking, is concerned with principles or indivisibles and not with relating or applying principles. In general, it is the *thinking* soul which judges that P is or is not Q, that asserts or denies P of Q, and that pursues what it asserts to be good but avoids what it asserts to be bad. Intuition merely apprehends the principles, and it is presupposed by the *thinking* soul.

11. Just as the sentient part, when affected by the sweet or bitter, is pleased or pained and hence pursues or avoids, respectively, so the *thinking* part, when affected by analogously opposed images of what is good or bad, asserts them as good or bad and hence pursues them or avoids them, respectively. Again, just as the sentient part is neither pleased nor pained without the presence of the corresponding sense impressions, so the *thinking* part does not assert goodness or badness without the corresponding images.

12. The grammatical structure is bad, perhaps because the text is corrupt; and the thought is highly abbreviated or not spelled out. I can only interpret, and the translation given is in accord with and follows my interpretation.

Just as the air affects the eye, which in turn affects ultimately the sentient part, so something (perhaps the active intellect) affects the images, which in turn affect the thinking part; and just as the sentient part is a mean which is affected by and judges differently different sense impressions coming under the same genus (e.g., sweet and bitter) or under different genera (e.g., sweet and white), so the thinking part is a mean which is affected by and judges differently different corresponding images. Again, just as the sentient part and its different affections are numerically one but different in essence and in definition, so are the thinking part and its corresponding affections.

What kind of affections in the *thinking* part correspond to the affections in the sentient part? Perhaps thoughts are to the *thinking* part as sensations are to the sentient part. Do sensations as felt differ from sense impressions? When one is sensing, of course, there is a difference between the physical affection of the sense organ and the corresponding mental affection of the soul; and the latter affection exists only during the process of sensation, whereas the former remains in the organ after the sensation and even when one is asleep.

13. Just as a boundary is like a mean between things, so is the *thinking* soul; and just as a point, which is a boundary within a straight line, separates one part of that line from the other, so the *thinking* soul is a sort of mean which judges whiteness to be different from blackness or sweetness.

14. Many similarities or analogies are suggested. Just as there is one sentient part — the common faculty of sensation — which acts as a boundary and discriminates different things under one genus or under different genera, so there is one *thinking* part which discriminates in images corresponding different things. Thus the *thinking* part is to the sentient part as the different images or the universals in those images are to the corresponding different sensibles or the corresponding sensations, respectively, produced by those sensibles. Again, just as the discriminations made by the sentient part belong to that part and so are numerically one with it, although different in essence and in definition, so, in a similar way, are the discriminations made by the *thinking* part. Once more, different images and the corresponding concepts which the thinking soul thinks in them are, respec-

tively, analogous to the different sensibles and the sensations produced by those sensibles, whether those sensibles and their corresponding sensations come under the same genus or under different genera.

15. Many if not most manuscripts omit the Greek word for "not"; but the text which follows this omission makes no sense.

16. What do A, B, C, and D stand for? If C and D are to belong to one subject and so be numerically one with it, as the text which follows seems to indicate, the same would apply to A and B. It seems, then, that A and B are not the sensibles, whether these be the attributes qua sensed or the subjects underlying those attributes (e.g., colors or the colored bodies), but the sensations or the sense impressions produced by the corresponding sensibles, and that C and D are the corresponding images or the corresponding concepts.

17. Evidently, if A:B :: C:D, then A:C :: B:D. But why introduce this alternation? Perhaps in order to suggest other analogies which follow. For example, the sensation of whiteness is to the image of whiteness or the concept of whiteness as the sensation of blackness is to the image of blackness or the concept of blackness, respectively; and if A and B are not contraries but come under different genera, like the sensation of whiteness and that of sweetness, a similar analogy follows.

18. Why speak of the thinking power and not of the *thinking* power? But the former is a genus of the latter and is concerned with both concepts (or intuitions), which are principles, and judgments, which are combinations of concepts; and the statement up to here is true and a principle. Consequently, the *thinking* power, too, *thinks* (i.e., judges) its objects in the images.

Aristotle often states a principle, which serves as a cause, and then proceeds to apply it to an instance, leaving it up to the reader to perceive the principle as applied as well as a cause. For example, a triangle has two right angles; hence a right triangle has two right angles, because it is a triangle; and the principle and cause is the triangle. If the statement "a triangle has two right angles" is taken as the principle, then it is a qualified principle, for it is demonstrable. Perhaps the statement "the thinking power thinks the forms in the images" is indemonstrable and hence an unqualified principle.

19. What does "it" refer to? Perhaps to the thinking part or the desiring part, but I am inclined to take the thinking part, which here seems to be the passive and not the active intellect; for (a) it is the thinking part which is mentioned at the start, and (b) the expression "is moved", grammatically in the passive mood, rules out the active intellect. As for that which moves this part, whether the appetitive or some other part, it is another problem; and as to whether the thinking part is moved to pursuit or avoidance, this depends on what it thinks to be pleasurable or painful, but that which makes it so think is determined by the sensations which are received and the consequent images aroused by what those sensations indirectly imply. The first of the two examples which follow illustrates these points.

20. The color of the beacon is directly sensed, the subject underlying that color is indirectly sensed as being a beacon with fire, the motion of this beacon (or better, of the fire's color) is sensed as a common sensible, this motion arouses an image of an approaching enemy and so something painful which must be avoided, and retreat caused by that part of a man which initiates motion follows.

21. Why not only images? But judgments and deliberations require thoughts, and thoughts are impossible without images (for the thinking part thinks its objects in images); so images alone are not sufficient. Images, of course, differ from thoughts. For example, in an image of a triangle the angles appear to have definite magnitudes, and the sides appear to have definite directions relative to us, but in the thought of a triangle the magnitude of the angles and the directions of the sides are indefinite; and this is evident from the fact that the definition of a triangle does not specify the definiteness of the angles and the directions, and this is because the thought of a triangle leaves out (or abstracts, if you wish) this definiteness which is present in the image. 449b30-450a7. The same applies to all thoughts in their relation to their corresponding images. So perhaps in the judgments and deliberations concerning the future, the pleasurable which is to be pursued and the painful which is to be avoided may necessitate images with or without corresponding thoughts.

22. This is the second example in which only images with or without thoughts determine pursuit or avoidance. Images or thoughts, by means of judgments and deliberations, ultimately lead to other images or thoughts of things which are pleasurable or painful, and these finally lead to pursuit or avoidance, as in the case of the first example.

23. All *actions* are performed for the sake of happiness and hence necessitate the pursuit of the pleasurable or the good and the avoidance of the painful or the bad, or else, the pursuit of the most pleasurable or the least painful of the given alternatives.

24. In what sense are the true and the false good and evil, respectively, in a qualified way? As an end in itself, the true is good without qualification, and the false is bad in a similar way. In a qualified way, however, the true may be instrumental and hence pursued for the sake of something else. Thus engineers study mathematics and physics for the sake of producing things; and men of *action* pursue truths for the sake of *action*, and this is evident when they judge and deliberate before they *act*.

Hicks has a different interpretation and so translates the text differently. He thinks that the term "they" in "they differ" refers to the true and the qualified good, the qualified good being good for someone and not good without qualification. If so, truth would always be good without qualification; but neither is this the case, as I have indicated above, nor does the text support his translation, for Aristotle would have inserted the word τι or τινì if he were thinking of the qualified good.

25. These are the mathematical objects.

26. The phrase "thinking of the snub-nose" here, from what follows, may mean (a) thinking of the snub-nose qua snub-nose or (b) thinking of the snub-nose qua concave.

27. An alternative to "snub-nose" is "snubness", and snubness is to a nose which has snubness as oddness is to a number which has oddness. Further, just as oddness must have "number" in its definition (for oddness is defined as indivisibility of a number into two equal parts), so "snubness" must have "nose" in its definition. So since a nose must include flesh in its definition, snubness too must include flesh in its definition. Concavity, on the other hand, although belonging to snubness or to a snub nose, can be thought apart from flesh, for it may exist in other things also. Further, it can be abstracted from and studied apart from physical objects or physical matter.

28. The intellect studies mathematical objects (numbers and magnitudes) and whatever belongs to them apart from the physical objects in which they exist. In so treating them, however, it does not judge them as existing apart from physical objects; it gives definitions of them and investigates properties of them without considering the manner in which they exist. The consideration of their manner of existence belongs to first philosophy (metaphysics). 1077b17-8a31.

29. These are the objects as existing in the soul, i.e., the potential intellect when actualized; for this intellect, whether of indivisible objects or of objects as *known*, is one with those objects, as stated before.

30. No treatise on this subject is known to exist; so either it was written and lost or it was not written.

8

1. According to some thinkers, like is known by like; so since all things are composed of elements, the soul too would have to be composed of all elements if it can know all things (404b8-18). The difficulties facing this position have been enumerated in Book A. There is a sense, however, in which the soul can be all things, not literally but in some other way. So the position of these thinkers has some truth, and this truth is stated in a general way in what follows. But first, things are either sensible or intelligible, and they are known by the corresponding parts of the soul, the sentient and the cognitive. Accordingly, sensation is of the sensible but *knowledge* is of the *knowable,* and sensation and *knowledge* are two species of knowledge. What about the thinking of indivisibles? Perhaps they are somehow included under knowledge; for one who has *knowledge* must have also thoughts of such indivisibles, for *knowledge* is a combination of such thoughts, as in the *knowledge* that a triangle's altitudes are concurrent.

2. Is the term "potentially" used in just one sense here? The same applies to "actually". As stated in 429b5-9, a scientist who is asleep is potentially

in activity; and so is a child prior to learning science, but in a different way. Similarly, a scientist is actually a scientist when he is exercising his science; but he is actually a scientist even if he is asleep, although in a different way, for he has science, which is a quality and is actual. What if a scientist is using his science on an individual? But then he is applying what he already knows universally on an individual and is not just thinking universally as a scientist. Anyway, the correspondence of *knowledge* to the *knowable* things is the same in the two cases, or else analogous, whether one is exercising his *knowledge* or not, and whether he has that *knowledge* or not.

3. An alternative to "forms" is "species", which signifies the sensible or *knowable* objects as existing in the soul and not in the things themselves. This will become clearer as we proceed.

4. The stone is a composite of matter and form, and it is certainly not in the soul. Further, it is not the stone's form as such which is in the soul, but a likeness of it, so to say (οιον αυτό, 418a3-6, 424a1-2); otherwise the soul, having the form of redness as existing in a red object would itself be red, having the form of a triangle would itself be triangular, and having many forms would be actually many and not just one. We may liken the form of a thing as existing in the soul to the form of a tree as existing in the picture of a tree, and the analogy would be as follows: the triangle's form as existing in the soul is to the triangle's form as existing in the triangle as the tree's form as existing in the picture is to the tree's form as existing in the tree.

5. Some things exist apart from sensible objects, e.g., the prime mover. But the things discussed here are those which presuppose sensation and exist in some way in sensible objects which have magnitude and are external to the soul; or else, they exist in our knowledge of these objects, but our knowledge is not separable from our bodies, and bodies have magnitude.

6. There seems to be some difficulty in getting the meaning from the text taken literally; so we interpret.

Affections and dispositions of sensible objects as well as quantities exist in things which are sensible; but colors and sounds and other sensible objects are sensed directly whereas quantities are sensed indirectly, as stated in Book B. Now if the phrase "in the forms of sensible objects" means in the forms of the sensible objects which are external to the soul, there is no dispute; but this meaning does not seem to be relevant to what follows. If, however, it means the forms as existing in the soul, then the intelligible objects are objects of thought, each such object being numerically one with the thought of it, as already stated, and each such thought being *of* an object by abstraction—e.g., *of* a quantity—or *of* an affection or a disposition of a sensible object external to the soul. Now just as the external objects corresponding to the intelligible objects are not separate from magnitudes or bodies, so when we sense them we do so as not being separate, and our sense impressions as well as our images of those objects represent these as similarly related. Further, without sensations there can be no corresponding sense impressions and no corresponding images, and without these images there can be no corresponding thoughts. Hence without sensations there can be no corresponding thoughts; and if sensations do not exist, neither can one understand the corresponding terms when read or expressed by another person, nor can further thinking which requires these thoughts occur. 81a38-b9.

7. Assertions and denials are combinations of concepts and are true or false, and they are accompanied by belief; images, on the other hand, need not be combinations, and when we imagine A as being or not being B, we need not believe or disbelieve in that combination. As for primary concepts, we have discussed how they differ from the corresponding images in Comm. 21 of the preceding Section by taking a triangle as an example. It is true, however, that thoughts require images; and one may add that some animals (e.g., dogs) have images but no thoughts.

9

The kind of locomotion discussed here is (a) that of the whole living thing and not that of its parts, 253a14-15, and it is (b) initiated by the living thing itself. This motion is also called "travelling". Locomotion of the parts of a living thing occurs in such motions as heartbeat and breathing, and such motions are caused by external movers and are discussed elsewhere. In general, a thing which changes, whether by increasing or decreasing or altering or being generated or being destroyed, requires locomotion of parts of itself. Thus locomotion is prior in existence to all other changes, that is, it is presupposed by all other changes, 260a20-261b26, 320a19-25.

In this Section the question is raised as to the nature of the part of the soul which causes locomotion in animals. The discussion is exploratory and is limited to going over some difficulties in answering the question. The answer is given in the next Section.

1. Judgment is an attribute of sensation or of *thought*, 427a17-21. In seeing, for example, one judges that this color is white and that color is red, and there is no mistake in seeing colors; in *thinking*, on the other hand, one may be mistaken, e.g., one may judge 39 to be a prime number.

The phrase "has been defined" in line 432a15 refers to the definition as given by others, 403b25-7, 405b10-2, 427a17-9, not to that given by Aristotle; for Aristotle (a) would not exclude the nutritive power, 413b1-2, (b) would not regard locomotion as a requirement, since some animals are stationary, 413b2-4, and (c) would not include the thinking power for the same reason. To be an animal, then, a living thing must have, in addition to the nutritive part, a power of sensation as a minimum, 413b2.

Hicks seems to be right in saying that the discussion of locomotion by animals should follow the discussion of sensation and of *thinking*. Evidently, no such motion can occur without the power of sensation or of *thought*, and some animals (i.e., men) initiate such motion sometimes without *thinking* and sometimes with *thinking*. So if a discussion of such motion is not to be duplicated, it should follow the discussion of sensation and of *thought*. Again, not all animals can initiate motion; and things common to all animals should be discussed before things which belong to some animals are discussed.

2. Parts P and Q of a whole are said to be separable in magnitude if, as material parts or as attributes or powers of material parts, they exist or can exist in separate places. Parts P and Q are said to be separable in definition if their definitions differ, even if P and Q are not separable in magnitude. Thus the convexity and concavity of an arc differ in definition but are inseparable in magnitude, for they exist of necessity in the same arc.

3. The parts which have been enumerated are listed in 413a23-5, b10-3, 414a31-2, and elsewhere; the parts usually discussed during Aristotle's time were perhaps those which the Platonists were considering, namely, the rational and those of temper and *desire*, or, the rational and the irrational (or nonrational) parts. 432a24-6, 1102a26-8, 1182a23-6.

4. Perhaps this would be the appetitive part, for it is this which appears to initiate or to partake in causing motion.

5. The term "part" has many senses, 1023b12-25, and problems concerning the sense in which the soul has parts were raised in 402b1-3, 413b13-16, and 414b19-415a13. It is also evident that the number of the parts of the soul depends on the sense or senses in which one uses the term "part" in discussing the soul.

6. If the parts of the soul are differentiated specifically, they become more numerous than if they are differentiated generically. For example, corresponding to the appetitive part, taken as one genus, there are three parts, those of wish, of *desire*, and of temper. In general, then, as we descend to the lower species, the number of parts becomes greater.

7. An alternative to "irrational" is "nonrational". The Greek term is used sometimes in the first sense and sometimes in the second.

8. If the parts of the soul are reached by a dichotomy into the part which has reason and the part which has no reason (such division was used in Plato's Academy), then those who divide the soul into the rational part and the part or parts without reason, whether the latter be the nonrational part or, specifically, the parts concerned with temper and *desire*, there will appear other parts whose differences from the parts as given by these thinkers is greater than those among the parts given by these thinkers. For example, the nutritive part of the soul differs from the rational and the spirited and the *desiring* parts more than these parts differ from each other, but the nutritive part is not mentioned by these thinkers.

9. Vision, which belongs to the sentient part, is of proper sensibles, and

one is not mistaken in seeing, say, red color. But reason takes the form of discourse or thought in which the soul combines or separates, whether truly or falsely, as in "five is odd" or "five is even". On the other hand, since vision cannot be mistaken about its proper objects, it apprehends those objects truly, in one of the senses of the term "truth", 1051b33-1052a4, for truth in the main sense is an attribute of a *thought* in which a predicate is combined with or is separated from a subject. Again, there is sensation of proper sensibles, of common sensibles, and of accidental sensibles. So it is evident that one cannot easily say that the sentient part of the soul is rational or nonrational.

10. If the parts of the soul are posited as separate in magnitude, there is much difficulty in seeing how the imaginative part, which differs in definition from all the other parts, can be so separate from the sentient and all the other parts, for the imaginative part is very closely related to the sentient part, 429a1-2.

11. The appetitive part, which is thought (perhaps by these thinkers) to differ from all the other parts in its power and definition, gives rise to an absurdity if its species are taken into account; for these species are concerned with wish, *desire*, and temper. But whereas the latter two species come under the nonrational part, whether partly or wholly, the species concerned with wish comes under the rational part, for wish uses *thought*. Consequently, the appetitive part would be partly rational and partly irrational; and this situation violates the scientific principle according to which a genus must be subdivided if scientific knowledge through the cause is to be acquired. According to this principle, scientific knowledge of greatest generality or with necessary and sufficient conditions is knowledge through the cause, and such knowledge is of properties and leaves out irrelevant or accidental causes; and if such knowledge is to be acquired, the various species under a genus should not overlap, that is, they should be exclusive and exhaustive and have nothing in common except their genus. Scientific knowledge through the cause is discussed at length in the *Posterior Analytics*, 71a1-100b17.

12. If the soul is divided into the rational, the spirited, and the *desiring* parts, the latter two parts will be appetitive, and so will the part that wishes, which uses *thought;* hence the appetitive part, being a genus of the parts concerned with wish, *desire*, and temper, cannot be separated from these parts in magnitude, for a genus does not exist apart from its species, 999a5-10.

13. This sentence implies that only animals travel from one place to another. What about algae and tumble-weeds? Three questions arise. Do these living things initiate their own locomotion or are they caused to so move by external movers? Do these things have sensation? Was Aristotle aware of such living things? From what follows later, the kind of locomotion

discussed by Aristotle is initiated by an animal and presupposes at least the faculty of sensation. Such locomotions would appear to exclude those occurring by chemical and physical actions and reactions, in which there is no sensation or any other kind of awareness.

14. 253a7-21, 259b1-16, 453b11-458a32.

15. The nutritive part of the soul does not cause animals to travel; for if it did, plants, too, having only one power, the nutritive, would travel and hence have organic parts to do so. But plants by their nature have no such parts. Now we observe that, when animals travel, they do so for the sake of something: to pursue what is pleasurable, e.g., food or shelter or the like, or to avoid what is painful, e.g., harm of one sort or another; further, they desire to do these things or imagine doing them prior to pursuing or avoiding them. In short, desire and imagination are observed to be two candidates as movers which cause animals to travel. Locomotion by force is excluded, for force is an external and indefinite and therefore an accidental cause but a mover in the animal itself is sought. Dialectically, then, Aristotle uses observation to name desire and imagination or the corresponding abilities as possible movers which cause an animal to travel.

16. Animals which are stationary live in water, e.g., testaceous animals in water. 487b6-8, 683b4-5.

17. Nature and the intellect act for the sake of something, for the best; so they do nothing in vain. This is Aristotle's teleological hypothesis induced from observation. 271a33, 415b16-7, 434a31-2, 788b20-4.

18. If nature is to achieve its end, things which are necessary to bring about that end must exist and be put into operation. For example, if happiness is to be achieved, the virtues must be possessed and therefore acquired; if an animal is to travel, it must have the kind of bodily parts which make travelling possible; and if wood is to be cut, instruments for that cutting must exist and be put into operation.

19. Defect differs from incompleteness. That which is not yet developed fully is said to be incomplete, e.g., a two-year old child. But that which is defective cannot develop fully for one reason or another. A baby born with no arms is defective, and so is a man who has lost his vision. A whole species, too, may be defective, when nature failed to reach its end for that species, as in the case of moles, which cannot see; for here nature has failed to perfect the organ of vision. 533a2-7.

20. Since stationary animals reach maturity and reproduce and deteriorate, they have the kind of completeness which is proper to them. Hence they would have had the organs necessary to travel if sensation were the moving cause of travelling.

21. See 429a22-3.

22. The speculative intellect seeks truth and stops at truth as its purpose. But a problem arises with respect to truths in practical and productive

sciences, for the ultimate aims there are *action* and production, respectively. Knowing the truths in each of these sciences, however, should be distinguished from acting in accordance with them; further, those truths and the
truths of the sciences in general are universal, whereas what is produced or
acted upon is not universal but a particular. It appears, then, that the pursuit
of truths alone in the productive and practical sciences is speculative and
instrumental, whereas the *actions* and productions according to those truths
require (a) minor premises which are concerned with individuals and are
not parts of a science and also (b) a moving cause to act on these individuals,
even if action on these individuals presupposes those truths. For example,
let "a man should avoid excessive drinking" be a scientific premise in ethics,
and let "James is a man" and "drinking this amount of whiskey is excessive"
be the minor premises. Then the last two premises are minor and James's
avoidance of drinking this whiskey is an *action;* but neither the two premises nor the *actual* avoidance are parts of ethics as a science, for they are
individuals and not universal.

23. Is this matter an individual or universal, and if an individual, is it
something in the present or possibly in the future and even in the past or
else imagined? Perhaps it is an individual. The heart, of course, may be
moved even if one thinks of something fearful in the past or something
imagined. Anyway, there are cases in which speculation by the part which
is called "intellect" does not cause travelling; so that intellect cannot be the
mover.

24. In this case, the intellect may give the order and *thought* may assert
that something should be pursued or avoided, but the *action* which follows
is not that ordered by the intellect or asserted by *thought* but that which
is ordered by *desire.* Here two possible movers are indicated, (a) the intellect
along with *thought,* and (b) *desire. Desire* often overrules the intellect or
thought, and this happens with the incontinent man; for this man knows
what he should do, e.g., to avoid excessive drinking, but his *desire* to drink
excessively clouds or overpowers his *thought* of avoiding such drinking. So,
dialectically, it appears that the intellect or *thought* is not the mover.

25. This is another argument against the intellect or *thought* as the mover,
but it is given from the point of view not of *action* but of production. A
physician has medical science but does not necessarily cure; and this seems
to indicate that something else is needed to cause the doctor to cure, e.g.,
desire or intention or something else.

26. We are left with desire as the possible mover; but another difficulty
seems to appear. A continent man *desires* something bad, e.g., excessive
drinking, but avoids pursuing such drinking, for his thought, which regards
excess as harmful, is stronger than his desire (which here is *desire*) and
overrules it.

10

1. From what follows in the remaining part of this sentence, the term "intellect" here is used in a sense even wider than that in 429a22-3 (see Comm. 5 of Section 4), for it includes both imagination and thought. Why? According to Aristotle, two kinds of movers are needed for locomotion, an unmoved and one which is movable. From the text which follows, the movable mover is desire and the unmoved mover is the object of desire. But before a thing becomes an object of desire it must be perceived, whether by thought or imagination or in some other way. So just as "desire", being a genus, has species signifying different kinds of movable movers, so Aristotle uses "intellect" here like a genus with "thought" and "imagination" as species from which the different kinds of unmoved movers will be elicited.

A question may be raised. Should Aristotle use "intellect" to include in its meaning also sensation, or, does he so use it? For one may argue that the object of desire may also be sensed, as in the case of a painting which is seen and desired to be bought and owned. In 701a29-36, Aristotle mentions imagination, thought, and sensation as the three possible things by which a man acts to attain the object desired. But if this be the case, certain difficulties seem to arise. One difficulty is the meaning of "object of desire". Does this term signify a mover which must be in the man who desires or may it be outside of the man also? The problem will be discussed in Comm. 24.

2. *Actions* by men are meant. For the other animals cannot violate what they cannot *know*, but some men, e.g., the incontinent, do violate *knowledge* which they possess. The expression "the other animals" in the second part of this sentence confirms the position that *actions* by men are meant. Perhaps the word πολλά is corrupt and should be πολλοί, in which case the translation becomes: "many men who *act* against *knowledge* follow imagination".

3. The term "thinking" here is not used as in line 433a10 but in the main sense, which excludes imagination without thought (in the limited sense).

4. According to Hicks, the term "desire" here is restricted to irrational desire, which excludes wish. But it seems to me that Aristotle's thought would be more continuous if "intellect" here is used as in Comm. 1 and "desire" is used in its wide sense; for in this way each of these two terms would still make room for both the unmoved and movable movers, which will be distinguished as the discussion continues.

5. In this paragraph, distinctions within the terms "intellect" and "desire" taken in their wide sense as in Comms. 1 and 4 begin to appear, and the term "intellect" here excludes mere imagination and is used as in lines 429a22-3.

6. Not every intellect, as used in the last Commentary, is a cause of locomotion; for the theoretical intellect does not cause such motion since its

activity is an end in itself and its object exists of necessity. The activity of the intellect which causes locomotion, on the other hand, is not an end in itself but a process of thinking out the means leading to an end; and since such means are actions for that end, which does not exist of necessity but may or may not be realized, that intellect is practical, for what is practicable may or may not be or come to be.

7. Desire is relative to that which is desired, i.e., to the object of desire, and while it lasts, the object desired, which is the end of desire, has not yet been attained; so desire qua an affection or an activity is not an end in itself or complete but is incomplete. As incomplete and for the sake of something else, then, it resembles the practical intellect when in activity.

8. The object of desire considered here is that whose attainment requires *thought*, for the object of desire in a nonrational animal cannot be a starting-point of practical *thought* because such an animal has no thinking faculty. In man, then, let the object of desire be a house to be built for comfort. Practical *thought* in a man starts with this object and proceeds, let us say, as follows: "If a house is to be built, a loan must be obtained; if a loan is to be obtained, collateral must be deposited with the bank; such collateral is available". Then the man goes to the bank with collateral, gets the loan, and builds the house. Thus the starting-point of practical *thought* is the house to be built (or the comfort of living in that house, if you wish), and the last step of this *thought* is the availability of collateral. *Action* now begins with this last step and we have the following successive steps: taking the collateral, going to the bank, getting the loan, and building the house, this last step (or the comfort of living in it, if you wish) being the object which is desired.

9. Some manuscripts have the Greek term for "object of desire" instead of the Greek term for "the appetitive [soul]" here and also in lines 433a20 and 433a21 which follow. The two Greek terms come from the same root and differ very little. In a way, both alternatives are right, but in different ways. For (a) one may say that the object of desire so moves the appetitive soul that this soul's motion becomes a desire of that object, then that desire starts the *thinking* of the steps to be taken, and finally *action* begins; or (b) one may omit the object of desire and start with the appetitive soul in the act of desiring as the mover of *thought* followed by *action*.

It seems, however, that the discussion up to line 433a27 is concerned with the movable mover and that the unmoved mover starts there. If the unmoved mover is considered as starting here, the continuity of thought seems broken. Further, in lines 433a20-1, where imagination instead of practical *thought* is suggested as the movable mover, what is stated is that imagination, too, cannot cause motion without desire. So if locomotion of an animal always requires desire but sometimes occurs with imagination without *thought* but at other times occurs with *thought*, it would follow that desire, which is the common element, as stated in 433a20-2, is the movable mover. One might assert that desire is always accompanied with imagination, for even *thought* requires images. To anticipate, we may say that, in the case of imagination without *thought*, it is the object of imagination which moves desire, and then desire immediately or directly causes the animal to travel; but in the case of *thought*, it is the object of *thought*, while the images and the objects imagined appear to be only instrumental to the *thought* and to the object of that *thought*, and then desire uses *thought* before causing the animal (a man) to travel.

10. It has just been stated that imagination does not cause locomotion without desire; so it now remains to consider if the intellect as such causes locomotion. Since imagination as such excludes desire and hence cannot by itself cause locomotion, it makes no difference whether the term "intellect" here includes imagination in any way or not. Perhaps "intellect" here is taken in the restricted sense which excludes imagination.

11. Perhaps the kind of motion meant here is locomotion. Anyway, if both the intellect and desire cause motion, then "that which causes motion" would apply to each not qua intellect or qua desire but qua something which is common to both, for the differentia in each of them would not contribute to the locomotion which is caused. Now if *desire* and the intellect are opposed, it is in view of their differentiae and not their genus, for locomotion still occurs; but we should use the term "practical intellect" and not just "intellect".

12. The theoretical intellect does not cause motion, as already stated in 432b27-9, for it is not concerned with practical matters, which require motion; and its activity is an end in itself, and as such it is complete and not a motion, for a motion is an incomplete activity, 1066a20-1. So if the intellect causes locomotion, it is practical, whether directly or indirectly (for what is productive is indirectly practical since a thing produced, being useful, is ultimately for the sake of an end), and as such it requires wish; for the practical intellect uses judgment, and when it judges something to be good, it wishes to act in order to attain that good. But wish is defined as desire of the good; and this good is not a means to an end but an end in itself, and it is not only pleasurable or pleasure, or appearing to be so, but also requires *thought* to be attained. Hence the intellect which causes motion, in wishing the good, desires it and so cannot cause locomotion without desire. But wish is also of that which appears to be good but is not good, 146b36-147a4; for those who use judgment, e.g., thieves and sometimes even good men, may be mistaken as to what is good. Nevertheless, judgment is used even here; for judgment in the main sense is of that which is good, but in a secondary sense it is of that which appears to be but is not good, as in the case of the use of stolen money which is mistakenly thought to be a good, 1113a15-b2, 1235b25-6.

13. In nonrational animals, which have no judgment, desire takes the form of *desire*, which is of the pleasant, and the pleasant may or may not be good; in a man, who has intellect, desire takes the form of *desire* whenever he *acts* incontinently, and such desire is in violation of his right judgment.

It is now evident that the movable mover which causes locomotion is taken generically; for in nonrational animals such a mover can only be *desire*, which is a species of desire, and in rational animals it cannot be the intellect as such, for the theoretical intellect does not cause locomotion at all, while the practical intellect cannot cause such motion without wish, which is a species of desire.

14. Perhaps the term "intellect" here needs clarification, for it has been used in many senses. In the main sense, the intellect is always right, but in a secondary sense, it may be right or wrong. And when it is wrong, it is something called "positive ignorance", as in the case of a mistaken *thought*, 73b23-9. Here it is used in the main sense. Now to be right, the intellect must be (a) either of indivisibles or of composites and also (b) of what is good or true. Since in this context it is practical, it is of what may or may not be or come to be; since it is of what is good, it must perceive the good as good and the bad as bad; and if it is to attain the good, it must *think* out the right steps to do so. Perhaps the term is limited to true principles of what is good or bad.

15. Among animals, in general, that which is imagined to be pleasant or good or true may or may not be so, and what is desired may or may not be good or pleasant. For example, an object desired by a nonrational animal may be beneficial or harmful, by an incontinent man it is bad, and by a virtuous man it is good.

16. The object of desire introduced here is the immovable mover in all animals, and it is either the object of *thought* or the object imagined, 433b12. It will be discussed in Comm. 24.

17. The apparent good may be good or bad, but very often Aristotle uses the term "apparent good" to mean that which appears to be good but is not.

There are many kinds of goods, and they come under all the categories, 1096a19-29. But some goods are impossible to attain. For example, a man cannot become God; nor, as a composite, can he be or become immortal, 128b35-6, for his body is composed of elements and is therefore destructible. Thus not every kind of good is practicable, 1111b4-26.

If this sentence is intended to apply to all animals (and perhaps it is), then the word "practicable good" here, which signifies that which may or may not be or come to be and not that which exists of necessity, does not apply only to what is achievable by man but also to what is achievable by nonrational animals; and the word "good", too, which applies to what is actually or apparently good, is not limited to the object of wish, in which *thought* is required, but includes also the object of *desire*, for the term "good" has many senses. So the good here is either the object of wish or the object of *desire*, assuming that also temper is included. In short, the good here is the object of desire, as stated.

18. The Greek term for "desire" was used in two senses: as a power, which is the appetitive part of the soul, and as the activity of that power. As a power, it can cause locomotion, but when in activity causing locomotion, it is a mover which is movable, for it itself is caused to be moved by the object of desire, as already stated in Comm. 16.

19. Aristotle here points out that, in the *Republic*, Plato's subdivision of the soul into its parts or powers is limited and is based on a wrong principle; for the soul's parts or powers are inferred from their functions, and the principle of subdivision should be difference in function, that is, difference in what the parts can do. Plato divides the soul into the parts concerned with thinking, *desiring*, and temper, but he makes no mention of the nutritive and the sentient parts. Further, the *desiring* part and that of temper are species of one part, the appetitive part, whose function is to cause locomotion, and they differ from each other much less than, let us say, the nutritive does from the sentient part, whose functions differ. The thinking and the deliberative parts mentioned here are perhaps the scientific and the estimative parts, respectively, 1139a3-15, the first being concerned with thinking for its own sake about things which cannot be otherwise (i.e., with *knowledge* of necessary things for its own sake), the second with thinking not for its own sake but for the sake of *action* and production, which are about what may or may not come to be through man himself.

20. The reason meant is right reason, and the corresponding desire takes the form of a wish, which in its primary sense is of the really good (using the word "really" for emphasis). Contrary desires occur in continent and incontinent men, and such desires are implied in 433a1-3, 6-8.

21. Men, of course, are such animals.

22. Bad *desires* and the wishes opposed to them compete in a continent and an incontinent man; but this is not the case in a temperate man, for he has no bad *desires*, and so his wishes and *desires* are in harmony. An intemperate man qua such, on the other hand, has no wishes in the primary sense, which are of the good; so he follows bad *desires* by regarding them as good, although they appear to him to be good without being so, or else his wishes are bad, for they are of what appears to be good but is bad. But what is pleasurable or good without qualification?

Perhaps the pleasurable which is meant here is that which gives pleasure to the senses, and the good is that which is wished in the primary sense and requires intellect and a sense of time to be perceived. Then a man, perhaps without much thought about the future or with mistaken thought of what the good is or what the right means in acquiring it are, may regard that which is now pleasurable to be pleasurable without qualification, that is, pleasurable without being harmful in the long run, and if so, to be also good without qualification. Of course, that which is good without qualification, too, is pleasurable (in the wide sense), for good activities are virtuous activities, and these are pleasant, 1156b22-3. An example of what is pleasurable without qualification in the limited sense indicated is wholesome and tasty food appropriately taken, for such food, so taken, has no nonaccidental harmful effects in the long run and so contributes to one's happiness. Examples of what is good without qualification are activities in accordance with virtue, such as a generous act and philosophical activity.

23. This is the movable mover, generically taken, for it includes desire, wish, (and perhaps) temper.

But how can desire, which is an affection and an alteration and so a motion, 433b17-8, be movable, if there can be no motion of motion, 225b13-6? An affection, of course, exists in something affected, and this is a physical substance or a part of it, such as an organ in a man. So if the appetitive part as something affected be taken as being a physical part (i.e., a part with matter) and not desire as such, then perhaps it is that part which is movable; and that part as a mover causes motion not in virtue of its matter but in virtue of the desire in it.

24. We may now turn to the problem raised in Comm. 1, for difficulties seem to arise with the meaning of the term "object of desire".

First, desire and the object of desire are related to each other as an object moved to its mover, and these two are related to each other as an object caused to its cause. But an object caused and its cause when in activity must exist simultaneously, 95a10-24, whereas desire in activity and the object of desire do not appear to exist simultaneously, as in the case of a house yet to be built and the desire of building it. Again, is it necessary for an object of desire to be immovable or motionless? If one desires an apple and goes to the kitchen to fetch it, the apple, being a physical substance, is movable even if it is motionless; and a man may desire to possess an object which is in motion or desire it if it is in motion. Again, the object of desire in the above examples is external to the man, but that which first initiates locomotion in an animal is thought to be in the animal and not external to it, 699b34-700a17; and, besides, it seems absurd to regard as unmoved movers the desired apple and the house yet to be built and not the man who desires these, for no inanimate physical substance can initiate motion, 700b6-7. Other difficulties may be mentioned.

If the above difficulties are to be avoided, perhaps the meaning of the term "object of desire" should be reexamined. Let the following hypotheses be laid down: (a) if an animal desires something, the unmoved mover while the desire is being fulfilled is in that animal and not external to it; (b) desire and the object of desire, when in activity, are simultaneous, whether the animal is desiring prior to initiating travelling or during travelling; (c) the intellect and the intelligible object are numerically one, and so is *knowledge* and the object of *knowledge*, 430a3-5, 431a1-2, b21-3, 1072b20-3, 1074b38-1075a5.

Now *knowledge* and the object of *knowledge* are one in a way analogous to that in which the concavity and the convexity of a curved line are one, i.e., numerically one, for both these are in the line and cannot be separated, although they are distinguishable; and it is in this manner that *knowledge* and the object of *knowledge* are numerically one. Further, the object of *knowledge* is universal or of a universal and is not a particular or of a particular; for it is of, or is applicable to, an indefinite number of things, actual or possible, regardless of time, and it exists in or with *knowledge*. It is with *knowledge*, if the latter is considered as a relation or a relative, for *knowledge* and its object are correlatives, together, and numerically one; it is in *knowledge*, if *knowledge* is considered as a quality, like mathematics, for mathematics as *knowledge* of the mathematically *known* is like a composite which includes the object *known*. The same applies to the intellect and its object or to any thought and the object of that thought.

If we turn to sensation and imagination, a similarity exists, although there is a difference. In the case of sensation, the sensible object is outside, e.g., it may be a colored object or a sounding object, and in the case of imagination, the imagined object may be outside or even nonexistent. Yet in these, too, we have two things which are numerically one, namely, sensation and the object of sensation, imagination and the object of imagination. The object of sensation differs from the sensible object, for it is something like the sensible object, but not that object itself; it is a sense impression, like an imprint of the sensible object on the power of sensation when in activity; it exists as a form or a species in sensation but without matter, like the face in a picture of a man, for that face as such is not the face of the man himself but is something like it, a configuration or arrangement or a sort of form without matter, 424a18-9, and it exists not outside of the picture but in the picture. Similar remarks apply to the object imagined or object of imagination, whether the imagined object has existence or not (here, too, the terms "object imagined" and "imagined object" must be distinguished in their meaning, like the terms "object of sensation" and "sensible object"), for if the imagined object does not exist, there is still something, the object imagined or the object of imagination of which we are aware and which is in or with the image.

Let us now consider the immovable and movable movers keeping in mind the distinctions just made. The object of desire is an object imagined or an object thought and is of what is good or of what appears to be good; and, since it exists in the thinking or imaginative part of an animal, it exists in the animal and not outside of it. Further, it is not in motion, in fact, it is immovable; for, not being with matter, it cannot be moved (for no form or part of a form or attribute is movable, 224b11-3, 1067b9-10), or if it is moved at all, it is only indirectly or accidentally that it is moved and not essentially, as in the case of the soul, 405b31-407b26. Moreover, it is a mover by causing the appetitive part of the animal to be in motion, whether this motion be an alteration or some other kind of motion, 701a4-6, and this part in turn causes the animal to travel. Does the object of desire move desire as such or the appetitive part of an animal? But desire is an alteration and a motion, and as such it is only indirectly movable, whereas that which is essentially or directly movable has matter; hence that which is essentially movable by the object of desire here is the appetitive part of an animal which has matter, i.e., the organ in which desire exists.

If the remarks just given are right, a problem arises in connection with the motion of the first or outermost heaven (or sphere) of the universe in its relation to the prime mover, i.e., to God or Intellect. Does the prime mover cause the motion of that sphere as a man who is external to a chair causes the motion of that chair, or does He cause that motion in the same way in which an animal's object of desire, as described, causes the appetitive part to move? It would appear that it is the prime mover as such that causes the motion, for lines 1072a23-26 state "and since that which is moved and is a mover is thus an intermediate, there is something which causes motion without being moved, and this is eternal, a substance, and an *actuality.*" But lines 1072a26-7 which follow state "And this is the way in which the object of desire or the intelligible object moves, namely, without itself being moved". Further, if the essence of God is Thinking, which is of itself (1074b33-5), would being a mover of the outer sphere be a part of God's essence or a property of God? In either case, would not God's essence depend on the motion of the outermost sphere? The converse would appear to be the case or more likely to be the case, for it is the motion that would depend on God. If, on the other hand, God moves the outermost sphere not as such but as an object of desire (1072a23-7) or as an object loved (1072b1-4), then the immovable mover as an object of desire would exist in the outermost sphere just as the object of an animal's desire exists in that animal and is not external to it, or else that mover would exist in an immaterial and separate substance distinct from God but somehow associated with the outermost sphere. If this be granted, it would appear that each of the eternal spheres of the universe is a thinking substance, but not sentient, or else that it is associated with a separate and immaterial thinking substance which is not God but some other immaterial substance whose activity is eternal and the same. That no sphere can be a sentient substance is clear from the fact that alteration and hence sensing cannot belong to an eternal object, for such changes necessitate locomotion of parts in the object, and such object would then be a composite and hence destructible. Further, positing the prime mover as an object of desire or an object loved seems to do away with the problem of how God, being immaterial, can cause a material substance (the outermost sphere) to move with respect to place, if imparting locomotion is possible only by contact.

The above Commentary may be viewed not necessarily as the solution to the problems raised but as my own difficulties and manner of trying to understand Aristotle's position.

25. In one sense there are two movers, one being immovable and the other movable; in another, there are still many movers, i.e., wish, *desire*, and temper. In either case, there are many movers. Generically, of course, there is only one movable mover, the appetitive part, and only one immovable mover, the object of desire.

26. 256b14-20. The mover in (1) is the immovable mover, as in (a), and that by which motion is caused in (2) is that which causes motion (i.e., travelling, which is locomotion) but is also moved by the immovable mover, as in (b). The motion produced in the movable mover is desire, which is an affection and hence an alteration, but the motion which the movable mover produces in the animal is travelling, which is a locomotion. 700b35-701a6.

27. This is the same as the object of desire. In other words, the object of desire and the practicable good are numerically one but distinct in essence or definition; for to be an object of desire is to be something which is related to desire, whereas to be a practicable good is to be a good which can be brought about by man's *action*. The two expressions are like the expressions "George Washington" and "the first President of the U.S.A.", which signify the same person but differently. Perhaps the apparent good is included under "good".

28. That which is moved essentially is a material thing, and "the appetitive part" here would be the material part or organ which can be affected essentially and through which the animal desires. When it is said that desire is moved, (700b35-701a1), it is only indirectly that it is moved and not essentially, for desire is a motion, and no motion can be moved essentially; it is moved in the same way in which the soul is moved, for the soul is moved indirectly by being in a composite of matter and form, and it is this composite that is moved essentially, 405b31-407b26.

29. If desire is considered potentially, as when we say that a man has desires, it is not a motion, but if it is considered as an activity, it is a motion.

Manuscripts differ. An alternative translation to "taken as an activity" is "or as an activity". There is a difference between a motion and an activity: a motion is an incomplete activity, but an activity need not be incomplete, as in the case of pleasure for its own sake.

I am not sure which of these two alternatives Aristotle had in mind.

30. This is (3), which is moved but is not a mover, and its motion in this context is locomotion.

31. The manner in which the bodily parts of an animal operate by desire

so as to cause locomotion come under functions common to the body and soul. Some discussion of this appears in *Motion of Animals* and *Locomotion of Animals*, 698a1-714b23.

32. If convex surface S_1 and concave surface S_2 of bodily parts A_1 and A_2, respectively, coincide, where A_1 is in motion but A_2 is at rest, then S_1 and S_2 are in the same place and so not separate; but S_1 is in A_1 and hence definable in terms of A_1, and S_2 is likewise definable in terms of A_2, for a part is definable in terms of the whole of which it is a part. For example, a hand is defined as such and such a part of man or of the body with such and such functions.

33. The mechanical principles of causing motion are pushing and pulling, and all the other kinds are referred to these two, 243a16-b17, 703a19-21.

34. In summary, then, the appetitive part is both movable and a mover, and it is moved by the practicable good (or apparent good), which is immovable; and this good, whether apprehended with judgment or not, exists (if the interpretation in Comm. 24 is right) in the sentient part, for judgment requires images and so presupposes sensation and the sentient part. It should be noted, too, that actual desire presupposes the apprehension of the practicable good, which is the immovable mover in animals, but that the converse is not necessarily so; hence this mover is in this sense prior to desire. 1072a29.

11

1. There are animals which, when fully developed, have by their nature only the sense of touch. They are perfect with respect to their nature in the sense that they have reached their goal without hindrance, but they are imperfect with respect to the possible powers which some animals can have, such as that of seeing and that of thinking.

2. The problem whether such animals can have imagination was raised in 414b14-6.

3. In other words, just as the movements of such animals are indefinite or indeterminate, so are their *desires* and their imagination. The indefiniteness of those movements is a matter of observation, and perhaps it is more apparent than that of their *desires*. But these animals appear to have *desires*, for they appear to pursue some things and to avoid others. Imagination in them, on the other hand, is less apparent, for its existence appears to be a matter of inference from their movements and *desires* or by analogy from higher animals.

4. 433b29-30.

5. A man who deliberates posits an end and comes to the conclusion by comparing and using a unit or standard; so reasoning is used to make the choice of the means, 1112b12-21. Thus if A exceeds B, whether numerically or in magnitude or in value or in some other way, it is so perceived by a

comparison of A with B. For example, 6 is greater than 4 by 2 units; and if this relation is perceived and the greater is posited as the end, 6 will be chosen. If A and B are not numbers or cannot be numbered, comparison and choice are still possible by the use of, say, A or something belonging to A as the unit or standard. For example, if comparison is made with respect to value, which is a quality, A's value may be taken as the standard, and then B will be perceived as falling short of that value, as in the preference of one painting over another, even when their numerical value in cost is not considered.

6. In comparing, one must use more than one image; hence in concluding through deliberation, one must choose by using more than one image.

7. Sense imagination as existing in nonrational animals cannot connect images to form opinions. But a man can form opinions, which are beliefs, and when he does this, he must use images, 427b14-6; for he must use universals or concepts, which are impossible without images. 432a3-10.

8. The desire indicated here is that of nonrational animals, or else that which is common to all animals as a genus; it may be temper or *desire*, but it cannot be wish.

9. Wish is basically of the good, but a *desire* may be good or may be bad. So there are good and bad *desires*. It follows, then, that a wish in a man may be opposed by the corresponding bad *desire*, as in a continent or an incontinent man, who knows and wishes the good (e.g., drink to moderation) but *desires* what is bad (e.g., drink to excess). In a continent man, wish overpowers the corresponding bad *desire*; in an incontinent man, bad *desire* overpowers the corresponding wish.

10. Some commentators interpret a sphere to be a heavenly sphere, believed by the Greeks and Aristotle to move around the Earth in a certain manner, e.g., the sphere of the fixed stars and that of the planets; others interpret it to be a ball in a game played by two players. I prefer the second interpretation but I differ in the manner in which the analogy is explained. Now in a continent or an incontinent man, the *desire* is bad and its direction is opposed to that of the corresponding wish; and the stronger of these two desires, which may be either the wish or the *desire*, overpowers the weaker and continues in its original direction to achieve its end. By analogy, if two balls with different weights travel towards each other, their directions are opposed and the heavier overpowers the lighter and continues in its original direction till it comes to a stop.

11. Here, again, some commentators think that "the higher" modifies a higher heavenly sphere, for the motion of such sphere always affects the motion of a lower sphere but is not affected by the motion of that sphere; others think that it refers to wish, for wish is a desire of the good and, using thought, is a higher desire than temper or *desire*.

12. What are the three kinds of locomotions or what are their causes? Some alternatives may be listed.

(a) According to Eudoxus, the motion of the Sun or the Moon is resolved into the motions (as causes) of three heavenly spheres, 1073b17-21.

(b) The three kinds of locomotions are caused by reason, *desire*, and the combination of these two, as in continent and incontinent men.

(c) The locomotions are caused by continence, incontinence, and temperance.

(d) The locomotions are caused by the three kinds of desires, that is, by wish, temper, and *desire*.

Perhaps there are other alternatives.

If the locomotions meant are those of the heavenly spheres or bodies, then their similarities to those of animals are implied. Now it appears that temper may be a cause of locomotion in a man, for anger causes men to *act*. If so, then alternatives (b) and (c) seem inadequate. Alternative (a) is faced with some difficulties. For one thing, Aristotle does not quite agree with the theory of Eudoxus. Alternative (d) is plausible, but I am not quite sure.

13. The *knowing* part of the soul qua *knowing* is concerned with truth for its own sake and not for the sake of *action* or production, except indirectly, but locomotion in a man occurs essentially in *action* or production.

14. Perhaps the Greek text for the parenthetical expression, if not corrupt, may be analyzed as follows. "A man of type X should do a thing of type Y; John is a man of type X, and doing so-and-so is doing a thing of type Y; therefore John should do so-and-so". This is a syllogism in Aristotle's form, although it may not appear to be. One may also use the following. "*Action* of type Y by a man of type X should be performed; this intended *action* by me is an *action* of type Y by a man of type X; therefore, this intended *action* by me should be performed".

Now the conclusion "this intended *action* by me should be performed" is a belief or opinion and not an *action*, and it does not imply that the *action* is being performed; but if the *action* is being performed, then that belief or opinion is functioning as a mover. The sentence which follows brings this out.

15. Perhaps this statement needs some analysis, or else an interpretation. Just as sensation is of particulars, so *action* is on particular matters. If the universal opinion were the moving cause, it would be a mover of all or of most of the particulars to which it is applicable. But it is not such a mover; for a person's *action* is not a set of actions by such-and-such persons but a single *action* by one person of such-and-such a kind.

There is a sense, however, in which the universal opinion participates in an *action* performed by a person. The *action* is a particular in time and is caused by a particular mover in time; but it will not occur unless something else is presupposed or implied, namely, that such-and-such a person should do such-and-such a thing. This presupposition is universal and changeless, but particular instances of it which cause that *action* require or imply it, and in this sense the universal participates in the *action* although it does not directly cause it in time.

12

1. The argument is as follows. Whatever has a soul must, during its lifetime, grow and mature and deteriorate; to do so, it must take in food; to take in food, it must have a power; this power is the nutritive power; therefore, whatever has a soul must, during its lifetime, have the nutritive power, which may be the whole soul, as in plants, or a part of the soul, as in animals. By definition, the nutritive power is the minimum which a living thing must have, 412a14-5, and some living things, i.e., plants, have this power but no other power, 414a32-3. It follows, then, that the nutritive power is prior in existence to all other powers which living things may have.

2. Some living things do not have a power of sensation, and such things are plants. For touch requires an organ composed of all the other material elements if it is to receive the corresponding sense impressions of external objects (or their forms without the matter), 423a11-7, but a plant is composed of earth alone or mostly of earth, 435a24-b2, 477a27-8, 761b13, and so it cannot have an organ of touch to receive the corresponding sense impressions; and without touch, the other senses cannot exist, for they presuppose touch, 414b3, 415a3-6.

3. By definition, animals are living things with the power of sensation; and animals are either (a) stationary and live in water, 487b6-8, or (b) capable of travelling. Now stationary animals appear to be higher than plants but lower than animals which can travel, and they take in food from the spot on which they grow. But such animals are not discussed here. So one may raise the problem whether those animals have a power of sensation for the sake of just living or for the sake of living well; for if they do not need a sense for the sake of taking in food and preservation, that sense would appear to be either useless or for the sake of living well; and if that sense exists for the sake of living well (for nature would not have it exist in vain), one may raise the problem whether the loss of that sense destroys the animal altogether or allows it to live only like a plant.

The expression "nature does nothing in vain" seems to imply that "nature" in the primary sense means the form of a composite thing (of an animal in this case), as discussed in the *Physics*, 192b8-193b21; for an animal is a composite and not a nature, and a composite has a nature or exists *by nature*, and nature in the main sense is a principle as form existing *in* the composite which has it, 1015a13-9. Further, in a composite, it is its nature as form that *does* or *acts* and not nature as matter, which is passive or a principle capable of being acted upon but not of acting. It appears, then, that an animal acts by its form and that its activity is its function or final cause and not something indeterminate, which could be something in vain.

4. Coincidences or accidents arise not because of the nature of a thing but because of the plurality of things having matter; for at times a composite is prevented by other composites from being in activity according to its nature and then accidents or coincidences arise. For example, a man's function or purpose may be thwarted by another man's purpose or by lightning or by some other agent and not by himself or his nature, and a falling rock may be prevented from reaching its natural place.

5. The higher stage of living things presented now is that of animals which can travel. Such animals must travel to get their food, which is necessary for living and their preservation, and living is their nature's function.

6. In some manuscripts the question is, "For why should it not have it?", and we have a problem. Another problem is Aristotle's position concerning ungenerable bodies, e.g., the Sun and the planets, whether they have the power or activity of sensation or not. Again, the text as it stands does not spell out the thought. Finally, perhaps the text is corrupt, for there seems to be no continuity of thought, regardless of which of the two questions is taken. This situation has given rise to various interpretations. We shall give two of our own, with reasons.

If the question raised is the translation as given and is about a celestial body, such a body cannot have a power of sensation. For sensation is an affection, which is an alteration, i.e., a motion with respect to quality, and this motion presupposes a locomotion of some parts of the body, 260a26-b26. But a body with parts is a composite and hence destructible, whereas a celestial body according to Aristotle is simple, indestructible, and not subject to alteration or change with respect to quantity, 269a2-7, 270a12-4.

If the question is the variant "For why should it not have it?" and is about an ungenerable composite (Aristotle would deny the possibility of an ungenerable body which is a composite, but he may be allowing it here as a hypothesis which others may adopt), such composite would be no better off (in fact, it would be worse off) without sensation. For, (a) since ungenerable substances are also indestructible and hence eternal, 281a28-283b22, the absence of the power of sensation would have no adverse effect on the eternality of that composite, and, (b) since thinking without any sensation at all is simple and belongs only to simple substances which are immaterial and eternal (e.g., to God, 1072a19-1075a10), thinking by that composite substance would still require images and hence the power of sensation in spite of its indestructibility or eternality.

The second interpretation is preferable, for it gives greater continuity to the thought in the paragraph. Then the translation within the parentheses should be as follows: "Moreover, nor can an ungenerable [composite which can travel be without a power of sensation]. For, why should it not have it? Perhaps [because it would be] better for its body or for its soul. But, as it is, this cannot be the case; for neither will its soul think any more [without sensation], nor will its body, [being ungenerable], exist more because of [lack of sensation]."

7. It is necessary for an animal to have the sense of touch if it has a power of sensation, and the medium and organ of touch must be not an element but a blend of elements, as stated in 423a11-7 and 434a27-9. A fuller account of that necessity will now be given.

8. External media of sense may be elements or blends of elements. Air is such a medium in seeing a color or hearing a sound, but water and glass and other objects, too, may be such media. In sensing by touch, on the other hand, the medium is flesh, which is a part of the animal's body, and so is the corresponding organ, and these must be blends and not elements, as already stated; and the objects touched must be sensed directly by the animal's body and not through an external medium. Now in sensing by touch, the animal is so affected that it receives the forms of the objects without their matter, as stated in 424a17-19, and by using those forms to distinguish beneficial from harmful objects, the animal accepts or pursues the beneficial but rejects or avoids the harmful objects for the sake of its preservation.

9. Harmful objects of touch may be such extremes as fire and cold and intense pressure, which tend to destroy the animal, but they may be also the contraries of food, which do not contribute to the growth and sustenance of animals. Similar remarks apply to beneficial objects of touch. So one species of objects of touch is food and its contraries, and taste is the corresponding sense which discriminates those objects. It is by contact, then, that taste distinguishes food from its contraries, and it does this by receiving the corresponding forms without the matter of those objects; and the attribute of those objects which causes those forms is their flavor. In short, taste is touch of nutritive objects; so both (a) taste as a species and (b) touch which is not taste are necessary for the preservation of an animal. "Touch", it may be added, may be used in two senses, either generically to include "taste" as a species of it or specifically to exclude "taste".

10. Vision, hearing, and smell are necessary for animals which can travel, but they may be used also for living well. Vision may be used to behold beautiful objects, hearing to listen to beautiful music and for communication, which imparts knowledge, and smell to sense perfumes and odors of good food. The tongue, which is used for tasting, may be used also for the sake of living well, for it is used for communication.

11. To survive, animals which can travel must avoid danger and seek food and shelter, and to do these they must use, besides touch, also vision and hearing and smell.

12. The mover in alteration, whether it is unmoved or is an intermediate mover and so also moved, need not move with respect to place in order to

act, for it may be in activity while remaining in the same place, as in the case of a stationary sounding object which is heard or as still air which is heated by fiery coal and warms a man at a distance. Some parts of such mover, of course, may undergo locomotion, and it is in this sense—a qualified sense, for alteration necessitates locomotion in some sense—that a mover which causes alteration may be said to undergo locomotion. The air next to a sounding bell, activated by the bell, does not travel towards the man but activates the air next to it, which in turn activates the air next to it, etc., till the air in contact with the ear is activated. Thus the whole air which is activated by the bell does not travel but the parts of it are activated in a temporal succession. In modern times, those parts undergo longitudinal locomotion to and fro without actually travelling towards the ear. One might say that it is the activation of the parts which travels towards the ear but not the parts themselves, but such travelling is indirect or accidental; for there is no motion of motion (225b10-226b17) because motion belongs only to a body which can move and not to an attribute of a body, and attributes as such cannot move except indirectly (224b11-3), as already stated.

In sensing an object at a distance, then, that object is not sensed directly but causes an alteration or some other activity of the medium (or series of mediums) which in turn directly acts on the animal by contact and causes an alteration or affection in that animal; and that affection is sensing.

13. Perhaps this long sentence lists the kinds of bodies as possible intermediate movers and the manner in which they act on the object moved; and it states that (a) air, as an intermediate mover which causes alteration without travelling, remains unified as explained in 419b21-420a2, and that (b) it does so further from the unmoved mover than water does.

14. If a man stands at a distance from a mirror in daylight, his color and shape act on the air which, being affected and remaining unified without travelling, acts on the smooth surface of the mirror. The mirror itself, so acted, acts in turn on the air in a similar manner but in the contrary direction. Then the air, so acted, remains unified and, again without travelling, affects the man's vision and causes him to see himself.

15. The words "as if" appear to suggest a similarity and also a difference. The theories of Plato and Aristotle are similar in one respect but different in another. In both there is a direction to and from a mirror, but Plato uses man's vision as the starting point and actual travelling of rays from the eye as the manner, whereas Aristotle uses man's shape and color as the starting point but a medium which is uniformly affected without travelling as the manner.

13

1. 423a12-7, 434b10-24.

2. Perhaps "the other elements" refers to air and water, as stated in 425a3-9, and the intervening medium is external to the animal's body. The sensation of the color of a body at a distance, for example, occurs through an external medium, air or water or even glass, 424b27-30.

3. In other words, the sensation of touch occurs when the external body is contacted by the animal's body, in which case there is no intervening medium external to the animal's body.

4. The Greek terms for the sense of touch and of contact or touching come from the same root.

5. The colored body, being in contact with the air, activates the air, and the activated air comes in contact with the eye. So seeing occurs not by direct contact with the colored body or its color but by way of the activated intervening medium.

6. The phrase "is thought" refers to the general opinion, which in this case is only roughly right. Aristotle would state the fact more accurately as follows: the sensation of touch alone occurs when an external object is touched directly by the animal's body and not indirectly by an external medium. The flesh which touches the object is not the organ of touch but a medium, but it is not an external medium. 423b20-6.

7. 410a30-b2, 423a12-7.

8. See 423b31-424a10 and the corresponding Commentaries.

9. Neither inanimate things nor plants, which have life, have the sense of touch, but this sense is both necessary and sufficient for a living thing to be what we call "an animal". So the definition of an animal, generically taken as a living thing with a sense of touch, is real and not nominal.

10. The sense of touch is prior in existence to the other senses, i.e., those senses cannot exist without the sense of touch, but the sense of touch can exist without any or all of the others. So if any of the other senses in a living thing is destroyed, the sense of touch in that thing is not necessarily destroyed; and this priority of the senses further supports the definition of an animal which includes only touch. If a sense other than that of touch is destroyed by the corresponding agent, the sense of touch may be destroyed by that agent; but this occurs whenever that agent has an additional effect which destroys the organ of touch. But if a tangible agent destroys the sense of touch, it must destroy also the other senses in view of the priority just mentioned.

It may be added, a sense organ and the corresponding sense always exist together, that is, if either of the two ceases to exist, so does the other. 424a24-8.

11. There is a problem. In this paragraph it is stated that animals which possess the senses other than that of touch do so not for the sake of existing (that is, not because those senses are necessary for the preservation of those animals), but for the sake of living well, the implication being that those

animals could exist even without those senses; and this statement seems to be confirmed by lines 434b21-9. Lines 436b10-437a5, on the other hand, state that touch and taste are necessary for animals if they are to be preserved but that, in the case of travelling animals, also the senses of sight and of smell and of hearing (perhaps not necessarily all three, for bees do not hear, 980b22-4) are necessary for preservation, the implication being that those animals could not exist without those senses.

Perhaps the difficulty is only apparent. The senses of taste and touch are necessary for all animals, taken as a genus. But when we come to a species of that genus, additional necessities arise, as in the case of travelling animals; so those animals require also the senses of sight and hearing and smelling for preservation, although not necessarily all three, as in the case of bees. Further, a species of travelling animals, e.g., men, possess the senses of sight and of hearing and of taste (not necessarily all three) not only for mere existence, but also to live well, for these senses or their organs may be used, in addition to what is necessary for existence, also for the sake of living well. Thus the tongue is used also to talk to others, hearing to listen to others, and vision to distinguish things; and all these three functions are for the sake of knowledge and prudence, which in the case of men contribute to their happiness. This interpretation seems to be confirmed by lines 434b24-6; and if it is correct, then the word ἕνεκά (= "for the sake of") in line 435b21 should be understood as a final cause in which living well and the existence of the corresponding senses and organs when used properly are convertible, and δὲ in line 435b24 should be translated as "but", which is one of its main translations. Causation from the scientific point of view, it may be added, is discussed at length in the *Posterior Analytics*, 71a1-100b17.

GLOSSARY

The meaning of most terms in the translation are made clear in the English-Greek Glossary by means of a definition or a property or a description or examples, and references are often given to the page and lines according to the Bekker text. If an English term is not always used in the same sense, its various meanings are listed and are separated by a semicolon or a period. A few terms appear sometimes in Roman and sometimes in italic letters, but they differ in meaning. For example, the terms "desire" and *"desire"* differ in meaning, and so do the terms "substance" and *"substance"*. Synonyms are indicated.

In the Greek-English Glossary, English synonyms used for the same Greek term are separated by a comma; for example, the Greek term σημαίνειν is translated sometimes as "to signify" and sometimes as "to mean", and these two synonyms are separated by a comma. But if the English terms are separated by a semicolon, they are not synonyms; for example, the term οὐσία is translated sometimes as "substance" and sometimes as *"substance"*, and the term αἴσθησις is translated sometimes as "sensation" and sometimes as "faculty of sensation", but the two English terms in each case differ in meaning and are separated by a semicolon.

ENGLISH-GREEK

absolutely ἁπλῶς Synonyms: "simply", "unqualified", "without qualification".

abstract, v. ἀφαιρεῖν To attend to an attribute or element as a thing in
itself without reference to the subject to which it belongs. For example, a geometrician abstracts surfaces from bodies to which they
belong and attends to them as such without making any reference
to those bodies. 1061a28-b3, 1077b2-14.

accident συμβεβηκός A thing which belongs to another thing neither
always nor for the most part, but sometimes, e.g., sickness in a man,
and finding a coin when walking. 1025a14-30.

accidentally κατὰ συμβεβηκός Synonyms, see "by accident".

according to κατά See "in virtue of", "by virtue of".

account λόγος

accurate ἀκριβής

acted upon, be πάσχειν This is one of the ten categories, and so an
ultimate genus. 1b25-7, 1017a24-7. Syn: "affected, be".

acting ποιεῖν This is one of the categories. 1b25-2a10.

action πρᾶξις An action by man, usually chosen with a purpose. 1105a28-
33.

activity ἐνέργεια A term with a wide meaning, having as species such
things as action, thinking, sensing, awareness, and so on. 1045b27-
1052a11. Synonyms: "*actuality*", "exercise" (sometimes).

actuality ἐνέργεια Same as "activity".

actuality ἐντελέχεια existing, the opposite of potentiality.

affected, be πάσχειν Same as "acted upon"

affection πάθημα; πάθος.

affirmation κατάφασις A statement signifying that something belongs to
something else, e.g., such forms as "every A is B", "some A is B",
and "some A is not-B". 17a25.

air ἀήρ For the meaning, see "water".

alteration ἀλλοίωσις Motion with respect to quality; e.g., becoming sick
or changing color. 226a26-9, 270a27-30, 319b10-4.

always ἀεί

analogy ἀναλογία Sameness of relation between two pairs; e.g., if A is
to B as C is to D, then the first two terms in the order given are
analogous to the last two terms in the order given. A proportion is
a special case of analogy. 74a17-25, 76a37-40, 98a20-3, 99a8-16.

anger ὀργή

animal ζῷον A living thing having as a minimum the power of sensing.
Hence it includes man.

animal, nonrational θηρίον An animal which has no reason, that is, one
which cannot make statements or think by using universal terms.

animate ἔμψυχον Having a soul.

appear, v. φαίνεσθαι

appetitive part ὀρεκτικόν That part of an animal, whether of the soul or of the body or of the composite, which has the power of desiring.

apprehend κρίνειν; θιγεῖν

apprehension θίξις

appropriate οἰκεῖος Syn: "peculiar"

argument λόγος

art τέχνη Acquired ability to produce something in accordance with true reason. 1140a6-23.

as ῇ Sometimes, same as "insofar as". See "qua".

as an accident   See "by accident".

as far as ῇ See "insofar as".

attribute, n. συμβεβηκός A thing which, having no matter, is present in a subject, whether demonstrable from that subject or not, and whether an accident or not. For example, color belongs to a surface and is an attribute of the surface; similarly, sickness is an attribute of man, the equality of the sum of the angles of a triangle to two right angles is an attribute of a triangle, and being in the office is an attribute of a man (if he is there). 1025a14-34. An attribute of a subject may be a subject of another attribute, e.g., surfaces are attributes of bodies but are subjects of colors.

attribute πάθος An attribute belonging to a thing in virtue of that thing.

authoritative κύριος See "dominant".

basic κύριος See "dominant".

because διά To say that A is C because of B is to say that B causes C to belong to A. For example, greater specific gravity than a liquid causes a substance to sink in the liquid, so it sinks because of such gravity. 73b25-74b4. Synonyms: "through", "by means of", "by" (sometimes).

become, v. γίγνεσθαι See "generation".

beginning ἀρχή See "principle".

be in ἐνυπάρχειν

being, n. ὄν, πρᾶγμα Synonyms: "thing", "that which exists", "fact".

belief ὑπόληψις The term is generic. It is an affection or *thought* about what is or what is not the case. Its species are "knowledge", "opinion", "prudence", and their contraries. 426b24-7.

belong ὑπάρχειν The term is wider in meaning than the term "be predicable of". 48a40-49a10.

blend, n. μῖξις A union of bodies, readily adaptable in shape, which have acted upon and so altered each other; for example, a union of coffee and cream, not of salt and pepper. 327a30-328b32.

body σῶμα

boundary   ὅρος; ἄκρον
breathing   ἀναπνοή
by   ᾗ   See "qua".
by accident   κατὰ συμβεβηκός   P is said to belong to Q by accident if it
   does so neither necessarily nor for the most part but occasionally.
by itself   καθ' αὑτό
by means of   ᾗ; διά   See "qua", "because".
by nature   φύσει   P is said to exist by nature if, being a composite, it has
   in itself a principle of motion or of rest; e.g., animals, earth, and
   water exist by nature. 192b8-193a1.
by virtue of   See "in virtue of".
can, v.   ἐνδέχεσθαι   That which may or may not be or come to be. Syn:
   "may".
carpentry   τεκτονική
category   κατηγορία   Any one of the highest ten genera of things. 1b25-7,
   83b13-7, 103b20-3, 225b5-7, 1017a22-7, 1032a14-5, 1068a8-9.
cause   αἴτιον, αἰτία   Syn: "reason". 94a20-b26, 194b16-5b30, 983a24-32,
   1013a24-1014a25.
chance thing   τυχόν
chance   αὐτόματον   A moving cause which is accidental and hence varia-
   ble or indefinite. 195b31-198a13.
change   μεταβολή   This is a generic term, and its species are "generation",
   "destruction", and "motion"; and the kinds of motion are locomotion, alteration, increase, and decrease. 225a1-b9.
cold, n. or adj.   ψυχρόν
Cold   ψυχρόν   For Parmenides, a principle of sensibles. 986b31-987b2.
color   χρῶμα
come to be   Same as "become". See "generation".
common   κοινός
common sensible   κοινόν   418a7-20.
complete   τέλειος   (a) That of which no part is outside or missing; (b) that
   whose virtue within its genus cannot be exceeded, as a perfect doctor
   or a perfect fluteplayer. 1021b12-1022a3. Syn: "perfect".
composite   σύνθετος
composite, n.   σύνολον   Composed of matter and form, or of substance and
   attribute; e.g., a statue, whose parts are, let us say, bronze and shape,
   and a white man, who is a man and has whiteness. 995b34-5, 999a32-
   3, 1037a29-31, 1060b23-5, 1077b7-9.
concept   νόημα
conclusion   συμπέρασμα   A statement or thought which follows logically
   from premises.
contact, n.   ἁφή, θίξις
contemplate   θεωρεῖν

continence ἐγκράτεια

continuous συνεχής A and B are said to be continuous if their limits (not necessarily all) are one; a property of a continuous thing is infinite divisibility. 227a10-7, 1069a5-9, 232b24-5, 268a6-7.

contrariety ἐναντίωσις complete difference; the two contraries taken together. See "contrary".

contrary ἐναντίον The primary meaning is: contraries are the most different under the same genus, e.g., whiteness and blackness, oddness and evenness, justice and injustice. For secondary meanings, see 1018a25-35, 1055a3-b29.

conviction πίστις A strong belief; an attribute of a belief, admitting the more and the less. 125b28-126a2, 126b13-30, 428a19-23, 1146b24-31.

courage θάρσος

darkness σκότος

decrease, n. φθίσις The lessening of a thing's quantity.

defect πήρωμα A privation in a living thing, whether due to failure of nature or violence, which cannot be corrected; e.g., permanent blindness.

define, v. ὁρίζειν

definition ὅρος, λόγος (sometimes) Perhaps this term is wider than the term "definition". Lines 93b29-94a14 seem to imply that what is given as a definition may be nominal, and hence even of a nonbeing, whereas a definition as defined is of the essence or whatness of a thing, and a thing exists (90b3, 16, 30, 91a1, 1031a11-4). Further, only three kinds of definitions are listed in 94a11-4.

definition ὁρισμός A formula of the essence or whatness of a thing. 90b3-4, 94a11-4, 1031a11-4.

deliberation βούλευσις Inquiry into the means needed to bring about a desired end, usually in practical matters. 1112a18-3a2.

deliberative part βουλευτικόν

demonstration ἀπόδειξις A syllogism, mainly through the cause, of that which is of necessity true. 71b9-18.

denial ἀπόφασις A statement signifying that something does not belong to something else; for example, the forms "no A is B" and "some A is not B".

desire, n. ὄρεξις The three species of desire are wish, desire, and temper.

desire, object of ὀρεκτόν

desire, n. ἐπιθυμία Desire through sensation of pleasure or of what appears to be pleasant but is not. 146b36-7a4, 414b2-14.

desiring part ἐπιθυμητικόν The appetitive part which is limited to desire. See "appetitive part".

destruction φθορά Change from being to nonbeing. Such a change is said to be unqualified if it is with respect to substance, e.g., the death of a man, but it is said to be qualified if it is with respect to an attribute, e.g., quantity or place or quality. 225a12-20, 1067b21-5.

deterioration   φθίσις

dialectics   διαλεκτική   A discipline dealing effectively but logically with any problem, whether attacking or defending a thesis, starting from generally accepted beliefs. 100a18-b23, 101a25-8, 1004b17-26.

difference   διαφορά

different   διάφορος   A and B are said to be different if, being the same in species or genus or by analogy, but not numerically the same, they are distinct. 1018a12-5, 1054b23-31, 1058a6-8.

different   ἕτερον   Same as "distinct".

differentia   διαφορά   If A and B are different but under the same genus, the elements in their definition which make A and B distinct are said to be their differentiae.

dimension   μέγεθος

directly   See "in virtue of itself".

discourse   λόγος

discriminate   κρίνειν   To distinguish or apprehend by sensation or by thought, 432a15-6. Syn: "distinguish", "apprehend".

disposition   διάθεσις   8b26-9a13, 1019b5, 1022b1-3.

distinctness   ἑτερότης   This term is a genus of "difference", taken in the narrow sense.

distinguish   Same as "discriminate".

divine   θεῖος   Honorable and eternal, or almost so; god-like.

division   διαίρεσις

doctrine   δόξα   A hypothesis of considerable weight.

dominant   κύριος   That which gives orders or upon which something else depends. Syn: "authoritative", "basic", "main".

earth   γῆ   For meaning, see "water".

element   στοιχεῖον   The first constituent in each thing. Thus, the material components which are indivisible in kind into other kinds are elements, and so are the letters of words, and the indefinable terms, and the syllogisms which are used as forms in geometrical and other demonstrations. 1014a26-b15.

end   τέλος   1021b25-1022a13.

equality   ἰσότης   Sameness or oneness in quantity. 1021a11-2.

error   ἀπάτη

especially   μάλιστα   Syn: "most of all", "in the highest degree".

essence   τὶ ἦν εἶναι   (a) That which, usually being in a category, is in the thing and in virtue of which the thing remains the same and is univocally called by the same name, for example, the form of a statue or the whiteness of whatever is white insofar as it is white; (b) that in the soul which exists as knowledge and by which we know a thing's essence taken in sense (a). 1029b1-1030b13.

essentially   See "in virtue of itself".

estimative part   λογιστικόν   That part or soul of man which *thinks* and concludes about things that may or may not be, 1139a6-15.

eternal   ἀΐδιος

evil   κακόν

excess   ὑπερβολή

exercise   ἐνέργεια   Syn: "activity", "*actuality*".

extension   μέγεθος

extreme   ἄκρον

extreme term   ἄκρον

extremity   ἔσχατον

fact   τὸ ὅτι

faculty   δύναμις   A mental power of an animal.

falsity   ψεῦδος   A statement or a thought which is contrary to fact. 1011b25-7, 1051b3-5.

fear   φόβος

figure   σχῆμα   Syn: "shape".

final cause   οὗ ἕνεκα   That for the sake of which something exists or becomes. This is not limited to animals but extends to plants and even inanimate things. 194b16-195b30, 983a24-b1, 1013a24-b28.

fire   πῦρ   For meaning, see "water".

finite   πεπερασμένος

flavor   χυμός   The quality of a thing which is the object tasted or object of taste.

food   τροφή

force   βία

for the sake of something   ἕνεκά του

form   εἶδος   This is the immaterial principle of a composite which has also matter. Some forms exist by themselves, i.e., without matter. Man's form is his soul, the form of a house is its structure, the form of a sphere is its surface, and God is a form without matter.

Form   εἶδος   For Plato, Forms are posited as immovable, immaterial, changeless, more real than sensible things, and the causes of sensible and destructible things; and each Form is posited as being separate from other Forms, like an animal, which is separate from a tree or an automobile. Syn: "Idea". 987b29-b22.

form   μορφή   It is not clear whether the terms "*form*" and "form" are used synonymously or not. Syn: "*shape*".

formula   λόγος   Any thought or expression which has parts each of which has significance; a definition (sometimes); a form or structure with parts.

Friendship φιλία   For Empedocles, a principle which causes things to come together. 984b27-985a10.

general   καθόλου   Same as "universal".

generation   γένεσις   A change from not-being to being. If the generation is to a substance, as when a baby is born, it is called "simple generation" or "unqualified generation", but if to something belonging to a substance, as from not-white to white, it is called "qualified generation". 225a12-7, 1067b21-3. Syn: "becoming".

genus   γένος   In the whatness or definition of a thing, a genus is a constituent as matter or subject to which the addition of a differentia produces a species under that genus.

God   θεός   Syn: "prime mover", for Aristotle.

god   θεός   The term is used if many gods are posited.

good   ἀγαθόν   That which is chosen or apprehended by the intellect as an end in itself or as a means to an end. 1096a19-29, 1362a21-1363b4.

good temper   πραότης   See "temper, good".

growth   αὔξησις

habit   ἕξις   A disposition which is hard to displace, whether it be acquired, like a virtue or scientific knowledge, or natural, such as strength or a disposition to illness. 8b25-9a13, 1022b4-14.

harmony   ἁρμονία; συμφωνία   The second term applies to voice or sounds; the first term is more general.

hearing   ἄκουσις   Actual hearing, as when one is listening to music.

hearing   ἀκοή   *hearing*; faculty of hearing.

heaven   οὐρανός

honorable   τίμιος

hot, n. or adj.   θερμόν   329b24-32, 378b10-26, 388a20-4, 1070b10-5.

Hot   θερμόν   For Parmenides, a principle of sensibles. 986b31-7a2.

Idea   ἰδέα   Same as "Form".

ignorance   ἄγνοια   No thought at all about a thing; false thought about a thing, as when one believes that something is the case when such is not the case. 79b23-8.

image   φάντασμα

imagination   φαντασία

immortal   ἀθάνατος

immovable   ἀκίνητος

impassive   ἀπαθής   Not capable of being affected.

imperfect   Same as "incomplete".

impossible   ἀδύνατον

impression   σημεῖον   For example, the impressions left by footsteps.

impression, sense   See "sense impression".

inanimate   ἄψυχον

included, be ἐνυπάρχειν
incomplete ἀτελής Not yet reached perfection. Syn: "imperfect".
inconsistency ὑπεναντίωσις A contradiction which is implied by a number of statements or *thoughts*.
incontinent ἀκρατής A man who has bad *desires* and knows that they are bad, but he yields to them because his *desires* overpower his wishes or his reason. 1145b8-1152a33.
increase, n. αὔξησις
indefinite ἀόριστος; ἄπειρον
indirectly κατὰ συμβεβηκός, καθ᾽ ἕτερον
indivisible ἀδιαίρετος
inferior χεῖρον
infinite ἄπειρον
inhaling ἀναπνοή
in itself See "in virtue of itself".
insofar as ᾗ Same as "qua". See "qua".
instrument ὄργανον
intellect νοῦς The power which acquires concepts or true principles; the concepts or the true principles which exist in the mind; any thinking or thought, sometimes including imagination. By definition, intellect in the second sense is always true.
intellect, passive and active 430a10-25.
Intellect νοῦς Plato's first principle. Syn: "the *One*", "the *Good*".
intelligence σύνεσις Ability to use thoughts in judging well objects of prudence, when someone else speaks about them. 1142b34-1143a18. Syn: "good intelligence".
Intelligence νοῦς For Anaxagoras, a moving principle and cause of things. 984b11-20.
intelligible object νοητόν the object of thought, as opposed to the object of sensation. Syn: "object of thought".
intention προαίρεσις A choice of the apparently best of the alternatives deliberated upon. 1113a2-7. Syn: "deliberative choice".
intermediate object μέσον
intervening medium μεταξύ
intervening space μεταξύ
in the highest degree μάλιστα Syn: "most of all", "especially".
investigate θεωρεῖν
in virtue of κατά A is said to belong to B in virtue of B, or to C in virtue of B, if it is a part of the essence or whatness of B (as animality is a part of man), or if it is demonstrable through B (as the equality of vertical angles through the definition of vertical angles), or if it is an attribute of B and is definable in terms of B (as oddness, which is defined as indivisibility of a number into two equal numbers). Syn: "according to", "by virtue of", "essential", 73a28-b24, 1022a14-36.

in virtue of itself   καθ' αὐτό
irrational   ἄλογον   The contrary of "rational" in the sense of having bad
   or false reason.
judge   κρίνειν
judge rightly   φρονεῖν
judgment   λογισμός   Reasoning with conclusion about things whose existence is of the possible but not of the necessary or impossible.
kind   εἶδος; γένος
know, v.   γιγνώσκειν, γνωρίζειν, εἰδέναι   It is not clear whether the three
   terms are synonyms or not. The first term is generic and includes
   sensations, 731a33-4. The third term appears to be limited to knowledge of things through their causes in the *Metaphysics* (981a24-30,
   983a25-6); but perhaps it is not so limited in the *Posterior Analytics*
   (98b21) but, like *knowing*, excludes sensations or accidents of individuals and is limited to knowledge taken universally, with or without causes.
knowable   ἐπιστητόν   That which can be *known*; object of *knowledge*.
knowing part   ἐπιστημονικόν   The part of man that *knows* or can *know*,
   whether it be a part of the soul or of that which has that part.
knowledge   γνῶσις
knowledge   ἐπιστήμη   Knowledge through the cause or causes, whether
   demonstrable or indemonstrable, of that which is necessarily so, like
   the equality of vertical angles or the product of the sides as the area
   of a rectangle, or like the definition of a thing through its causes.
   71b9-12, 72a18-22, 88b36-7. Syn: "science", "scientific knowledge".
   By definition, then, *knowledge* is always true.
last, adj.   ἔσχατον
length   μῆκος
life   ζωή   In a living thing, plants included, the taking in of food, growing,
   and deteriorating.
light, n.   φῶς
like, adj.   ὅμοιος   Syn: "similar".
limit   πέρας
line   γραμμή
live, v.   ζῆν
locomotion   φορά   Motion with respect to place.
magnitude   μέγεθος
main   κύριος   Same as "dominant".
make   ποιεῖν   Syn: "produce".
man   ἄνθρωπος   An animal which has reason. It includes both sexes.
materials   ὕλη   Syn: "matter".
mathematical objects   μαθηματικά
mathematics   μάθημα   The science of quantities.

matter ὕλη

may,v. ἐνδέχεσθαι That which may be or is possible to be. Its contrary is "cannot" or "impossible".

mean,n. μέσον, μεσότης

mean,v. σημαίνειν Syn: "signify".

medical science ἰατρική

medium μέσον

memory μνήμη

metaphor μεταφορά

method μέθοδος Systematic inquiry.

middle term μέσον If all A is B and all B is C, B is said to be the middle term.

mistaken. ἀπάτη Syn: "error".

moist,adj. ὑγρός

more μᾶλλον Comparative of "much". Syn: "to a higher degree".

mortal being θνητός

most of all μάλιστα

motion κίνησις It is a generic term having as its species "locomotion" or "motion with respect to place", "alteration" or "motion with respect to quality", and "increase" and "decrease", which signify motions with respect to quantity.

motionless ἀκίνητος

must,v. ἀνάγκη Syn: "it is necessary".

natural φυσικός Syns: "physical".

natural philosopher φυσιολόγος

nature φύσις The form of a physical substance; the matter of a physical substance; the moving cause of a thing; the final cause of a thing; sometimes, in any category, the essence of a thing. 192b8-193b21, 1014b16-1015a19.

nature, according to κατὰ φύσιν 192b8-193b21, 199b14-8.

nature, by φύσει 192b8-193b21, 199b14-8.

nature, contrary to παρὰ φύσιν

necessary ἀναγκαῖον Syn: "must".

negation ἀπόφασις The term is wider than "denial", for it is applied also to terms, e.g., to "not-white".

noble καλόν That which, being chosen for its own sake, is praiseworthy; that which is good and pleasant by being good. 1366a33-5.

nonrational ἄλογον The contradictory of what is rational. Thus rocks and the nutritive soul are nonrational.

nourish τρέφειν

number ἀριθμός A plurality measured by a unit, that is, a natural number greater than the number 1 (in modern mathematical language). 4b20-31, 1020a8-9, 1057a2-4, 1085b22, 1088a5-8.

Number ἀριθμός For the later Plato, a Number, such as Seven, is also an
    Idea, and it is generated ultimately from the two principles, the *One*
    and the *Dyad* (also called *"Indefinite Dyad"*). 1075b37-1076a4,
    1084a3-7, 1090b13-9.
numerically one ἀριθμῷ ἕν
nutritive part θρεπτικόν That power in a living thing which causes that
    thing to take in food and grow and mature and deteriorate; the
    material organ having that power.
object ὑποκείμενον Syn: "subject", which usually underlies an attribute.
    Sometimes the term "object" is used to signify something discussed
    or thought, whether a being or a nonbeing, but there is no Greek
    term for it.
object of desire ὀρεκτόν
object of thought νοητόν Same as "intelligible object".
odor ὀσμή That attribute in a thing which causes a smell in a living thing.
one ἕν Syn: "unity".
One ἕν A principle posited by some ancient philosophers. Plato regarded
    it as the first principle as form and a mover. 987a29-b22, 1084a3-7.
opinion δόξα A belief of something which may or may not be or come
    to be. 89a2-3, 100b5-7, 1039b31-1040a1, 1051b10-5.
opinion, be of the δοκεῖν
opposite ἀντικείμενον The main kinds of opposites are the contradictories,
    the contraries, the relatives, and privation and possession. 11b16-9,
    1018a20-b8
organ ὄργανον
other ἕτερον
pain λύπη
part μέρος, μόριον 1032b12-25.
partake of μετέχειν
passion πάθος Syn: "affection".
peculiar οἰκεῖος Same as "appropriate".
perfect τέλειος See "complete".
persuade πείθειν
philosophy φιλοσοφία The science of being qua being, that is, of the
    highest principles and causes and elements of things. 1003a21-32,
    1026a10-32, 1060b31-1061b17, 1064a28-b14.
physical φυσικός Same as "natural".
physician ἰατρός
physicist φυσικός
pity ἔλεος
place,n. τόπος
place,v. τίθεσθαι
place,n. τόπος The first inner motionless boundary of a containing body;
    for example, of a can of soup, the inner surface of that can. 212a20-1.

216

pleasure ἡδονή
point στιγμή
poor φαῦλος
posit τιθέναι, ποιεῖν To lay down something, usually a principle, as existing or as being true. 72a14-24.
position θέσις
possession ἕξις Syn: "habit".
posterior ὕστερον That which follows or comes after some other thing according to some principle. It is opposed to "prior".
potentiality δύναμις That which can be or become or do something else. 1019a15-1020a6.
potentially δυνάμει
power δύναμις
practicable πρακτόν
practical πρακτικός
predicate,v. κατηγορεῖσθαι
primarily πρώτως
principle ἀρχή The first thing from which something else is or becomes or is known. 1012b34-1013a23. Syn: "beginning", "starting point".
prior πρότερον It is the opposite of "posterior". 14a26-b23, 1018b9-1019a14.
privation στέρησις Not having, if by nature a thing should have, e.g., a blind man is deprived of vision, for by nature he should have vision; not having, whether simply or by nature, e.g., neither a blind man nor a stone has vision. 1022b22-1023a7.
produce ποιεῖν Syn: "make".
proper ἴδιον A is proper to B if B and only B can have A. Syn: "special".
proper sensible ἴδιον
proportion λόγος
prove συλλογίζεσθαι A is said to be proved from B if A, as a conclusion, follows from B, as premises, by means of logical principles.
prudence φρόνησις Generically (for all animals), the ability to look after one's own good, 1141a20-8; specifically (for men), a disposition by means of which one can deliberate truly concerning one's conduct for a good life. 1040a24-b30.
qua ᾗ An attribute C belongs to A qua B if it belongs to B but to no genus of B. For example, capability of motion belongs to a man and stone qua physical bodies, and infinite divisibility belongs to a straight line qua a magnitude. Syn: "insofar as", "as far as", "by", "by means of", "as". 73b25-74a3.
quality ποιόν This is one of the categories or highest genera. 8b25-11a38, 1020a33-b25.
quantity ποσόν This is one of the categories or highest genera. 4b20-6a35, 1020a7-32.

rather μᾶλλον   Syn: "more".

ratio λόγος

rational λόγον ἔχον   Having reason or thought, which is impossible without universal terms or concepts. Occasionally, that which has good
   or true reason.

reason,n. αἰτία, αἴτιον   Syn: "cause".

reason,n. λόγος   Any composite thought or expression, which includes
   universals; Sometimes, the term means good or true reason in the first
   sense.

reason,v. λογίζεσθαι   To use reason; to use reason of what is possible.

reason, contrary to παράλογον

reason, with good εὐλόγως

reasonable εὔλογον   Having good reason.

recollection ἀνάμνησις

regard   Same as "believe".

respiration ἀναπνοή   Syn: "breathing".

rest ἠρεμία

right,adj. ὀρθός

seeing ὅρασις

sensation αἴσθησις

sensation, faculty of   Same as "sense".

sense,n. αἴσθησις   Faculty of sensation. It may be a faculty of proper
   sensibles, or one that judges distinct sensibles.

sense,v. αἰσθάνεσθαι

sense impression αἴσθημα

sense of hearing ἀκοή

sense of smell ὄσφρησις

sense of taste γεῦσις

sense of touch ἀφή

sense organ αἰσθητήριον

sensible object αἰσθητόν   For example, colors, odors, flavors, etc.

sentient αἰσθητικόν   Having sense.

sentient part αἰσθητικόν   The part or soul of an animal which can sense.

separable χωριστός

shape σχῆμα

shape μορφή

share,v. κοινωνεῖν

side πέρας

sign,n. σημεῖον

signify σημαίνειν   Syn: "mean".

similar ὅμοιος   Things are said to be similar if their quality is one. 1018a15-
   9, 1021a11, 1054b3-14. Syn: "like".

simple ἁπλοῦς

simply ἁπλῶς   Syn: "unqualified", "without qualification", "absolutely".
single ἁπλοῦς
size μέγεθος
sky οὐρανός
smell,n. ὄσφρησις   Syn: "sensation of smell".
smell, sense of   See "sense of smell".
solid στερεόν
solution μῖξις   Syn: "blend".
sometime ποτέ   One of the categories. For example, in 1945.
soul ψυχή   The form of a living thing.
sounding ψόφησις   The actual sounding of an object.
sound ψόφος   The activity of air or a medium, caused by the impact of
   two bodies; the corresponding capacity of that medium.
space χώρα
special ἴδιον   Syn: "proper".
species εἶδος
speculate θεωρεῖν
spirited part θυμικόν   See "temper".
starting point ἀρχή   Syn: "beginning", "principle".
Strife νεῖκος   For Empedocles, a principle which causes things to separate
   from each other. 984b27-985a10.
subject ὑποκείμενον   A subject is relative to an attribute belonging to that
   subject. For example, color belongs to a body and sickness belongs
   to an animal, and color and sickness are attributes belonging, respectively, to a body and an animal, which are subjects.
substance οὐσία   Men and trees and chairs are examples of substances,
   and they exist as separate things, and all attributes belong to substances. 2a11-4b19. Some immaterial things, too, exist as separate
   things or are separable from other things, e.g., God and man's active
   intellect.
substance οὐσία   The *substance* of a thing is the nature as form of that
   thing, and it is applicable to all categories. For example, the *substance* of a triangle is to be a three-sided figure, and the *substance*
   of an animal is its soul.
succession ἐφεξῆς
syllogism συλλογισμός   An expression, verbal or written or in thought, in
   which a statement called "conclusion" follows necessarily from two
   other statements called "premises" which are posited as being so or
   true. 24b8-22, 100a25-7.
taste γεῦσις   Actual tasting; sense of taste.
taste, sense of   γεῦσις
temper θυμός   The spirited part of the soul, elicited, for example, in
   courage or retaliation; the activity of that part.

temper, good πραότης The virtue or right habit of exhibiting temper or anger.

term, extreme ἄκρον

that for the sake of which οὗ ἕνεκα Syn: "final cause".

theoretical θεωρητικός Concerned with the investigation or contemplation of universal truth. Syn: "speculative".

thing ὄν, πρᾶγμα Syn: "existent", "that which exists, actually or potentially".

think νοεῖν A mental activity contrasted with sensing, feeling, and imagining; sometimes Aristotle includes imagining in thinking, thus avoiding the coining of new words, 427b27-9.

think διανοεῖν Thinking which is combining concepts, and such thinking may be true or false.

think rightly φρονεῖν

thinking νόησις

thinking part νοητικόν Usually, the part of man that thinks.

thinking part διανοητικόν The part of man that *thinks*.

think that οἴεσθαι

this, a τόδε τι An individual thing, usually a primary substance, which one can point to.

thought διάνοια

thought to be δοκεῖν Syn: "be of the opinion".

thought, object of νοητόν Syn: "intelligible object".

through διά See "because".

time χρόνος

touch,n. ἀφή Syn: "contact".

touch, sense of ἀφή

trait An attribute or essential element of a thing. There is no Greek term for this term, unless perhaps the word κατηγορούμενον.

transparent (medium),n. διαφανές

travel φέρεσθαι

truth ἀληθές, ἀλήθεια A statement or thought which signifies a fact.

ultimate ἔσχατον

undivided ἀδιαίρετος

unit μονάς That which is indivisible with respect to quantity and has no position; sometimes, it is used as a genus to include also points, which have position. 1016b17-31, 409b6.

unity ἕν Syn: "one".

universal καθόλου That which by its nature belongs to an indefinite number of individuals, e.g., man or "man". The term is applicable to statements and to syllogisms also, e.g., to "every line is divisible". 17a38-b12, 1038b11-2.

universe, entire πᾶν

unqualified   ἁπλῶς   Syn: "simply", "without qualification", "absolutely".

unreasonable   ἄλογον   Syn: "irrational".

useful   χρήσιμος   It is a relative term. For example, A is useful to B if it is a means to B or for the sake of B. 101a25-8, 742a32, 1096a7.

virtue   ἀρετή

visible object   ὁρατόν

vision   ὄψις   The sense or faculty of seeing.

voice, vocal sound   φωνή

void   κενόν

water   ὕδωρ   As used by Aristotle, the term does not mean what we mean by "water". For him, in terms of attributes, it means a body which is cold, moist, and a liquid. Likewise, "fire" means a gaseous body which is hot and dry, "air" means a gaseous body which is hot and moist, and "earth" means a solid body which is cold and dry. These are the four material elements from which the other sensible bodies (not the heavenly) are composed. 330a30-b7, 382b13-5.

well,adv.   εὖ, καλῶς   Syn: "rightly".

wet   διερόν

whatness   τὸ τί ἔστι   A thing as indicated by its definition or by the answer to the question "what is it?". In a limited sense, a genus of that thing or of its definition. 92b4-8, 93a16-20, 103b27-37.

whole   ὅλον   A whole unity and also parts. The terms "whole" and "part" are correlatives, i.e., each is related to the other and both must be understood simultaneously.

whole (universe)   πᾶν

wish   βούλησις   Usually, desire of the good; desire of what appears to be good, whether it is good or not. 1113a15-b2.

with good reason   εὐλόγως

without qualification   ἁπλῶς   Syn: "absolutely", "simply", "unqualified".

wrongly   οὐκ ὀρθῶς

GREEK-ENGLISH

ἀγαθόν good
ἄγνοια ignorance
ἀδιαίρετος indivisible; undivided
ἀδύνατον impossible
ἀεί always
ἀήρ air
ἀθάνατος immortal
ἀΐδιος eternal
αἰσθάνεσθαι sense,v.
αἴσθημα sense impression
αἴσθησις sensation; faculty of sensation, sense
αἰσθητήριον sense organ
αἰσθητικόν sentient,adj.; sentient part
αἰσθητόν sensible object
αἴτιον, αἰτία cause, *reason*
ἀκίνητος motionless; immovable
ἀκοή hearing; sense of hearing
ἄκουσις *hearing*, actually hearing
ἀκρατής incontinent
ἀκριβής accurate
ἄκρον extreme; extreme term; boundary
ἀληθές true, truth
ἀλλοίωσις alteration
ἄλογον nonrational; unreasonable, irrational
ἀναγκαῖον necessary, must
ἀνάλογον analogous; analogy
ἀνάμνησις recollection
ἀναπνοή breathing, respiration; inhaling
ἄνθρωπος man (both sexes)
ἀντικείμενον opposite
ἀόριστος indefinite
ἀπάθεια impassivity
ἀπάτη mistake, error
ἄπειρον infinite; indefinite
ἁπλοῦς simple; single
ἁπλῶς simply, unqualified, absolutely, without qualification

ἀπόδειξις demonstration
ἀπόφασις denial; negation
ἀρετή virtue
ἀριθμός number; Number
ἀριθμῷ ἕν numerically one
ἁρμονία harmony
ἀρχή principle, beginning, starting point
ἀτελής incomplete, imperfect
αὔξησις increase; growth
αὐτόματον chance
ἀφαίρεσις abstraction
ἁφή sense of touch, touch, contact
ἄψυχον inanimate
βία force
βουλεύεσθαι deliberate
βουλευτικόν deliberative part
βούλησις wish
γένεσις generation, becoming
γένος genus; kind
γεῦσις taste,n.; sense of taste
γῆ earth
γίγνεσθαι come to be, become, arise, be formed
γιγνώσκειν know
γνωρίζειν know
γνῶσις knowledge
γραμμή line
διά because, through, by (sometimes), by means of.
διάθεσις disposition
διαίρεσις division
διαλεκτική dialectics
διανοεῖν *think*
διανοητικόν *thinking* part
διάνοια *thought*
διαφανές transparent (medium)
διαφορά difference; differentia
διερόν wet
δοκεῖν be thought, be of the opinion
δόξα opinion; doctrine

δυνάμει   potentially
δύναμις   faculty; power; potentiality
ἐγκράτεια   continence
εἰδέναι   know
εἶδος   species; form; kind; Form
ἔλεος   pity
ἔμψυχον   animate
ἕν   one, unity; *One*
ἐναντίον   contrary
ἐναντίωσις   contrariety, two contraries
ἐνδέχεσθαι   can,v., may
ἕνεκα, οὗ   that for the sake of which, final cause
ἕνεκά του   for the sake of something
ἐνέργεια   activity, *actuality*, exercise
ἐντελέχεια   actuality
ἐνυπάρχειν   be in, be included
ἕξις   habit; possession
ἐπιθυμία   *desire*
ἐπιθυμητικόν   *desiring* part
ἐπιστήμη   *knowledge*, scientific knowledge, science
ἐπιστημονικόν   *knowing* part
ἐπιστητόν   *knowable*, object of *knowledge*
ἔσχατον   extremity, last, ultimate
ἕτερον   distinct, different, other
εὔλογον   reasonable
εὐλόγως   with good reason
ἐφεξῆς   succession
ζῆν   live,v.
ζωή   life
ζῷον   animal
ᾗ   qua, as far as, insofar as, by means of, as, by
ἡδονή   pleasure
ἠρεμία   rest
θάρσος   courage
θεῖος   divine

θεός   god; God
θερμόν   heat; hot; *Hot*
θέσις   position
θεωρεῖν   investigate, contemplate, speculate; exercise *knowledge*; observe
θεωρητικός   theoretical, speculative
θηρίον   nonrational animal
θίξις   contact; apprehension
θνητός   mortal
θρεπτικόν   nutritive part
θυμικόν   spirited part (concerned with temper)
θυμός   temper
ἰατρική   medical science
ἰατρός   physician
ἰδέα   Idea
ἴδιον   proper, special; proper sensible
ἰσότης   equality
καθ᾽ αὐτό   in virtue of itself, essentially, in itself, directly; by itself
καθ᾽ ἕτερον   indirectly
καθόλου   universal, general (sometimes)
κακόν   evil
καλός   noble
κατά   in virtue of, by virtue of, according to
κατάφασις   affirmation
κατηγορεῖσθαι   predicate,v.
κατηγορία   category
κενόν   void
κίνησις   motion
κοινόν   common; common sensible; public; composite; shared
κοινωνεῖν   share,v.
κρίνειν   discriminate, distinguish, apprehend, judge
κύριος   main, dominant, basic, authoritative
λογίζεσθαι   to reason, especially of what is possible

λογισμός   judgment
λογιστικόν   estimative part or soul of man
λόγον ἔχον   with reason, having reason, rational
λόγος   discourse; argument; formula; definition; account; ratio; reason; discussion; doctrine; treatise; proportion
λύπη   pain
μάθημα   mathematics
μαθηματικά   mathematical objects
μάλιστα   most of all, especially, in the highest degree
μᾶλλον   more, rather, to a higher degree
μέγεθος   magnitude; size; extension; dimension
μέθοδος   method, systematic inquiry
μέρος, μόριον   part
μέσον   middle term; medium; intermediate object, mean
μεσότης   mean,n.
μεταβολή   change
μεταξύ   intermediate; intervening space; intervening medium
μεταφορά   metaphor
μετέχειν   partake of
μῆκος   length
μῖξις   blend; solution
μνήμη   memory
μονάς   unit
μορφή   shape, form
νεῖκος   Strife
νοεῖν   think
νόημα   concept
νόησις   thinking
νοητικόν   thinking part
νοητόν   object of thought, intelligible object
νοῦς   intellect; Intellect; Intelligence

οἰκεῖος   appropriate, peculiar
οἴεσθαι   think that
ὅλον   whole; universe
ὅμοιος   similar, like
ὄν   thing, being
ὅρασις   seeing
ὁρατόν   visible object
ὄργανον   organ; instrument
ὀργή   anger
ὀρεκτικόν   appetitive part
ὀρεκτόν   object of desire
ὄρεξις   desire,n.
ὀρθός   right,adj.
ὀρθῶς, οὐκ   wrongly
ὁρίζων   define
ὁρισμός   definition
ὅρος   definition; boundary
ὀσμή   odor
ὄσφρησις   sense of smell; smelling
ὅτι, τό   fact
οὐρανός   heaven; sky
οὐσία   substance; substance
ὄψις   vision
πάθημα   affection
πάθος   attribute; passion, affection
πᾶν   entire universe
παράλογον   contrary to reason
πάσχειν   be affected, be acted upon
πείθειν   persuade
πεπερασμένος   finite
πέρας   limit; side
πήρωμα   defect
πίστις   conviction
ποιεῖν   act; make, produce; posit
ποιόν   quality
ποσόν   quantity
ποτέ   sometime
πρᾶγμα   thing, fact, being
πρακτικός   practical
πρακτόν   practicable
πρᾶξις   action
πραότης   good temper

προαίρεσις   intention, deliberate choice
πρότερον   prior
πρώτως   primarily
πῦρ   fire
σημαίνειν   signify, mean
σημεῖον   sign; impression
σκότος   darkness
στερεόν   solid
στέρησις   privation
στιγμή   point
στοιχεῖον   element
συλλογίζεσθαι   prove
συλλογισμός   syllogism
συμβεβηκός   attribute; accident
συμβεβηκός, κατά   by way of an attribute; indirectly; accidentally, by accident, as an accident
συμπέρασμα   conclusion
συμφωνία   harmony, as applied to voice or sounds.
σύνεσις   intelligence
συνεχής   continuous
σύνθεσις   composition
σύνολον   composite
σχῆμα   shape, figure
σῶμα   body
τεκτονική   carpentry
τέλειος   complete, perfect
τέλος   end
τέχνη   art
τὶ ἔστι, τὸ   whatness
τὶ ἦν εἶναι   essence
τιθέναι   posit; place
τίμιος   honorable
τόδε τι   a this
τόπος   place
τρέφειν   nourish
τροφή   food
τυχόν   chance thing
ὑγρός   moist
ὕδωρ   water
ὕλη   matter, materials

ὑπάρχειν   belong
ὑπεναντίωσις   inconsistency
ὑπερβολή   excess
ὑποκείμενον   subject; object
ὑπολαμβάνειν   believe, regard
ὕστερον   posterior
φαίνεσθαι   appear; imagine (sometimes)
φαντασία   imagination
φάντασμα   image
φαῦλος   poor
φέρεσθαι   travel
φθίσις   decrease; deterioration
φθορά   destruction
φιλία   Friendship
φιλοσοφία   philosophy
φόβος   fear
φορά   locomotion; revolution (sometimes)
φρονεῖν   judge or think rightly
φρόνησις   prudence
φύσει   by nature
φυσικός   physicist; physical, natural
φύσιν, κατά   according to nature
φύσιν, παρά   contrary to nature
φυσιολόγος   natural philosopher
φύσις   nature
φωνή   voice, vocal sound
φῶς   light
χεῖρον   inferior
χρήσιμος   useful
χρόνος   time
χρῶμα   color
χυμός   flavor
χώρα   space
χωριστός   separable
ψεῦδος   falsity
ψόφησις   sounding
ψόφος   sound
ψυχή   soul
ψυχρόν   cold; Cold

Index